CW00694200

British Gene
Microfiche

Stuart A. Raymond

Published by the
Federation of Family History Societies (Publications) Ltd.,
The Benson Room, Birmingham & Midlands Institute,
Margaret Street, Birmingham, B3 3BS, U.K.

Copies also obtainable from:

S.A. & M.J.Raymond, P.O.Box 35, Exeter, EX1 3YZ, U.K.

First published 1999

ISBN: 1-86006-100-1

ISSN: 1033-2065

Printed and bound by the Alden Press, Oxford and Northampton.

Contents

Introduction

Genealogists need to consult a wide variety of original sources in their pursuit of ancestors. That may mean that they have to visit innumerable record offices to check out their holdings. However, increasingly, the sources needed have been microfilmed and are readily available for consultation at home. Family history societies have published thousands of original sources on fiche; they are listed in John Perkins' *Current publications on microfiche by member societies.* 4th ed. F.F.H.S., 1997. The present volume sets out to list the innumerable microfiche and microfilm issued by other bodies.

Commercial and private publishers, record societies, libraries and record offices have all contributed substantially to the publication of genealogical microfiche. A number of firms have specialised in fiche reprints of printed sources such as trade directories and record society publications. Others have transcribed and indexed innumerable parish registers and monumental inscriptions. There is a bewildering array of microfiche and microfilm publications available for the genealogist. Keeping track of what is currently available is not easy; there is no one source that can be checked for current information. This book is an attempt to remedy this situation, and to list all microfiche and microfilm likely to be of interest to the British genealogist which are currently in print.

There are a few exclusions: local histories on fiche have generally been omitted, as have many volumes of *miscellanea* issued by record societies. This volume does not purport to list everything available from the publishers included, but only their genealogical offerings; this applies with especial force to the publications of record societies reprinted by Chadwyck-Healey. Nevertheless, there is a great deal in this volume which will be of interest to local historian.

Geographically, this listing is confined to fiche and film published anywhere in the world relating to England, Scotland and Wales; Ireland is excluded. Scottish family history societies are not F.F.H.S. members, so a few of their publications have been listed here.

Arrangement of this listing is by publisher; however, there are also extensive indexes of authors, surnames, placenames, and subjects. The latter in particular provides the means to identify the titles being sought.

This volume has been compiled by means of a questionnaire sent to publishers — and therefore suffers from the faults of inconsistency common to such volumes. Accurate bibliographic citations are simply not to be had without checking all the actual microfiche oneself, an impossible task, especially given the fact that few libraries with on-line catalogues hold them. In general, I have had to rely on the information supplied by publishers, who rarely cite the titles of their fiche publications correctly in their publicity. In a few cases — especially in the case of record society publications — I have been able to verify information from other sources; however, this has not been possible in many other cases. Some relevant fiche have not been reported by their publishers at all. Complete accuracy is therefore unobtainable. A few publishers have not responded to inquiries, and I am aware of a number of titles that I have not been able to include due to lack of sufficient information. The prices quoted are as reported by publishers; where possible I have also indicated the cost of postage within or to the U.K. You should be aware that these prices are liable to change, and that neither I nor the Federation of Family History Societies are to be held respnsible for such changes.

This volume may be kept up to date by reference to the new book listings in journals such as *Family tree magazine, Family history news and digest,* and the *Genealogists' Magazine,* backruns of which were consulted to identify relevant publishers. Many publishers now have web sites; addresses of these have been given where known, and may also be checked for new titles.

Fiche listed here may generally be obtained direct from their publishers. Some may also be obtainable from family history society bookstalls, or from the Society of Genealogists. When ordering, please mention that you identified books in *British Genealogical Microfiche.*

This book has been typed by Mark Gant, Mary Raymond, Paul Raymond, and Cynthia Hanson; my thanks to them, and also to Bob Boyd, who has seen it through the press.

Stuart A. Raymond

PART 1

Commercial and Private Publishers

Ancestor Publishers
6166, Janice Way, Arvada, CO.,
80004-5160, U.S.A.
CHESTER, JOSEPH LEMUEL. *London marriage licences 1521-1869.* 1595pp. Fiche reprint (originally published 1887). $US46.00.

Arden Enterprises
Ashton Lodge, Church Road, Lyminge, Folkestone, CT18 8JA
Phone: (01303) 862368
HYDE, PATRICIA, & HARRINGTON, DUNCAN. *Faversham Hundred records, vol. 1, being an index and catalogue of 5257 original documents deposited at the Public Record Office, Centre for Kentish Studies, Canterbury Cathedral Archives and Lambeth Palace Library.* 0-9524563-03. 8 fiche. £8.50.

Brookes, Davies & Co.
Cambria House, 37 Pembroke Avenue, Hove, East Sussex, BN3 5DB
Phone: (01273) 328912
Pigot's Cheshire directory, 1822-3. 1 fiche. £1.70.
Pigot's Derbyshire directory, 1822-3. 1 fiche. £1.70.
Pigot's Gloucestershire directory, 1822-3. 1 fiche. £1.70.
Pigot's Herefordshire directory, 1822-3. 1 fiche. £1.70.
Pigot's Lancashire directory, 1822-3. 3 fiche. £5.10.
Pigot's Leicestershire directory, 1822-3. 1 fiche. £1.70.
Pigot's Lincolnshire directory, 1822-3. 1 fiche. £1.70.
Pigot's London directory, 1822-3. 6 fiche. £10.20.
Pigot's Monmouthshire directory, 1822-3. 1 fiche. £1.70.
Pigot's Rutland directory, 1822-3. 1 fiche. £1.70.
Pigot's Shropshire directory, 1822-3. 1 fiche. £1.70.
Pigot's Somerset directory (including Bristol) 1822-3. 2 fiche. £3.40
Pigot's Staffordshire directory, 1822-3. 1 fiche. £1.70.
Pigot's Warwickshire directory, 1822-3. 1 fiche. £1.70.
Pigot's Wiltshire directory, 1822-3. 1 fiche. £1.70.
Pigot's Worcestershire directory, 1822-3. 1 fiche. £1.70.
Pigot's Yorkshire directory, 1822-3. 2 fiche. £3.40
Pigot's North Wales directory, 1822-3. 1 fiche. £1.70.
Pigot's South Wales directory, 1822-3. 1 fiche. £1.70.
Pigot's Bedfordshire directory, 1823-4. 1 fiche. £1.70.
Pigot's Berkshire directory, 1823-4. 1 fiche. £1.70.
Pigot's Buckinghamshire directory, 1823-4. 1 fiche. £1.70.
Pigot's Cambridgeshire directory, 1823-4. 1 fiche. £1.70.
Pigot's Cornwall directory, 1823-4. 1 fiche. £1.70.
Pigot's Devon directory, 1823-4. 1 fiche. £1.70.
Pigot's Dorset directory, 1823-4. 1 fiche. £1.70.
Pigot's Essex directory, 1823-4. 1 fiche. £1.70.
Pigot's Hampshire directory, 1823-4. 1 fiche. £1.70.
Pigot's Hertfordshire directory, 1823-4. 1 fiche. £1.70.
Pigot's Huntingdonshire directory, 1823-4. 1 fiche. £1.70.
Pigot's Kent directory, 1823-4. 1 fiche. £1.70.
Pigot's London directory, 1823-4. 1 fiche. £11.90.
Pigot's Northamptonshire directory, 1823-4. 1 fiche. £1.70.
Pigot's Oxfordshire directory, 1823-4. 1 fiche. £1.70.
Pigot's Suffolk directory, 1823-4. 1 fiche. £1.70.

Brookes, Davies & Co. (*cont*)
Pigot's Surrey directory, 1823-4. 1 fiche.
£1.70.
Pigot's Sussex directory, 1823-4. 1 fiche.
£1.70.
*Pigot's Leicestershire and Rutland
directory, 1841.* 1 fiche. £1.70.
Pigot's Lincolnshire directory, 1841. 2 fiche.
£3.40.
Pigot's Northamptonshire directory, 1841.
1 fiche. £1.70.
Pigot's Nottinghamshire directory, 1841.
2 fiche. £3.40.
Pigot's Staffordshire directory, 1841.
2 fiche. £3.40.
Pigot's Warwickshire directory, 1841.
3 fiche. £5.10.
Pigot's Worcestershire directory, 1841.
1 fiche. £1.70.
Pigot's Yorkshire directory, 1841. 7 fiche.
£11.90.
Pigot's Derbyshire directory, 1842. 2 fiche.
£3.40.
Pigot's Herefordshire directory, 1842.
1 fiche. £1.70.
Pigot's Nottinghamshire directory, 1842.
2 fiche. £3.40.
Pigot's Shropshire directory, 1842. 1 fiche.
£1.70.
Pigot's Staffordshire directory, 1842.
2 fiche. £3.40.
Pigot's Warwickshire directory, 1842.
2 fiche. £3.40.
Pigot's Worcestershire directory, 1842.
1 fiche. £1.70.
Pigot's Yorkshire directory, 1842. 7 fiche.
£11.90.
Pigot's Dorset directory, 1842. 1 fiche.
£1.70.
Pigot's Gloucestershire directory, 1842.
2 fiche. £3.40
Pigot's Herefordshire directory, 1842.
1 fiche. £1.70.
Pigot's Monmouthshire directory, 1842.
1 fiche. £1.70.
Pigot's Oxfordshire directory, 1842. 1 fiche.
£1.70.
Pigot's Somerset directory, 1842. 2 fiche.
£3.40.
Pigot's Wiltshire directory, 1842. 1 fiche.
£1.70.
Slater's Berkshire directory, 1850. 2 fiche.
£3.40
Slater's Derbyshire directory, 1850. 2 fiche.
£3.40.

Slater's Gloucestershire directory, 1850.
3 fiche. £5.10.
Slater's Herefordshire directory, 1850.
1 fiche. £1.70.
Slater's Monmouthshire directory, 1850.
1 fiche. £1.70.
Slater's Shropshire directory, 1850. 1 fiche.
£1.70.
Slater's Staffordshire directory, 1850.
3 fiche. £5.10.
Slater's Warwickshire directory, 1850.
4 fiche. £6.80.
Slater's South Wales directory, 1850.
2 fiche. £3.40.
Post Office directory of London 1838.
15 fiche. £25.50.
Post Office directory of Lincolnshire 1855.
7 fiche. £11.90.
Post Office directory of Essex 1851. 3 fiche.
£5.10.
*Post Office directory of Hertfordshire,
1851.* 2 fiche. £3.40.
Post Office directory of Kent 1851. 4 fiche.
£6.80.
Post Office directory of Middlesex 1851.
2 fiche. £3.40.
Post Office directory of Surrey 1851.
2 fiche. £3.40.
Post Office directory of Sussex 1851.
3 fiche. £5.10.
*Post Office directory of Essex, Hertford-
shire, Kent, Middlesex, Surrey and
Sussex, 1851.* 7 fiche. £11.90
Post Office directory of Essex 1859. 6 fiche.
£10.20.
Post Office directory of Hertfordshire 1871.
3 fiche. £5.10.
Post Office directory of Hertfordshire 1859.
3fiche. £5.10.
Post Office directory of Kent 1859. 9 fiche.
£15.30.
Post Office directory of Middlessex 1859.
4 fiche. £6.80.
Post Office directory of Surrey 1859.
5 fiche. £8.50.
Post Office directory of Sussex 1859.
6 fiche. £10.20.
Post Office directory of Essex 1871. 7 fiche.
£11.90.
Post Office directory of Middlesex 1871.
7 fiche. £11.90.
Post Office directory of Surrey 1871.
10 fiche. £17.00.
Post Office directory of Sussex 1871.
6 fiche. £13.60.

Gore's directory of Liverpool 1761, 1 fiche. £1.70.

SEAGRAVE, J. *The Chichester guide and directory, 1804*. 1 fiche. £1.70.

Holden's triennial directory of London, 1805/6/7. 14 fiche. £23.80.

Holden's triennial directory of 85 provincial towns in Great Britain and Ireland, 1805/6/7. 7 fiche. £11.90.

Baines & Parsons' directory of Lancashire, 1824-5. 21 fiche. 21 fiche. £35.70.

Pigot & Dean's Directory of Manchester, Salford, etc., 1824-5. 8 fiche. £13.60.

Parson & White's directory of the counties of Durham and Northumberland, 1828. 8 fiche. £13.60.

Parson & White's directory of Cumberland, 1829. 8 fiche. £13.60.

Parson & White's directory of Westmorland 1829. 4 fiche. £6.80.

Mannix & Whellan's directory of Cumberland, 1847. 11 fiche. £18.70.

Mathew's directory of Bristol & Clifton, 1851. 6 fiche. £10.20.

BILLING, M. *Directory of Worcestershire 1855*. 8 Fiche. £13.60.

Francis White & Co's directory of Cheshire, 1860. 15 fiche. £25.50.

Edward Cassey & Co's directory of Berkshire, 1868. 5 fiche. £8.50.

Gore's directory of Liverpool, 1868. 14 fiche. £23.80.

Edward Cassey & Co's directory of Oxfordshire, 1868. 5 fiche. £8.50.

Kelly's directory of Cambridgeshire, 1883. 4 fiche. £6.80.

Hulley's directory of Birmingham, 1893-4. 23 fiche. £39.10.

Hampshire poll book, 1734. 3 fiche. £5.10.

Norfolk poll book, 1768. 3 fiche. £5.10.

Sussex poll book, 1774. 3 fiche. £5.10.

Lewes poll books, 1802, 1812 & 1826. 1 fiche. £1.70.

Gloucestershire poll book, 1811. 1 fiche. £1.70.

Westminster poll book, 1818. 4 fiche. £6.80.

Lincolnshire poll book, 1824. 4 fiche. £6.80.

Wiltshire poll book, 1818. 2 fiche. £3.40.

East Kent poll book, 1832. 3 fiche. £5.10.

East Sussex poll book, 1832. 2 fiche. £3.40.

Brighton poll book, 1847. 1 fiche. £1.70.

Brighton poll book, 1818. 1 fiche. £1.70.

Terry Burns
39 Bolton Lane, Hose, Melton Mowbray, LE14 4JE

BURNS, TERENCE E. *Census 1861: Pancras (District 9) RG9/94-124. Surname index.* 6 pts.1994-7. Contents:

Regents Park RG9/094-099. 3 fiche. 1997. £2.66.

Tottenham Court RG9/100-103. 3 fiche. 1997. £2.66.

Grays Inn Lane RG9/104-208. 30 fiche. 1997. £2.66.

Somers Town RG9/109-114. 4 fiche. 1996. £3.46.

Camden Town RG9/115-118. 3 fiche. 1994. £2.66.

Kentish Town RG9/119-124. 4 fiche. 1994. £3.46.

N.B. A consolidated index of Pancras 1861 is in preparation.

BURNS, TERENCE E. *Surname index, Hampstead 1861. RG9/091-093*. 3 fiche. 1998.

Chadwyck-Healey Ltd.
The Quorum, Barnwell Road, Cambridge, CB5 8SW

ANDERSON, MICHAEL, ed. *1851 census enumerators' returns*. 145 fiche. £545.00. A 10% sample of the returns.

HOUSTON, RAB, ed. *Records of a Scottish village: Lasswade, 1650-1750*. 6 fiche. £52.00.

JONES, DAVID LEWIS, ed. *British and Irish biographies, 1840-1940*. 14,287 fiche. £37,265.00. Microfiche reprint of 272 biographical dictionaries in 1200 volumes.

KEEN, DEREK, & HARDING, VANESSA, eds. *Historical gazetteer of London before the Great Fire. Part 1. Cheapside*. 50 fiche. £285.00. Traces innumerable house descents.

MACFARLANE, ALAN, et al, eds. *Records of an English village: Earls Colne, 1400-1750*. 126 fiche. £510.00.

MARTIN, G.H., ed. *Husting rolls of deeds and wills, 1252-1485*. 30 microfilm reels. £2010.00. Transcripts of 22,600 deeds and wills enrolled in the principal court of medieval London.

MYERS, ROBIN, ed. *Records of the Stationers Company, 1554-1920*. 115 microfilm reels. £7,275.00.

9

Chadwyck-Healey Ltd. (*cont.*)
British trials, 1600-1900. c.48,000 fiche when complete. Price on application. Republication of unofficial first-hand accounts of trials.
Calendars of charters and rolls in the manuscript collections of the Bodleian Library. 327 fiche. £1260.00.
Calendars of charters and rolls in the manuscript collections of the British Library. 19 microfiche reels. £1320.00.
Index of manuscripts in the British Library. 10 vols. 5,603pp. 0-85964-140-6. 1985. £2,300.00.
National inventory of documentary sources in the United Kingdom and Ireland. Fiche. Prices on application. Massive.
Publications of the English record societies, 1835-1972, and the Index Library. 5,136 fiche. £17,640.00. See under particular societies in pt. 2 for details of individual volumes.
Records of the Court of Arches 1554-1911: Lambeth Palace Library. 12,437 + 308 fiche; 105 microfilm reels. £30,870.00.

Barbara J. Chambers
39 Chatterton, Letchworth Garden City, Hertfordshire, SG6 2JY
CHAMBERS, BARBARA J. *Regimental service returns for 1806: PRO WO25/871-1120.* 3 vols. Fiche or booklet. 1998-.
  v.1 *1st & 3rd & 4th battalions 1st (Royal) Regiment of Foot.* 1998. £4.00.
  v.2 *1st batallion 2nd (Queens) Regiment of Foot; 1st and 2nd batallions 3rd (Buffs) Regiment of Foot; 1st & 2nd batallions 4th (Kings) Regiment of Foot.* 1998. £3.00.
  v.3. *1st & 2nd Life Guards; Royal Horse Guards; 1st, 2nd & 3rd Dragoon Guards.* Forthcoming.

Jill Chambers
4 Quills, Letchworth, Hertfordshire, SG6 2RG
Email: jchambers@sprynet.co.uk
CHAMBERS, JILL. *Criminal petitions index.* Pt.1. HO17/40-49. 80pp. 1997. Also available in printed form. Pt.2. HO17/50-59. Forthcoming.

R.G. Cotterell
19 Bellevue Road, Bexleyheath, Kent, DA6 8ND
Email: RJCindex@aol.com
Cheques payable to Trueflare Ltd. please.

Thames Riverside parish series.
1. *Christchurch, East Greenwich: 1868-1912 baptisms.* 5 fiche. £5.75 + p&p 30p.
2. *Christchurch, East Greenwich: 1868-1913 marriages.* 2 fiche. £2.75 + p&p 30p.
3. *St. Botolph, Northfleet: 1775-1837 baptisms and marriages, plus 1813-1837 burials.* 3 fiche. £3.50 + p&p 30p.
4. *St. Peter & Paul, Milton next Gravesend 1845-1876: baptisms and marriages.* 2 fiche. £2.75 + p&p 30p. See also vol. 28.
5. *Holy Trinity, Milton next Gravesend 1845-1876: baptisms and marriages.* 1 fiche. £1.50 + p&p 30p. Also includes St. Andrews Waterside Mission.
6. *St. John the Baptist, Erith: 1801-1812 & 1830-1873 baptisms; 1801-1858 burials; 1801-1863 marriages.* 4 fiche. £4.25 + p&p 30p. See also vol. 11.
7. *St. George, Gravesend: 1775-1837 baptisms and marriages, also 1813-1837 burials.* 3 fiche. £3.75 + p&p 30p. See also vol. 16.
8. *Holy Trinity, Dartford: 1813-1839 baptims, marriages and burials.* 2 fiche. £2.75 + p&p 30p. See also vol. 10.
9. *St. James, Gravesend: 1852-1878 baptisms.* 1 fiche. £1.50 + p&p 30p.
10. *Holy Trinity, Dartford: 1840-1843 baptisms, marriages and burials plus 1900-1902 baptisms.* 1 fiche. £1.50 + p&p 30p. See also vol. 8.
11. *St. John the Baptist, Erith: 1813-1845 baptisms, marriages and burials.* 2 fiche. £2.75 + p&p 30p. See also vol. 6.
12. *St. Paulinus, Crayford: 1813-1851 baptisms, marriages and burials.* 2 fiche. £2.75 + p&p 30p.
13. *St. Peter and St. Paul, Shorne: 1800-1875 baptisms and burials; 1800-1835 marriages.* 2 fiche. £1.75 + p&p 30p.
14. *St. Mary, Chalk: 1768-1876 baptisms, marriages and burials.* 2 fiche. £2.75 + p&p 30p.
15. *St. Margaret's, Plumstead: 1813-1853 baptisms; 1820-1853 burials; 1820-1836 marriages.* 2 fiche. £2.75 + p&p 30p. See also vol. 7.

16. *St. George, Gravesend: 1837-1876 baptisms.* 2 fiche. £2.75 + p&p 30p.
17. *St. Michael's, East Wickham. (chapelry in Plumstead) 1813-1846 baptisms and burials; 1813-1837 marriages.* 1 fiche. £1.75 + p&p 30p.
18. *St. Mary, Higham: 1813-1877 baptisms and burials; 1813-1851 marriages; also St. John, Higham: 1862-1877 baptisms.* 2 fiche. £2.25 + p&p 30p.
19. *St. Luke's, Charlton: 1813-1840 and 1867-1872 baptisms; 1813-1839 and 1866-1869 burials; 1813-1837 marriages.* 2 fiche. £2.75 + p&p 30p.
20. *St. Peter and St. Paul, Dagenham: 1800-1842 baptisms, marriages and burials.* 2 fiche. £2.75 + p&p 30p.
21. *St. Peter and St. Paul, Grays Thurrock: 1813-1825 baptisms, marriages and burials.* 1 fiche. £1.00 + p&p 30p.
22. *St. Mary the Virgin, Stone next Dartford: 1750-1851 baptisms and marriages; 1750-1864 burials.* 2 fiche. £2.75 + p&p 30p.
23. *St. Mary's, Greenhithe: 1857-1887 baptisms; 1858-1919 marriages.* 1 fiche. £1.50 + p&p 30p.
24. *St. Mary's, Putney: 1799-1812 baptisms, marriages and burials.* 1 fiche. £1.75 + p&p 30p.
25. *St. Peter and St. Paul, Swanscombe: 1750-1862 baptisms, marriages and burials.* 4 fiche. £4.25 + p&p 30p.
26. *St. Mary's, Rotherhithe: 1834-1870 baptisms and marriages; 1834-1855 burials.* 6 fiche. £6.75.
27. *St. Margarets, Barking: 1813-1851 baptisms, marriages and burials.* 4 fiche. £4.50 + p&p 30p.
28. *St. Peter and St. Paul, Milton next Gravesend: 1775-1812 baptism, marriages and burials.* 2 fiche. £2.75.
29. *St. Mary Magdalene, East Ham, Essex: 1813-1841 baptisms, marriages and burials.* 1 fiche. £1.75 + p&p 30p.
30. *All Saints, West Ham, Essex, Essex: 1813-1835 baptisms, marriages and burials.* 4 fiche. £4.50 + p&p 30p.

The Company of Watermen and Lightermen of the River Thames series

1. *Apprenticeship bindings 1692-1716.* 3 fiche. £3.75 + p&p 30p.
2. *Apprenticeship bindings 1716-1742.* 3 fiche. £3.75 + p&p 30p.
3. *Apprenticeship bindings 1742-1783.* 3 fiche. £3.75 + p&p 30p.
4. *Apprenticeship bindings 1783-1823.* 3 fiche. £3.75 + p&p 30p.
5. *Apprenticeship bindings 1823-1861.* 3 fiche. £3.75 + p&p 30p.
6. *Apprenticeship bindings 1861-1884.* 2 fiche. £2.75 + p&p 30p.
7. *Apprenticeship bindings 1884-1908.* 2 fiche. £2.75 + p&p 30p.
8. *Index of contract licences for over-aged boys articled to a freeman for a two year period 1865-1926.* 1 fiche. £1.75 + p&p 30p.
9. *Apprenticeship bindings and affidavit birth proofs 1898-1949.* 3 fiche. £3.75 + p&p 30p.

Harry Galloway Publishers and Booksellers

Orders: The Cottage, Manor Terrace, Paignton, Devon, TQ3 3RQ
Email: bernard__welchman__ familyhistorian@compuserve.com
Correspondence: "Staverton", 19 Kirke Grove, Taunton, Somerset, TA2 8SB,
Phone: (01823) 282267

CRISP, F.A., ed. *Abstracts of Somersetshire wills etc., copied from the manuscript collections of the late Rev. Frederick Brown, M.A., F.S.A.* 18 fiche. Originally published 1887-1890. £22.50.

GREEN, E. *The preparations in Somerset against the Spanish Armada 1558-1588.* 3 fiche. 1-873931-65-4. 1995 (originally published 1888). £6.00.

HAWKINGS, DAVID T., ed. *Index to Somerset Estate Duty office wills ... 1805-[1857].* 2 pts. 2 + 6 fiche. 1-873931-28-X(pt.1). 1-873931-29-8(pt.2). 1995. £10.00.

HOWARD, A.J., & STOATE, T.L., eds. *The Somerset protestation returns and lay subsidy rolls, 1641-2.* 7 fiche. 1-873931-07-7. £9.95. 1993 (originally published 1975).

HUMPHREYS, A.L., ed. *Materials for the history of the town and parish of Wellington in the county of Somerset. Part one: wills (Wellington & West Buckland) 1372-1811.* 3 fiche. Originally published 1908. £5.50.

Harry Galloway Publishers and Booksellers (cont.)

HUMPHREYS, A.L., ed. *Materials for the history of the town and parish of Wellington in the County of Somerset, part two: manorial court rolls 1277-1908.* 3 fiche. Originally published 1910. £5.50.

JEWERS, A.J., ed. *Marriage allegation bonds of the bishops of Bath and Wells from their commencement to the year 1755.* 9 fiche. 1-873931-11-5. 1909. £11.95.

KING, A.J., & WATTS, B.H., eds. *Municipal records of Bath 1189 to 1604.* 2 fiche. 1-873931-64-6. 1995 (originally published 1885). £4.00.

KNOX, GEORGE, ed. *Surname index for the 1891 census of North Somerset.* Vols.1-8 are available in hard copy; see *British Genealogical Books in Print.*
v.9. *Bedminster.* 6 fiche. £9.00.
v.10. *Harptree, Chew Magna and Clutton.* 1 fiche. £2.20.
v.11. *Long Ashton, St. George and Yatton.* 3 fiche. £5.00.

MEDLYCOTT, MERVYN, SIR. *Somerset wills index: printed and manuscript copies.* 4 fiche. 1-873931-27-1. 1993. £5.95.

PHIPPS, H.R., ed. *Abstracts of Bath & Wells diocesan records: marriage licences & allegations 1583-1681.* 30 fiche. 1-873931-12-3. £25.00.

STOATE, T.L. *Cornwall gazetteer.* 4 fiche. 1996. £5.50.

STOATE, T.L., ed. *The Cornwall protestation returns 1641.* 6 fiche. 1-873931-57-3. 1994. Originally published 1974. £8.50.

STOATE, T.L., ed. *Devon taxes 1581-1660.* 5 fiche. 1-873931-58-1. 1995 (originally published 1988). £9.00.

STOATE, T.L., ed. *Dwelly's index to the Somerset hearth tax exemption certificates of 1670 and 1674 with a completion of part 5 of Dwelly's national records volume 2.* 2 fiche. 1976. £4.00.

SYMONS, R. *Geographical dictionary or gazetteer of the county of Cornwall.* 6 fiche. Originally published 1884. £7.50.

WEAVER, F.W., ed. *Somerset incumbents.* 8 fiche. 1-873931-13-1. Originally published 1889. £7.95.

WEAVER, F.W., ed. *The visitations of the County of Somerset, in the years 1531 and 1573, together with additional pedigrees, chiefly from the visitation of 1591.* 4 fiche. 1-873931-38-7. 1994 (originally published 1885). £6.95.

WEAVER, F.W., ed. *Wells wills arranged in parishes, and annotated.* 6 fiche. 1-873931-39-5. Originally published 1890. £8.50.

WORTHY, C., ed. *Devonshire wills.* 8 fiche. £12.95.

The Acland estate act 1834. 1 fiche. Originally published Bemrose & Sons, 1896. 1-86241-000-3. £2.40.

An act for enlarging and repairing the parish churches of East and West Teignmouth, in the County of Devon; and for authorizing the sale of divers hereditaments in East and West Teignmouth, Ilsington, and Highweek, in the said County; and for discharging the expences to be occasioned thereby, 1815. 1 fiche. £2.40. Many names.

A bill for improving several roads, and making certain new roads, in the Counties of Devon and Somerset, leading to and from the town of Tiverton; and for amending an act of his present majesty, for repairing several roads leading from and through the town of Wiveliscombe 11 Geo. IV, 1830. 1 fiche. 1-873931-63-8. £1.80. Many names of landowners and occupiers in Rackenford, Knowstone, East Anstey, Molland, Stoodleigh, Tiverton, Cruwys Morchard, Witheridge, Thelbridge, East Worlington, Chawleigh, Exeter St. Sidwell, Heavitree, Exeter St. David, Stoke Canon, Halberton, Cullompton, Willand, Uffculme, Kentisbeer, Uplowman, Sampford Peverell, Holcombe Rogus, Thorne St. Margaret and Sampford Arundell.

Directories

Pigot & Co's directory of Somerset 1844. 2 fiche. £3.75.

Kelly's directory of Dorset 1895. 6 fiche. £9.95.

Kelly's directory of Somerset & Bristol 1889. 16 fiche. £14.95.

Kelly's directory of Somerset & Bristol 1875. 18 fiche. 1993. 1-873931-35-2. £16.95.

A general directory for the county of Somerset. 7 fiche. Originally published William Bragg, 1840. 1-873931-46-8. £8.50.

Parish Registers

HAYWARD, D.L., ed. *The parish registers of Bruton, Co. Somerset volume I, 1544-[1812].* 2 vols. 5 + 6 fiche. 1-873931-92-1 (v.1). 1-873931-96-4 (v.2). Originally published 1907-11. £10.95.

STOATE, T.L., ed. *Carhampton parish registers and civil papers.* 3 fiche. £4.50.

DANIEL, W.E., ed. *The parish registers of Horsington, 1558-1836.* 4 fiche. Originally published 1907. £7.50.

STOATE, T.L., ed. *Luccombe parish registers and poor rates, & Stoke Pero parish registers.* 2 fiche. £3.50.

STOATE, T.L., ed. *Selworthy parish registers and civil papers.* 3 fiche. £4.50.

JEWERS, A.J., ed. *The parish registers of Street, in the county of Somerset: baptisms and marriages to 1755, burials to 1762.* 2 fiche. 1-873931-62-X. Originally published 1898. £3.95.

STOATE, T.L., ed. *Timberscombe parish registers.* 2 fiche. £3.50.

SPENCER, J.H., ed. *Wilton parish registers, 1558-1837.* 6 fiche. Originally published 1890. £8.50.

STOATE, T.L., ed. *Wootton Courtenay parish registers.* 2 fiche. £3.50.

Nick Vine Hall

P.O.Box 581, Collaroy Beach, N.S.W., 2097, Australia.

Bedfordshire

Pigot's directory of Bedfordshire, 1823. 1 fiche. £3.00; $A9.00.

Pigot's directory of Bedfordshire, 1830. Forthcoming.

Pigot's directory of Bedfordshire, 1839. 2 fiche. £6.00; $A15.00.

Slater's directory of Bedfordshire, 1850. 1 fiche. £3.00; $A9.00.

Kelly's directory of Bedfordshire, 1864. 4 fiche. £12.00; $A27.00.

Kelly's directory of Bedfordshire, 1877. Forthcoming.

Kelly's directory of Bedfordshire, 1894. 4 fiche. £12.00; $A27.00.

Kelly's directory of Bedfordshire, 1898. 5 fiche. £15.00; $A33.00.

Kelly's directory of Bedfordshire, 1910. Forthcoming.

Kelly's directory of Bedfordshire, 1924. Forthcoming.

Berkshire

Pigot's directory of Berkshire, 1823. 1 fiche. £3.00; $A9.00.

Pigot's directory of Berkshire, 1830. Forthcoming.

Pigot's directory of Berkshire, 1844. 3 fiche. £9.00; $A21.00.

Kelly's directory of Berkshire, 1848. Forthcoming.

Slater's directory of Berkshire, 1852. 3 fiche. £9.00; $A21.00.

Kelly's directory of Berkshire, 1864. 4 fiche. £12.00; $A27.00.

Kelly's directory of Berkshire, 1877. Forthcoming.

Kelly's directory of Berkshire, 1891. 4 fiche. £12.00; $A27.00.

Kelly's directory of Berkshire, 1915. Forthcoming.

Kelly's directory of Berkshire, 1920. Forthcoming.

Kelly's directory of Berkshire, 1931. Forthcoming.

Pigot's directory of Buckinghamshire, 1823. 1 fiche. £3.00; $A9.00.

Pigot's directory of Buckinghamshire, 1830. Forthcoming.

Robson's directory of Buckinghamshire, 1839. 2 fiche. £6.00; $A15.00.

Pigot's directory of Buckinghamshire, 1844. 2 fiche. £6.00; $A15.00.

Musson's directory of Buckinghamshire, 1853. Forthcoming.

Kelly's directory of Buckinghamshire, 1854. Forthcoming.

Kelly's directory of Buckinghamshire, 1864. 4 fiche. £12.00; $A27.00.

Kelly's directory of Buckinghamshire, 1877. 3 fiche. £9.00; $A21.00.

Kelly's directory of Buckinghamshire, 1891. 4 fiche. £12.00; $A27.00.

Kelly's directory of Buckinghamshire, 1899. 5 fiche. £15.00; $A33.00.

Kelly's directory of Buckinghamshire, 1915. Forthcoming.

Kelly's directory of Buckinghamshire, 1920. Forthcoming.

Cambridgeshire

Holden's directory of Cambridge, 1805. 1 fiche. £3.00; $A9.00.

Pigot's directory of Cambridgeshire, 1823. 1 fiche. £3.00; $A9.00.

Pigot's directory of Cambridgeshire, 1830. 1 fiche. £3.00; $A9.00.

Pigot's directory of Cambridgeshire, 1839. 2 fiche. £6.00; $A15.00.

Kelly's directory of Cambridgeshire, 1846. Forthcoming.

Gardner's directory of Cambridgeshire, 1851. 6 fiche. £18.00; $A39.00.

Kelly's directory of Cambridgeshire, 1858. Forthcoming.

Nick Vine Hall (*cont.*)
Cassey's directory of Cambridgeshire, 1864. 4 fiche. £12.00; $A27.00.
Kelly's directory of Cambridgeshire, 1879. 3 fiche. £9.00; $A21.00.
Kelly's directory of Cambridgeshire, 1883. Forthcoming.
Kelly's directory of Cambridgeshire, 1900. 6 fiche. £18.00; $A39.00.
Kelly's directory of Cambridgeshire, 1912. Forthcoming.
Kelly's directory of Cambridgeshire, 1925. Forthcoming.

Channel Islands
Kelly's directory of the Channel Islands, 1911. 5 fiche. £15.00; $A33.00.
Kelly's directory of the Channel Islands, 1931. Forthcoming.

Cheshire
Holden's directory of Chester, Stockport & Macclesfield, 1805. 1 fiche. £3.00; $A9.00.
Pigot's directory of Cheshire (part), 1816. Forthcoming.
Pigot's directory of Cheshire, 1822. Forthcoming.
Baines' directory of North East Cheshire, 1825. 1 fiche. £3.00; $A9.00.
Pigot's directory of Cheshire, 1830. Forthcoming.
Pigot's directory of Cheshire, 1834. Forthcoming.
Pigot's directory of Cheshire, North East, 1832. 1 fiche. £3.00; $A9.00.
Pigot's directory of Cheshire (part), 1841. Forthcoming.
Slater's directory of Cheshire, 1848. 1 fiche. £3.00; $A9.00.
Bagshaw's directory of Cheshire, 1850. 4 fiche. £12.00; $A27.00.
Slater's directory of Cheshire, 1855. Forthcoming.
Morris's directory of Cheshire, 1874. 8 fiche. £24.00; $A51.00.
Kelly's directory of Cheshire, 1896. Forthcoming.
Kelly's directory of Cheshire, 1914. Forthcoming.
Kelly's directory of Cheshire, 1928. Forthcoming.

Cornwall
Holden's directory of Falmouth, Truro and Penryn, 1805. 1 fiche. £3.00; $A9.00.

Pigot's directory of Cornwall, 1823. 1 fiche. £3.00; $A9.00.
Pigot's directory of Cornwall, 1830. 1 fiche. £3.00; $A9.00.
Pigot's directory of Cornwall, 1844. 3 fiche. £9.00; $A21.00.
Slater's directory of Cornwall, 1852. 3 fiche. £9.00; $A21.00.
Kelly's directory of Cornwall, 1889. Forthcoming.
Venning's directory of East Cornwall, 1901. Forthcoming.
Kelly's directory of Cornwall, 1902. Forthcoming.
Kelly's directory of Cornwall, 1910. 7 fiche. £21.00; $A45.00.
Kelly's directory of Cornwall, 1923. 7 fiche. £21.00; $A45.00.
Kelly's directory of Cornwall, 1930. Forthcoming.

Cumberland
Holden's directory of Carlisle and Whitehaven, 1805. 1 fiche. £3.00; $A9.00.
Pigot's directory of Cumberland, 1820. Forthcoming.
Pigot's directory of Cumberland, 1828. Forthcoming.
Pigot's directory of Cumberland, 1834. Forthcoming.
Slater's directory of Carlisle, 1837. 1 fiche. £3.00; $A9.00.
Mannix's directory of Cumberland, 1847. 4 fiche. £12.00; $A27.00.
Slater's directory of Cumberland, 1855. Forthcoming.
Slater's directory of Cumberland, 1879. 3 fiche. £9.00; $A21.00.
Patterson's directory of Whitehaven, 1883. Forthcoming.
Bulmer's directory of East Cumberland, 1884. Forthcoming.
Kelly's directory of Cumberland, 1897. 7 fiche. £21.00; $A45.00.
Bulmer's directory of Cumberland, 1901. Forthcoming.
Kelly's directory of Cumberland, 1925. Forthcoming.
Kelly's directory of Cumberland, 1929. Forthcoming.

Derbyshire
Holden's directory of Chesterfield and Derby, 1805. 1 fiche. £3.00; $A9.00.
Pigot's directory of Derbyshire, 1822. Forthcoming.

Baines' directory of Glossop, 1825. 1 fiche.
£3.00; $A9.00.
*Pigot's directory of North West
Derbyshire, 1832.* 1 fiche. £3.00; $A9.00.
Pigot's directory of Derbyshire, 1835.
1 fiche. £3.00; $A9.00.
Kelly's directory of Derbyshire, 1848.
Forthcoming.
White's directory of Chesterfield, 1849.
Forthcoming.
Slater's directory of Derbyshire, 1850.
Forthcoming.
*White's directory of North Derbyshire,
1852.* 2 fiche. £6.00; $A15.00.
White's directory of Derbyshire, 1857.
5 fiche. £15.00; $A33.00.
*White's directory of North Derbyshire,
1868.* 1 fiche. £3.00; $A9.00.
Kelly's directory of Derbyshire, 1876.
6 fiche. £18.00; $A39.00.
Kelly's directory of Derbyshire, 1888.
Forthcoming.
Bulmer's directory of Derbyshire, 1895.
6 fiche. £18.00; $A39.00.
Kelly's directory of Derbyshire, 1908.
Forthcoming.
Kelly's directory of Derbyshire, 1916.
Forthcoming.
Kelly's directory of Derbyshire, 1928.
Forthcoming.

Devon
*Holden's directory of Exeter, Plymouth
and Tiverton, 1805.* 1 fiche. £3.00;
$A9.00.
Pigot's directory of Devon, 1823. 1 fiche.
£3.00; $A9.00.
Pigot's directory of Devon, 1830. 1 fiche.
£3.00; $A9.00.
Pigot's directory of Devon, 1844. 4 fiche.
£12.00; $A27.00.
White's directory of Devon, 1850. 5 fiche.
£15.00; $A33.00.
Slater's directory of Devon, 1852. 3 fiche.
£9.00; $A21.00.
White's directory of Devon, 1878.
Forthcoming.
Kelly's directory of Devon, 1889. 12 fiche.
£36.00; $A75.00.
White's directory of Devon, 1890. 15 fiche.
£45.00; $A93.00.
Kelly's directory of Devon, 1902.
Forthcoming.
Kelly's directory of Devon, 1910. 15 fiche.
£45.00; $A93.00.

Kelly's directory of Devon, 1923. 15 fiche.
£45.00; $A93.00.

Dorset
Holden's directory of Sherborne, 1805.
1 fiche. £3.00; $A9.00.
Pigot's directory of Dorset, 1823. 1 fiche.
£3.00; $A9.00.
Pigot's directory of Dorset, 1830. 1 fiche.
£3.00; $A9.00.
Pigot's directory of Dorset, 1844. 3 fiche.
£9.00; $A21.00.
Slater's directory of Dorset, 1852. 2 fiche.
£6.00; $A15.00.
Kelly's directory of Dorset, 1867. 4 fiche.
£12.00; $A27.00.
Kelly's directory of Dorset, 1875. 5 fiche.
£15.00; $A33.00.
Kelly's directory of Dorset, 1895.
Forthcoming.
Kelly's directory of Dorset, 1903.
Forthcoming.
Kelly's directory of Dorset, 1920.
Forthcoming.
Kelly's directory of Dorset, 1927.
Forthcoming.
Kelly's directory of Dorset, 1931.
Forthcoming.

Co.Durham
*Holden's directory of Gateshead &
Sunderland, 1805.* 1 fiche. £3.00; $A9.00.
*Pigot's directory of Darlington, Durham,
South Shields and Sunderland, 1820.*
Forthcoming.
Pigot's directory of Co. Durham, 1828.
1 fiche. £3.00; $A9.00.
Pigot's directory of Co. Durham, 1834.
1 fiche. £3.00; $A9.00.
Slater's directory of Co. Durham, 1848.
Forthcoming.
*Slater's directory of Gateshead & district,
1855.* Forthcoming.
Whellan's directory of Co. Durham, 1856.
6 fiche. £18.00; $A39.00.
Kelly's directory of Co. Durham, 1879.
7 fiche. £21.00; $A45.00.
Whellan's directory of Co. Durham, 1894.
14 fiche. £42.00; $A87.00.
Kelly's directory of Co. Durham, 1906.
9 fiche. £27.00; $A57.00.
Kelly's directory of Co. Durham, 1921.
Forthcoming.
*Ward's directory of North East Co.
Durham, 1928.* Forthcoming.

Nick Vine Hall (*cont.*)

Essex

Holden's directory of Colchester, 1805.
1 fiche. £3.00; $A9.00.

Pigot's directory of Essex, 1823. 2 fiche.
£6.00; $A15.00.

Pigot's directory of Essex, 1839.
Forthcoming.

Kelly's directory of Essex, 1846. 3 fiche.
£9.00; $A21.00.

White's directory of Essex, 1848. 4 fiche.
£12.00; $A27.00.

Kelly's directory of Essex, 1855. 9 fiche.
£27.00; $A57.00.

Kelly's directory of Essex, 1862.
Forthcoming.

White's directory of Essex, 1863. 5 fiche.
£15.00; $A33.00.

Kelly's directory of Essex, 1871.
Forthcoming.

Kelly's directory of Essex, 1896.
Forthcoming.

Kelly's directory of Essex, 1898. 9 fiche.
£27.00; $A57.00.

Kelly's directory of Essex, 1908.
Forthcoming.

Kelly's directory of Essex, 1933.
Forthcoming.

Gloucestershire & Bristol

Matthews' directory of Bristol, 1793.
Forthcoming.

Pigot's directory of Bristol, 1824.
Forthcoming.

Mathews' directory of Bristol, 1826.
Forthcoming.

*Pigot's directory of Gloucestershire (exc.
Bristol), 1822.* Forthcoming.

*Pigot's directory of Gloucestershire (inc.
Bristol), 1830.* Forthcoming.

Mathews' directory of Bristol, 1841.
Forthcoming.

*Pigot's directory of Gloucestershire (inc.
Bristol), 1844.* Forthcoming.

Mathews' directory of Bristol, 1846. 3 fiche.
£9.00; $A21.00.

Mathews' directory of Bristol, 1847.
Forthcoming.

Hunt's directory of Gloucester, 1847.
Forthcoming.

*Slater's directory of Gloucestershire
(inc. Bristol), 1852.* 3 fiche. £9.00;
$A21.00.

*Mathews' directory of Bristol & Clifton,
1854.* Forthcoming.

Slater's directory of Bristol, 1855.
Forthcoming.

*Slater's directory of Gloucestershire (inc.
Bristol), 1858.* 3 fiche. £9.00; $A21.00.

*Kelly's directory of Gloucestershire
(exc. Bristol), 1863.* 5 fiche. £15.00;
$A33.00.

*Kelly's directory of Gloucestershire (inc.
Bristol), 1870.* 6 fiche. £18.00; $A39.00.

*Deacon's directory of Gloucestershire (inc.
Bristol), 1880.* Forthcoming.

*Wright's directory of Bristol & Clifton,
1881.* Forthcoming.

*Kelly's directory of Gloucestershire (inc.
Bristol), 1889.* Forthcoming.

*Kelly's directory of Gloucestershire (exc.
Bristol), 1894.* 8 fiche. £24.00; $A51.00.

*Kelly's directory of Gloucestershire (exc.
Bristol), 1902.* 8 fiche. £24.00; $A51.00.

*Kelly's directory of Gloucestershire (exc.
Bristol), 1914.* 7 fiche. £21.00; $A45.00.

*Kelly's directory of Gloucestershire (inc.
Bristol), 1927.* 8 fiche. £24.00; $A51.00.

Kelly's directory of Bristol, 1932.
Forthcoming.

Hampshire

*Holden's directory of Portsmouth,
Winchester & Southampton, 1805.* 1 fiche.
£3.00; $A9.00.

*Pigot's directory of Hampshire (inc. Isle of
Wight), 1823.* 1 fiche. £3.00; $A9.00.

*Pigot's directory of Hampshire (inc. Isle of
Wight), 1830.* 1 fiche. £3.00; $A9.00.

*Pigot's directory of Hampshire (exc. Isle of
Wight), 1844.* Forthcoming.

Pigot's directory of the Isle of Wight, 1844.
Forthcoming.

*Slater's directory of Hampshire (exc. Isle of
Wight), 1852.* Forthcoming.

Slater's directory of the Isle of Wight, 1852.
Forthcoming.

*White's directory of the Isle of Wight,
1859.* 1 fiche. £3.00; $A9.00.

*White's directory of Hampshire (exc. Isle
of Wight), 1859.* 4 fiche. £12.00;
$A27.00.

*Kelly's directory of Hampshire (inc. Isle of
Wight), 1867.* 7 fiche. £21.00; $A45.00.

Kelly's directory of the Isle of Wight, 1867.
2 fiche. £6.00; $A15.00.

*Kelly's directory of Hampshire (exc. Isle of
Wight), 1875.* 7 fiche. £21.00; $A45.00.

Kelly's directory of the Isle of Wight, 1875.
2 fiche. £6.00; $A15.00.

White's directory of Hampshire (inc. Isle of Wight), 1878. 10 fiche. £30.00; $A63.00.
Kelly's directory of Hampshire (inc. Isle of Wight), 1895. 12 fiche. £36.00; $A75.00.
Kelly's directory of Hampshire (inc. Isle of Wight), 1903. Forthcoming.
Kelly's directory of Hampshire (exc. Isle of Wight), 1920. Forthcoming.
Kelly's directory of the Isle of Wight, 1920. Forthcoming.
Kelly's directory of Hampshire (exc. Isle of Wight), 1931. Forthcoming.
Kelly's directory of the Isle of Wight, 1931. Forthcoming.

Herefordshire
Pigot's directory of Herefordshire, 1822. Forthcoming.
Pigot's directory of Herefordshire, 1830. Forthcoming.
Pigot's directory of Herefordshire, 1835. 1 fiche. £3.00; $A9.00.
Pigot's directory of Herefordshire, 1842. Forthcoming.
Pigot's directory of Herefordshire, 1844. Forthcoming.
Hunt's directory of Hereford, Ross & Ledbury, 1847. Forthcoming.
Slater's directory of Herefordshire, 1850. Forthcoming.
Cassey's directory of Herefordshire, 1858. Forthcoming.
Directory of Herefordshire, 1863. Forthcoming.
Kelly's directory of Herefordshire, 1870. Forthcoming.
Kelly's directory of Herefordshire, 1885. Forthcoming.
Wells' directory of Herefordshire, 1888. Forthcoming.
Kelly's directory of Herefordshire, 1900. Forthcoming.
Kelly's directory of Herefordshire, 1909. Forthcoming.
Kelly's directory of Herefordshire, 1917. Forthcoming.
Kelly's directory of Herefordshire, 1926. Forthcoming.

Hertfordshire
Pigot's directory of Hertfordshire, 1823. 1 fiche. £3.00; $A9.00.
Pigot's directory of Hertfordshire, 1839. 2 fiche. £6.00; $A15.00.
Kelly's directory of Hertfordshire, 1846. Forthcoming.

Kelly's directory of Hertfordshire, 1855. 9 fiche. £27.00; $A57.00.
Kelly's directory of Hertfordshire, 1862. Forthcoming.
Cassey's directory of Hertfordshire, 1864. 4 fiche. £12.00; $A27.00.
Kelly's directory of Hertfordshire, 1874. Forthcoming.
Kelly's directory of Hertfordshire, 1886. Forthcoming.
Kelly's directory of Hertfordshire, 1899. Forthcoming.
Kelly's directory of Hertfordshire, 1908. Forthcoming.
Kelly's directory of Hertfordshire, 1933. Forthcoming.

Huntingdonshire
Pigot's directory of Huntingdonshire, 1823. 1 fiche. £3.00; $A9.00.
Pigot's directory of Huntingdonshire, 1830. 1 fiche. £3.00; $A9.00.
Pigot's directory of Huntingdonshire, 1839. 2 fiche. £6.00; $A15.00.
Slater's directory of Huntingdonshire, 1850. 2 fiche. £6.00; $A15.00.
Kelly's directory of Huntingdonshire, 1854. Forthcoming.
Kelly's directory of Huntingdonshire, 1864. 2 fiche. £6.00; $A15.00.
Kelly's directory of Huntingdonshire, 1877. Forthcoming.
Kelly's directory of Huntingdonshire, 1898. 3 fiche. £9.00; $A21.00.

Isle of Man
Pigot's directory of the Isle of Man, 1824. Forthcoming.
Slater's directory of the Isle of Man, 1837. 1 fiche. £3.00; $A9.00.
Post Office directory of the Isle of Man, 1936. Forthcoming.

Kent
Holden's directory of Canterbury, Chatham, Maidstone, Rochester & Strood, 1805. 1 fiche. £3.00; $A9.00.
Pigot's directory of Kent, 1823. 2 fiche. £6.00; $A15.00.
Kelly's directory of Kent, 1846. Forthcoming.
Bagshaw's directory of West Kent, 1847. 4 fiche. £12.00; $A27.00.
Bagshaw's directory of East Kent, 1847. Forthcoming.
Kelly's directory of Kent, 1855. 10 fiche. £30.00; $A63.00.

17

Nick Vine Hall (*cont.*)
Kelly's directory of Kent, 1862.
Forthcoming.
Kelly's directory of Kent, 1895. 13 fiche.
£39.00; $A81.00.
Kelly's directory of Kent, 1918.
Forthcoming.
Kelly's directory of Kent, 1922.
Forthcoming.
Kelly's directory of Kent, 1938.
Forthcoming.

Lancashire
Shaw's directory of Liverpool, 1769.
Forthcoming.
Raffald's directory of Manchester, 1773.
Forthcoming.
Gore's directory of Liverpool, 1796.
Forthcoming.
Holden's directory of Blackburn, Bolton,
Lancaster, Liverpool, Manchester,
Preston, Rochdale, Warrington & Wigan,
1805. 1 fiche. £3.00; $A9.00.
Pigot's directory of Manchester & Salford,
1813. Forthcoming.
Pigot's directory of Lancashire (part), 1816.
Forthcoming.
Pigot's directory of Lancashire, 1822.
Forthcoming.
Pigot's directory of Liverpool &
Manchester, 1824. Forthcoming.
Baines's directory of Lancashire (pt. 1),
1824. 4 fiche. £12.00; $A27.00. Includes
Liverpool.
Baines's directory of Lancashire (pt. 2),
1825. 5 fiche. £15.00; $A33.00. Includes
Manchester.
Parson's directory of North Lancashire,
1829. 2 fiche. £6.00; $A15.00.
Pigot's directory of Manchester & Salford,
1832. 4 fiche. £12.00; $A27.00.
Pigot's directory of Lancashire, 1834.
Forthcoming.
Slater's directory of Liverpool &
Manchester, 1837. 1 fiche. £3.00; $A9.00.
Pigot's directory of Manchester & Salford,
1841. 3 fiche. £9.00; $A21.00.
Slater's directory of Lancashire, 1848.
7 fiche. £21.00; $A45.00.
Mannex's directory of Furness & Cartmel,
1849. Forthcoming.
Gore's directory of Liverpool, 1851.
Forthcoming.
Mannex's directory of North Lancashire,
1851. 2 fiche. £6.00; $A15.00.

Slater's directory of Lancashire, 1855.
Forthcoming.
Slater's directory of Liverpool, 1858.
1 fiche. £3.00; $A9.00.
Kelly's directory of Lancashire (exc.
Liverpool), 1864. 6 fiche. £18.00;
$A39.00.
Mannex's directory of Furness & Cartmel,
1882. Forthcoming.
Barrett's directory of Preston, 1889. 4 fiche.
£12.00; $A27.00.
Town & County directory of Blackburn,
1900. Forthcoming.
Slater's directory of Prestwich, 1900.
Forthcoming.
Deacon's directory of Lancashire, 1903.
8 fiche. £24.00; $A51.00.
Bulmer's directory of Furness & Cartmel,
1910. Forthcoming.
Bulmer's directory of Lancashire, 1913.
Forthcoming.
Kelly's directory of Manchester, 1933.
Forthcoming.
Kelly's directory of Liverpool, 1934.
Forthcoming.

Leicestershire
Holden's directory of Hinckley & Leicester,
1805. 1 fiche. £3.00; $A9.00.
Holden's directory of Leicester, 1808.
Forthcoming.
Pigot's directory of Leicestershire, 1822.
Forthcoming.
Pigot's directory of Leicestershire, 1841.
1 fiche. £3.00; $A9.00.
Kelly's directory of Leicestershire, 1848.
Forthcoming.
Slater's directory of Leicestershire, 1850.
Forthcoming.
Melville's directory of Leicestershire, 1854.
Forthcoming.
White's directory of Leicestershire, 1862.
5 fiche. £15.00; $A33.00.
Pigot's directory of Leicestershire, 1862.
2 fiche. £6.00; $A15.00.
White's directory of Leicestershire, 1877.
10 fiche. £30.00; $A63.00.
Kelly's directory of Leicestershire, 1888.
Forthcoming.
Wright's directory of Leicestershire, 1896.
Forthcoming.
Kelly's directory of Leicestershire, 1916.
Forthcoming.
Kelly's directory of Leicestershire, 1928.
Forthcoming.

Kelly's directory of Leicestershire, 1932.
Forthcoming.

Lincolnshire
Holden's directory of Boston, Lincoln, Gainsborough & Stamford, 1805. 1 fiche. £3.00; $A9.00.
Pigot's directory of Lincolnshire, 1822. Forthcoming.
Pigot's directory of Lincolnshire, 1830. 1 fiche. £3.00; $A9.00.
Pigot's directory of Lincolnshire, 1841. 1 fiche. £3.00; $A9.00.
Kelly's directory of Lincolnshire, 1850. Forthcoming.
White's directory of Lincolnshire, 1856. 6 fiche. £18.00; $A39.00.
Johnson's directory of Lincolnshire, 1865. 4 fiche. £12.00; $A27.00.
Kelly's directory of Lincolnshire, 1876. Forthcoming.
Kelly's directory of Lincolnshire, 1889. Forthcoming.
Kelly's directory of Lincolnshire, 1913. Forthcoming.
Kelly's directory of Lincolnshire, 1922. Forthcoming.

London
Longman's directory of London, 1772. Forthcoming.
Holden's directory of London (pt. 1), 1805. 4 fiche. £12.00; $A27.00.
Holden's directory of London (pt. 2), 1805. 2 fiche. £6.00; $A15.00.
Critchett's directory of London, 1814. 4 fiche. £12.00; $A27.00.
Critchett's directory of London, 1817. Forthcoming.
Kent's directory of London, 1821. 3 fiche. £9.00; $A21.00.
Pigot's directory of London, 1822. Forthcoming.
Pigot's directory of London, 1823. 4 fiche. £12.00; $A27.00.
Pigot's directory of London, 1824. Forthcoming.
Critchett's directory of London, 1831. Forthcoming.
Robson's directory of London, 1833. 6 fiche. £18.00; $A39.00.
Critchett's directory of London, 1834. 5 fiche. £15.00; $A33.00.
Kelly's directory of London, 1842. 9 fiche. £27.00; $A57.00.

Kelly's directory of London, 1846. 23 fiche. £69.00; $A141.00.
Kelly's directory of London, 1850. 13 fiche. £39.00; $A81.00.
Kelly's directory of London suburbs, 1860. 9 fiche. £27.00; $A57.00.
Kelly's directory of London, 1862. 44 fiche. £132.00; $A267.00.
Kelly's directory of London, 1874. 49 fiche. £147.00; $A297.00.
Kelly's directory of London, 1880. 33 fiche. £99.00; $A201.00.
Coll'dge's directory of London, 1891. Forthcoming.
London Directory Co's directory of London, 1896. Forthcoming.
Kelly's directory of London, 1909. 48 fiche. £144.00; $A291.00.
Kelly's directory of London, 1916. Forthcoming.
Kelly's directory of London, 1922. Forthcoming.
Kelly's directory of London, 1934. Forthcoming.

Middlesex
Pigot's directory of Middlesex, 1823. 1 fiche. £3.00; $A9.00.
Pigot's directory of Middlesex, 1839. 1 fiche. £3.00; $A9.00.
Kelly's directory of Middlesex, 1846. 7 fiche. £21.00; $A45.00.
Kelly's directory of Middlesex, 1855. 9 fiche. £27.00; $A57.00.
Kelly's directory of Middlesex, 1862. Forthcoming.
Kelly's directory of Middlesex, 1882. 11 fiche. £33.00; $A69.00.
Kelly's directory of Middlesex, 1899. Forthcoming.
Kelly's directory of Middlesex, 1908. Forthcoming.
Kelly's directory of Middlesex (part), 1924. Forthcoming.
Kelly's directory of Middlesex, 1933. Forthcoming.

Monmouthshire
Pigot's directory of Monmouthshire, 1822. Forthcoming.
Pigot's directory of Monmouthshire, 1830. Forthcoming.
Pigot's directory of Monmouthshire, 1835. Forthcoming.
Pigot's directory of Monmouthshire, 1844. Forthcoming.

Nick Vine Hall (*cont.*)

Slater's directory of Monmouthshire, 1850. Forthcoming.

Slater's directory of Monmouthshire, 1858. 2 fiche. £6.00; $A15.00.

Slater's directory of Monmouthshire, 1880. 3 fiche. £9.00; $A21.00.

Kelly's directory of Monmouthshire, 1891. Forthcoming.

Kelly's directory of Monmouthshire, 1901. Forthcoming.

Kelly's directory of Monmouthshire, 1923. Forthcoming.

Norfolk

Holden's directory of Lynn Regis, Norwich & Great Yarmouth, 1805. 1 fiche. £3.00; $A9.00.

Pigot's directory of Norfolk, 1822. Forthcoming.

Pigot's directory of Norfolk, 1830. Forthcoming.

White's directory of Norfolk, 1836. Forthcoming.

Pigot's directory of Norfolk, 1839. 2 fiche. £6.00; $A15.00.

White's directory of Norfolk, 1845. 5 fiche. £15.00; $A33.00.

Kelly's directory of Norfolk, 1846. Forthcoming.

Slater's directory of Norfolk, 1850. 2 fiche. £6.00; $A15.00.

Kelly's directory of Norfolk, 1858. Forthcoming.

Kelly's directory of Norfolk, 1869. 7 fiche. £21.00; $A45.00.

Kelly's directory of Norfolk, 1875. Forthcoming.

Kelly's directory of Norfolk, 1879. Forthcoming.

White's directory of Norfolk, 1883. 13 fiche. £39.00; $A81.00.

Kelly's directory of Norfolk, 1896. Forthcoming.

Kelly's directory of Norfolk, 1912. Forthcoming.

Kelly's directory of Norfolk, 1916. Forthcoming.

Kelly's directory of Norfolk, 1925. Forthcoming.

Kelly's directory of Norfolk, 1937. Forthcoming.

Northamptonshire

Pigot's directory of Northamptonshire, 1823. 1 fiche. £3.00; $A9.00.

Pigot's directory of Northamptonshire, 1830. 1 fiche. £3.00; $A9.00.

Pigot's directory of Northamptonshire, 1841. 1 fiche. £3.00; $A9.00.

Kelly's directory of Northamptonshire, 1848. Forthcoming.

Slater's directory of Northamptonshire, 1850. 2 fiche. £6.00; $A15.00.

Kelly's directory of Northamptonshire, 1864. 4 fiche. £12.00; $A27.00.

Whellan's directory of Northamptonshire, 1874. 10 fiche. £30.00; $A63.00.

Kelly's directory of Northamptonshire, 1877. Forthcoming.

Kelly's directory of Northamptonshire, 1898. 6 fiche. £18.00; $A39.00.

Kelly's directory of Northamptonshire, 1910. Forthcoming.

Northumberland

Whitehead's directory of Newcastle, 1778. Forthcoming.

Holden's directory of Berwick, 1805. 1 fiche. £3.00; $A9.00.

Holden's directory of Newcastle, 1805. 1 fiche. £3.00; $A9.00.

Pigot's directory of Alnwick, Berwick on Tweed, Morpeth, Newcastle upon Tyne, & North Shields, 1820. Forthcoming.

Pigot's directory of Northumberland, 1828. Forthcoming.

Pigot's directory of Northumberland, 1834. Forthcoming.

Slater's directory of Newcastle & Gateshead, 1837. 1 fiche. £3.00; $A9.00.

Slater's directory of Northumberland, 1848. Forthcoming.

Whellan's directory of Northumberland, 1855. 11 fiche. £33.00; $A69.00.

Kelly's directory of Northumberland, 1879. 7 fiche. £21.00; $A45.00.

Bulmer's directory of Northumberland (West), 1886. Forthcoming.

Bulmer's directory of Northumberland (East), 1887. 6 fiche. £18.00; $A39.00.

Kelly's directory of Northumberland, 1914. Forthcoming.

Ward's directory of Newcastle etc., 1928. Forthcoming.

Ward's directory of Whitley Bay, Tynemouth, North and South Shields, Jarrow, Wallsend, Gosforth, Newcastle on Tyne, 1936. Forthcoming.

Nottinghamshire

Holden's directory of Newark & Nottingham, 1805. 1 fiche. £3.00; $A9.00.
Pigot's directory of Nottinghamshire, 1822. Forthcoming.
Pigot's directory of Nottinghamshire, 1828. 1 fiche. £3.00; $A9.00.
Pigot's directory of Nottinghamshire, 1841. 1 fiche. £3.00; $A9.00.
Kelly's directory of Nottinghamshire, 1848. Forthcoming.
Slater's directory of Nottinghamshire, 1850. Forthcoming.
White's directory of Nottinghamshire, 1852. 2 fiche. £6.00; $A15.00.
White's directory of Nottinghamshire, 1853. Forthcoming.
White's directory of Nottinghamshire, 1864. 5 fiche. £15.00; $A33.00.
White's directory of North Nottinghamshire, 1868. 1 fiche. £3.00; $A9.00.
Kelly's directory of Nottinghamshire, 1876. Forthcoming.
Kelly's directory of Nottinghamshire, 1888. Forthcoming.
Kelly's directory of Nottinghamshire, 1895. Forthcoming.
Kelly's directory of Nottinghamshire, 1916. Forthcoming.

Oxfordshire

Holden's directory of Oxford, 1805. 1 fiche. £3.00; $A9.00.
Pigot's directory of Oxfordshire, 1823. 1 fiche. £3.00; $A9.00.
Pigot's directory of Oxfordshire, 1830. 1 fiche. £3.00; $A9.00.
Pigot's directory of Oxfordshire, 1844. Forthcoming.
Kelly's directory of Oxfordshire, 1848. Forthcoming.
Kelly's directory of Oxfordshire, 1864. 4 fiche. £12.00; $A27.00.
Kelly's directory of Oxfordshire, 1877. Forthcoming.
Kelly's directory of Oxfordshire, 1887. Forthcoming.
Kelly's directory of Oxfordshire, 1891. 6 fiche. £18.00; $A39.00.
Kelly's directory of Oxfordshire, 1899. Forthcoming.
Kelly's directory of Oxfordshire, 1915. Forthcoming.

Kelly's directory of Oxfordshire, 1920. Forthcoming.
Kelly's directory of Oxfordshire, 1931. Forthcoming.

Rutland

Pigot's directory of Rutland, 1822. Forthcoming.
Pigot's directory of Rutland, 1828. 1 fiche. £3.00; $A9.00.
Pigot's directory of Rutland, 1835. Forthcoming.
Pigot's directory of Rutland, 1841. 1 fiche. £3.00; $A9.00.
Kelly's directory of Rutland, 1848. Forthcoming.
Slater's directory of Rutland, 1850. Forthcoming.
White's directory of Rutland, 1862. 1 fiche. £3.00; $A9.00.
White's directory of Rutland, 1877. 4 fiche. £12.00; $A27.00.
Kelly's directory of Rutland, 1888. Forthcoming.
Wright's directory of Rutland, 1896. Forthcoming.
Kelly's directory of Rutland, 1916. Forthcoming.
Kelly's directory of Rutland, 1928. Forthcoming.

Shropshire

Pigot's directory of Shropshire, 1822. Forthcoming.
Pigot's directory of Shropshire, 1828. Forthcoming.
Pigot's directory of Shropshire, 1835. Forthcoming.
Pigot's directory of Shropshire, 1842. Forthcoming.
Slater's directory of Shropshire, 1850. Forthcoming.
Bagshaw's directory of Shropshire, 1851. 5 fiche. £15.00; $A33.00.
Cassey's directory of Shropshire, 1871. Forthcoming.
Slater's directory of Shropshire, 1880. Forthcoming.
Porter's directory of Shropshire, 1888. 4 fiche. £12.00; $A27.00.
Kelly's directory of Shropshire, 1895. Forthcoming.
Kelly's directory of Shropshire, 1909. Forthcoming.
Kelly's directory of Shropshire, 1917. Forthcoming.

Nick Vine Hall (*cont.*)
Kelly's directory of Shropshire, 1926.
Forthcoming.

Somerset
*Holden's directory of Bristol, Bath,
Bridgewater & Frome, 1805.* 1 fiche.
£3.00; $A9.00.
Pigot's directory of Somerset, 1822.
Forthcoming.
Pigot's directory of Somerset, 1830.
Forthcoming.
Pigot's directory of Somerset, 1844.
Forthcoming.
*Hunt's directory of South West Somerset,
1848.* 1 fiche. £3.00; $A9.00.
*Hunt's directory of North West Somerset,
1850.* 1 fiche. £3.00; $A9.00.
*Hunt's directory of East central Somerset,
1850.* 1 fiche. £3.00; $A9.00.
Slater's directory of Somerset, 1852. 2 fiche.
£6.00; $A15.00.
*Kelly's directory of Somerset (inc. Bristol),
1861.* Forthcoming.
Kelly's directory of Somerset, 1875. 8 fiche.
£24.00; $A51.00.
*Deacon's directory of North East Somerset,
1888.* Forthcoming.
Kelly's directory of Somerset, 1889. 8 fiche.
£24.00; $A51.00.
*Kelly's directory of Somerset (inc. Bristol),
1894.* Forthcoming.
*Kelly's directory of Somerset (inc. Bristol),
1902.* 16 fiche. £48.00; $A99.00.
Lewis's directory of Bath, 1910.
Forthcoming.
*Kelly's directory of Somerset (inc. Bristol),
1923.* 11 fiche. £33.00; $A69.00.

Staffordshire
*Holden's directory of Leek, Walsall &
Wolverhampton, 1805.* 1 fiche. £3.00;
$A9.00.
*Pigot's directory of Leek &
Wolverhampton, 1816.* Forthcoming.
Pigot's directory of Staffordshire, 1822.
Forthcoming.
*Wrightson's directory of South East
Staffordshire, 1823.* 1 fiche. £3.00; $A9.00.
*Pigot's directory of South Staffordshire,
1829.* 1 fiche. £3.00; $A9.00.
Pigot's directory of Staffordshire, 1842.
Forthcoming.
Pigot's directory of Staffordshire, 1850.
Forthcoming.

White's directory of Staffordshire, 1851.
5 fiche. £15.00; $A33.00.
*White's directory of Burton-upon-Trent,
1857.* 1 fiche. £3.00; $A9.00.
Slater's directory of Staffordshire, 1862.
3 fiche. £9.00; $A21.00.
Kelly's directory of Staffordshire, 1872.
10 fiche. £30.00; $A63.00.
Kelly's directory of Staffordshire, 1900.
11 fiche. £33.00; $A69.00.
Kelly's directory of Staffordshire, 1924.
12 fiche. £36.00; $A75.00.

Suffolk
Holden's directory of Ipswich, 1805. 1 fiche.
£3.00; $A9.00.
Pigot's directory of Suffolk, 1823. 1 fiche.
£3.00; $A9.00.
Pigot's directory of Suffolk, 1830.
Forthcoming.
Pigot's directory of Suffolk, 1839.
Forthcoming.
White's directory of Suffolk, 1844. 5 fiche.
£15.00; $A33.00.
Kelly's directory of Suffolk, 1846.
Forthcoming.
Slater's directory of Suffolk, 1850. 2 fiche.
£6.00; $A15.00.
White's directory of Suffolk, 1855.
Forthcoming.
Kelly's directory of Suffolk, 1858.
Forthcoming.
Harrod's directory of Suffolk, 1864. 4 fiche.
£12.00; $A27.00.
White's directory of Suffolk, 1874.
Forthcoming.
Kelly's directory of Suffolk, 1883. 5 fiche.
£15.00; $A33.00.
Kelly's directory of Suffolk, 1896. 7 fiche.
£21.00; $A45.00.
Kelly's directory of Suffolk, 1900.
Forthcoming.
Kelly's directory of Suffolk, 1908.
Forthcoming.
Kelly's directory of Suffolk, 1912.
Forthcoming.
Kelly's directory of Suffolk, 1925.
Forthcoming.

Surrey
Pigot's directory of Surrey, 1823. 1 fiche.
£3.00; $A9.00.
Pigot's directory of Surrey, 1839. 2 fiche.
£6.00; $A15.00.
Kelly's directory of Surrey, 1846. 7 fiche.
£21.00; $A45.00.

Kelly's directory of Surrey, 1855. 9 fiche.
£27.00; $A57.00.
Kelly's directory of Surrey, 1862.
Forthcoming.
Church's directory of Sutton, 1880.
Forthcoming.
Kelly's directory of Surrey, 1895. 11 fiche.
£33.00; $A69.00.
Kelly's directory of Surrey, 1910.
Forthcoming.

Sussex
Holden's directory of Chichester, 1805.
1 fiche. £3.00; $A9.00.
Pigot's directory of Sussex, 1823. 1 fiche.
£3.00; $A9.00.
Pigot's directory of Sussex, 1832.
Forthcoming.
Pigot's directory of Sussex, 1839. 2 fiche.
£6.00; $A15.00.
Kelly's directory of Sussex, 1846.
Forthcoming.
Kelly's directory of Sussex, 1855. 9 fiche.
£27.00; $A57.00.
Melville's directory of Sussex, 1858. 4 fiche.
£12.00; $A27.00.
Kelly's directory of Sussex, 1862.
Forthcoming.
Kelly's directory of Sussex, 1913.
Forthcoming.
Kelly's directory of Sussex, 1871.
Forthcoming.
Kelly's directory of Sussex, 1895. 12 fiche.
£36.00; $A75.00.
Kelly's directory of Sussex, 1905.
Forthcoming.

Warwickshire
Pearson's directory of Birmingham, 1777.
2 fiche. £6.00; $A15.00.
*Holden's directory of Birmingham &
Coventry, 1805.* 1 fiche. £3.00; $A9.00.
Pigot's directory of Birmingham, 1816.
Forthcoming.
Pigot's directory of Warwickshire, 1822.
Forthcoming.
*Wrightson's directory of Birmingham,
1823.* 4 fiche. £12.00; $A27.00.
Pigot's directory of Birmingham, 1824.
Forthcoming.
Pigot's directory of Birmingham, 1829.
1 fiche. £3.00; $A9.00.
West's directory of Warwickshire, 1830.
9 fiche. £27.00; $A57.00.
Slater's directory of Birmingham, 1837.
1 fiche. £3.00; $A9.00.

Pigot's directory of Warwickshire, 1842.
Forthcoming.
Slater's directory of Warwickshire, 1850.
Forthcoming.
Slater's directory of Birmingham, 1852.
Forthcoming.
Kelly's directory of Warwickshire, 1854.
8 fiche. £24.00; $A51.00.
Slater's directory of Warwickshire, 1862.
3 fiche. £9.00; $A21.00.
Hulley's directory of Birmingham, 1870.
Forthcoming.
White's directory of Warwickshire, 1874.
8 fiche. £24.00; $A51.00.
Kelly's directory of Warwickshire, 1888.
Forthcoming.
Kelly's directory of Warwickshire, 1892.
Forthcoming.
Kelly's directory of Warwickshire, 1908.
Forthcoming.
Kelly's directory of Birmingham, 1912.
Forthcoming.
Kelly's directory of Birmingham, 1919.
Forthcoming.
Kelly's directory of Warwickshire, 1924.
7 fiche. £21.00; $A45.00.
Kelly's directory of Warwickshire, 1936.
Forthcoming

Westmorland
Holden's directory of Kendal, 1805. 1 fiche.
£3.00; $A9.00.
Pigot's directory of Kendal 1820.
Forthcoming.
Pigot's directory of Westmorland, 1820.
Forthcoming.
Pigot's directory of Westmorland, 1828.
Forthcoming.
Parson's directory of Westmorland, 1829.
2 fiche. £6.00; $A15.00.
Pigot's directory of Westmorland, 1834.
Forthcoming.
Mannex's directory of Westmorland, 1849.
Forthcoming.
Mannex's directory of Westmorland, 1851.
3 fiche. £9.00; $A21.00.
Slater's directory of Westmorland, 1855.
Forthcoming.
Bulmer's directory of Westmorland, 1885.
Forthcoming.
Bulmer's directory of Westmorland, 1905.
4 fiche. £12.00; $A27.00.
Kelly's directory of Westmorland, 1929.
Forthcoming.

Nick Vine Hall (*cont.*)
Wiltshire
Holden's directory of Bradford, Devizes,
  Salisbury & Trowbridge, 1805. 1 fiche.
  £3.00; $A9.00.
Pigot's directory of Wiltshire, 1822.
  Forthcoming.
Pigot's directory of Wiltshire, 1830.
  Forthcoming.
Pigot's directory of Wiltshire, 1844.
  Forthcoming.
Slater's directory of Wiltshire, 1852. 2 fiche.
  £6.00; $A15.00.
Kelly's directory of Wiltshire, 1867. 5 fiche.
  £15.00; $A33.00.
Kelly's directory of Wiltshire, 1875. 5 fiche.
  £15.00; $A33.00.
Kelly's directory of Wiltshire, 1889. 5 fiche.
  £15.00; $A33.00.
Kelly's directory of Wiltshire, 1899.
  Forthcoming.
Kelly's directory of Wiltshire, 1911.
  Forthcoming.
Kelly's directory of Wiltshire, 1920.
  Forthcoming.
Kelly's directory of Wiltshire, 1923.
  Forthcoming.
Kelly's directory of Wiltshire, 1927.
  Forthcoming.
Kelly's directory of Wiltshire, 1931.
  Forthcoming.
Kelly's directory of Wiltshire, 1939.
  Forthcoming.

Worcestershire
Holden's directory of Dudley &
  Kidderminster, 1805. 1 fiche. £3.00;
  $A9.00.
Pigot's directory of Worcestershire, 1822.
  Forthcoming.
Wrightson's directory of North
  Worcestershire, 1823. 1 fiche. £3.00;
  $A9.00.
Pigot's directory of North Worcestershire,
  1829. 1 fiche. £3.00; $A9.00.
Pigot's directory of Worcestershire, 1830.
  1 fiche. £3.00; $A9.00.
Bentley's directory of Worcestershire, 1840.
  Forthcoming.
Pigot's directory of Worcestershire, 1842.
  Forthcoming.
Hunt's directory of Worcester & Great
  Malvern, 1847. Forthcoming.
Slater's directory of Worcestershire, 1850.
  Forthcoming.

Kelly's directory of Worcestershire, 1854.
  5 fiche. £15.00; $A33.00.
Slater's directory of Worcestershire, 1862.
  2 fiche. £6.00; $A15.00.
Littlebury's directory of Worcestershire,
  1873. Forthcoming.
Wells' directory of Malvern, 1888.
  Forthcoming.
Kelly's directory of Worcestershire, 1892.
  Forthcoming.
Kelly's directory of Worcestershire, 1904.
  7 fiche. £21.00; $A45.00.
Kelly's directory of Worcestershire, 1912.
  Forthcoming.
Kelly's directory of Worcestershire, 1924.
  7 fiche. £21.00; $A45.00.

Yorkshire
Gales' directory of Sheffield, 1787.
  Forthcoming.
Wright's directory of Leeds, 1798.
  Forthcoming.
Holden's directory of Bradford, Halifax,
  Huddersfield, Hull, Leeds, Sheffield,
  Wakefield & York, 1805. 1 fiche. £3.00;
  $A9.00.
Pigot's directory of Yorkshire (part), 1816.
  Forthcoming.
Pigot's directory of Yorkshire, 1822.
  Forthcoming.
Baines' directory of Yorkshire West Riding,
  1822. Forthcoming.
Baines' directory of Yorkshire, East Riding,
  1823. Forthcoming.
Baines' directory of Yorkshire, North
  Riding, 1823. 2 fiche. £6.00; $A15.00.
Pigot's directory of Leeds & Sheffield,
  1824. Forthcoming.
Parson's directory of Leeds, 1826. 3 fiche.
  £9.00; $A21.00.
Pigot's directory of South West Yorkshire,
  1832. 1 fiche. £3.00; $A9.00.
Pigot's directory of Yorkshire, 1834.
  Forthcoming.
Pigot's directory of Hull, Leeds &
  Sheffield, 1837. 1 fiche. £3.00; $A9.00.
White's directory of Yorkshire, West
  Riding: pt. 1, 1837. 5 fiche. £15.00;
  $A33.00.
White's directory of Yorkshire, West
  Riding: pt. 2, 1838. 5 fiche. £15.00; $A33.00.
White's directory of Yorkshire, East &
  North Ridings, 1840. Forthcoming.
Pigot's directory of Yorkshire, 1841. 3 fiche.
  £9.00; $A21.00.

White's directory of Yorkshire, East Riding, 1846. Forthcoming.

Slater's directory of Yorkshire, 1848. 7 fiche. £21.00; $A45.00.

White's directory of Sheffield & Rotherham, 1849. Forthcoming.

White's directory of South Yorkshire (inc. Sheffield), 1852. 4 fiche. £12.00; $A27.00.

White's directory of West Yorkshire (inc. Leeds), 1853. 5 fiche. £15.00; $A33.00.

Slater's directory of Yorkshire, 1854. Forthcoming.

Slater's directory of Yorkshire, 1855. Forthcoming.

White's directory of Sheffield, 1857. 2 fiche. £6.00; $A15.00.

Jones' directory of Halifax, Dewsbury & Huddersfield, 1863. 3 fiche. £9.00; $A21.00.

White's directory of Yorkshire, East Riding, 1867. Forthcoming.

White's directory of South Yorkshire (inc. Sheffield), 1868. 6 fiche. £18.00; $A39.00.

Buchanan's directory of Kingston-Upon-Hull, 1872. Forthcoming.

Daily Chronicle's directory of the Huddersfield District, 1879. 3 fiche. £9.00; $A21.00.

Stevens' directory of the York District, 1881. Forthcoming.

Kelly's directory of Yorkshire, West Riding, 1889. Forthcoming.

Bulmer's directory of Yorkshire, North Riding, 1890. Forthcoming.

Bulmer's directory of East Yorkshire (exc. York), 1892. 7 fiche. £21.00; $A45.00.

Deacon's directory of Yorkshire, West Riding, 1900. Forthcoming.

Bulmer's directory of Sedbergh, Dent & Garsdale, 1905. 1 fiche. £3.00; $A9.00.

Town & County directory of Middlesborough, York & district, 1916. Forthcoming.

Directory of Yorkshire, West Riding, 1936. Forthcoming.

SCOTLAND

Findlay's directory of Scotland, 1843. Forthcoming.

Grant's directory of Scotland, 1868. Forthcoming.

Grant's directory of Scotland, 1872. 10 fiche. £30.00; $A63.00.

Scott's directory of Scotland, 1882. Forthcoming.

Grant's directory of Scotland, 1902. Forthcoming.

Massie's directory of Scotland, 1912. Forthcoming.

Slater's directory of Scotland, 1915. 9 fiche. £27.00; $A57.00.

Aberdeenshire

Pigot's directory of Aberdeen, 1820. 1 fiche. £3.00; $A9.00.

Slater's directory of Aberdeenshire, 1837. 1 fiche. £3.00; $A9.00.

Argyleshire

Slater's directory of Argyleshire, 1837. 1 fiche. £3.00; $A9.00.

Slater's directory of Argyleshire, 1915. 1 fiche. £3.00; $A9.00.

Ayrshire

Pigot's directory of Ayrshire (part), 1820. 1 fiche. £3.00; $A9.00.

Slater's directory of Ayrshire, 1837. 1 fiche. £3.00; $A9.00.

Slater's directory of Ayrshire, 1920. 2 fiche. £6.00; $A15.00.

Ayrshire Post's directory of Ayrshire, 1920. Forthcoming.

Browning's directory of central Ayrshire, 1934. 6 fiche. £18.00; $A39.00.

Banffshire

Slater's directory of Banffshire, 1837. 1 fiche. £3.00; $A9.00.

Slater's directory of Banffshire, 1915. 2 fiche. £6.00; $A15.00.

Berwickshire

Slater's directory of Berwickshire, 1837. 1 fiche. £3.00; $A9.00.

Buteshire

Slater's directory of Buteshire, 1837. 1 fiche. £3.00; $A9.00.

Caithness-shire

Slater's directory of Caithness-shire, 1837. 1 fiche. £3.00; $A9.00.

Slater's directory of Caithness-shire, 1852. 1 fiche. £3.00; $A9.00.

Clackmannanshire

Slater's directory of Clackmannanshire, 1837. 1 fiche. £3.00; $A9.00.

Dumbartonshire

Slater's directory of Dumbartonshire, 1837. 1 fiche. £3.00; $A9.00.

Nick Vine Hall (*cont.*)
Dumfriesshire
Pigot's directory of Dumfries & Annan,
1820. 1 fiche. £3.00; $A9.00.
Slater's directory of Dumfriesshire, 1837.
1 fiche. £3.00; $A9.00.
Slater's directory of Dumfriesshire, 1852.
1 fiche. £3.00; $A9.00.

Elginshire
Slater's directory of Elginshire, 1837.
1 fiche. £3.00; $A9.00.

Fifeshire
Pigot's directory of Dunfermline &
Kirkcaldy, 1820. 1 fiche. £3.00; $A9.00.
Slater's directory of Fifeshire, 1837. 1 fiche.
£3.00; $A9.00.

Forfarshire
Pigot's directory of Dundee & Montrose,
1820. 1 fiche. £3.00; $A9.00.
Slater's directory of Forfarshire, 1837.
1 fiche. £3.00; $A9.00.
Mathew's directory of Dundee, 1869.
4 fiche. £12.00; $A27.00.
Mathew's directory of Dundee, 1896.
Forthcoming.
Mathew's directory of Dundee, 1922.
Forthcoming.

East Lothian
Pigot's directory of Dunbar & Haddington,
1820. 1 fiche. £3.00; $A9.00.
Slater's directory of Haddingtonshire, 1837.
1 fiche. £3.00; $A9.00.

Inverness-shire
Slater's directory of Inverness-shire, 1837.
1 fiche. £3.00; $A9.00.

Kincardineshire
Slater's directory of Kincardineshire, 1837.
1 fiche. £3.00; $A9.00.

Kinross-shire
Slater's directory of Kinross-shire, 1837.
1 fiche. £3.00; $A9.00.

Kirkcudbrightshire
Pigot's directory of Kirkcudbrightshire,
1820. 1 fiche. £3.00; $A9.00.
Slater's directory of Kirkcudbrightshire,
1837. 1 fiche. £3.00; $A9.00.
Slater's directory of Kirkcudbrightshire,
1852. 1 fiche. £3.00; $A9.00.

Lanarkshire
Holden's directory of Glasgow, 1805.
1 fiche. £3.00; $A9.00.
Pigot's directory of Glasgow, Hamilton &
Lanark, 1820. 2 fiche. £6.00; $A15.00.
Lang's directory of Glasgow, 1826.
Forthcoming.
Slater's directory of Lanarkshire, 1837.
2 fiche. £6.00; $A15.00.
Graham's directory of Glasgow, 1840.
3 fiche. £9.00; $A21.00.
Khull's directory of Glasgow, 1845. 4 fiche.
£12.00; $A27.00.

Linlithgowshire
Slater's directory of Linlithgow, 1820.
1 fiche. £3.00; $A9.00.
Slater's directory of Linlithgowshire, 1837.
1 fiche. £3.00; $A9.00.

Midlothian
Denovan's directory of Edinburgh & Leith,
1804. Forthcoming.
Holden's directory of Edinburgh & Leith,
1805. 1 fiche. £3.00; $A9.00.
Abernethy's directory of Edinburgh &
Leith, 1814. 3 fiche. £9.00; $A21.00.
Pigot's directory of Edinburgh, Leith &
Dalkeith, 1820. 2 fiche. £6.00; $A15.00.
Shaw's directory of Edinburgh & Leith,
1823. Forthcoming.
Gray's directory of the Edinburgh district,
1833. 4 fiche. £12.00; $A27.00.
Slater's directory of Midlothian, 1837.
2 fiche. £6.00; $A15.00.
Slater's directory of Midlothian, 1852.
2 fiche. £6.00; $A15.00.
Murray's directory of Edinburgh & Leith,
1878. Forthcoming.
Morrison's directory of Edinburgh &
Leith, 1890. Forthcoming.
Morrison's directory of Edinburgh, 1911.
Forthcoming.
Directory of Edinburgh, 1923. Forthcoming.

Nairnshire
Slater's directory of Nairnshire, 1837.
1 fiche. £3.00; $A9.00.

Orkney
Slater's directory of the Orkney Isles, 1837.
1 fiche. £3.00; $A9.00.
Slater's directory of the Orkney Isles, 1852.
1 fiche. £3.00; $A9.00.
Slater's directory of the Orkney Isles, 1915.
1 fiche. £3.00; $A9.00.

Outer Hebrides
Slater's directory of the Outer Hebrides,
1915. 1 fiche. £3.00; $A9.00.

Peebles-shire
Slater's directory of Peebles-shire, 1837.
1 fiche. £3.00; $A9.00.
Slater's directory of Peebles-shire, 1915.
1 fiche. £3.00; $A9.00.

Perthshire
Slater's directory of Perth, 1820. 1 fiche.
£3.00; $A9.00.
Slater's directory of Perthshire, 1837.
1 fiche. £3.00; $A9.00.
Marshall's directory of Perth, 1860. 2 fiche.
£6.00; $A15.00.

Renfrewshire
Holden's directory of Greenock & Paisley,
1805. 1 fiche. £3.00; $A9.00.
Pigot's directory of Greenock, Paisley, &
Port Glasgow, 1820. 1 fiche. £3.00;
$A9.00.
Fowler's directory of Renfrewshire, 1836.
4 fiche. £12.00; $A27.00.
Slater's directory of Renfrewshire, 1837.
1 fiche. £3.00; $A9.00.
Hutchinson's directory of Greenock, 1903.
Forthcoming.
Blair's directory of Greenock, 1864.
Forthcoming.

Ross & Cromarty
Slater's directory of Ross & Cromarty,
1837. 1 fiche. £3.00; $A9.00.
Slater's directory of Ross & Cromarty,
1852. 1 fiche. £3.00; $A9.00.

Roxburghshire
Slater's directory of Roxburghshire, 1837.
1 fiche. £3.00; $A9.00.
Rutherford's directory of Roxburghshire,
1866. 4 fiche. £12.00; $A27.00.

Selkirkshire
Slater's directory of Selkirkshire, 1837.
1 fiche. £3.00; $A9.00.
Rutherford's directory of Selkirkshire,
1866. 2 fiche. £6.00; $A15.00.

Shetland
Slater's directory of the Shetland Isles,
1837. 1 fiche. £3.00; $A9.00.
Slater's directory of the Shetland Isles,
1915. 1 fiche. £3.00; $A9.00.

Stirlingshire
Pigot's directory of Falkirk,
Grangemouth & Stirling, 1820.
1 fiche. £3.00; $A9.00.
Slater's directory of Stirlingshire, 1837.
1 fiche. £3.00; $A9.00.
Slater's directory of Stirlingshire, 1915.
2 fiche. £6.00; $A15.00.

Sutherland
Slater's directory of Sutherland, 1837.
1 fiche. £3.00; $A9.00.
Slater's directory of Sutherland, 1852.
1 fiche. £3.00; $A9.00.
Slater's directory of Sutherland, 1915.
1 fiche. £3.00; $A9.00.

Wigtownshire
Slater's directory of Newton Stewart,
Stranraer, & Wigtown, 1820. 1 fiche.
£3.00; $A9.00.
Slater's directory of Wigtownshire, 1837.
1 fiche. £3.00; $A9.00.
Slater's directory of Wigtownshire, 1852.
1 fiche. £3.00; $A9.00.

WALES
Pigot's directory of Wales, 1822.
Forthcoming.
Pigot's directory of North Wales, 1822.
Forthcoming.
Pigot's directory of North Wales, 1835.
1 fiche. £3.00; $A9.00.
Pigot's directory of North Wales, 1844.
Forthcoming.
Slater's directory of North Wales, 1858.
2 fiche. £6.00; $A15.00.
Slater's directory of North Wales, 1880.
Forthcoming.
Pigot's directory of South Wales, 1822.
Forthcoming.
Pigot's directory of South Wales, 1830.
1 fiche. £3.00; $A9.00.
Pigot's directory of South Wales, 1835.
Forthcoming.
Pigot's directory of South Wales, 1844.
Forthcoming.
Slater's directory of South Wales, 1852.
Forthcoming.
Slater's directory of South Wales, 1858.
2 fiche. £6.00; $A15.00. £6.00; $A15.00.
Slater's directory of South Wales, 1880.
4 fiche. £12.00; $A27.00. £12.00.
Kelly's directory of South Wales, 1891.
Forthcoming.

Nick Vine Hall (*cont.*)
Denbighshire
Porter's directory of Wrexham, 1886.
1 fiche. £3.00; $A9.00.

Glamorganshire
*Western mail directory of Cardiff,
Penarth, Llandaff, Whitchurch, & Ely,
1910.* Forthcoming.
Western Mail directory of Cardiff, 1929.
Forthcoming.

Mrs S.M. Hay
13, Martin Road, Fairfield, Dunedin,
9006, New Zealand.
Available in U.K. from: Denis R. Hall,
375, Liverpool Road, Islington,
London, N1 1NL.
*Tallis's London street views: a stranger's
guide to London. Inner London
directory, 1838-40 & 1847.* 5 fiche. £5.00.
Indexes over 10,000 surnames in *A
stranger's guide to London,* published
by the London Topographical Society, 1969.

M.M. Publications
75, Thomas More House, The Barbican,
London, EC27 8BT.
Return of owners of land 1873.
Reprinted on fiche. £1.50 per English
or Welsh county; £50.00 the set (English
& Welsh); 20% discount on orders for
5 or more counties. Scotland 4 fiche £5.00.
Harts army lists.
 1844. 6 fiche. £6.25.
 1861. 7 fiche. £7.00.
 1875. 3 fiche. £3.75.
 1884. 3 fiche. £3.75.
Fiche for 1852, 1862, 1863, 1866, 1871 and
1872 forthcoming.
Army lists.
 1761. 3 fiche. £3.75.
 1773. 3 fiche. £3.75.
 1776. 1 fiche. £1.75.
 1826. 4 fiche. £3.75.
Monthly army lists.
 1853 August. 1 fiche. £1.50.
 1858 January. 1 fiche. £1.50.
 1881 September. 2 fiche. £2.50.
 1882 August. 2 fiche. £2.50.
 1883 June. 3 fiche. £3.75.
 1885 January. 3 fiche. £3.75.
 1891 April (quarterly). 25 fiche. £17.50.
 1905 July. Forthcoming.
 1914 August. Forthcoming.

Indian Army & Civil Service list.
 1861 July. 4 fiche. £3.75.
 1881 July. Forthcoming.
 1914 February. 4 fiche. £3.75.
Navy lists.
 1821. 2 fiche. £2.50.
 1851. 2 fiche. £2.50.
 1920. 41 fiche. £32.75.
O'BYRNE, WILLIAM R. *A naval biographical
dictionary.* Fiche reprint; originally
published 1849. Lives of c.5000 naval
officers.
East India Co. register & directory.
 1808. 1 fiche. £1.75.
 1811. 2 fiche. £2.50.
 1821. 2 fiche. £2.50.
 1831. 2 fiche. £2.50.
 1851. 2 fiche. £2.50.
*Parish register abstract, England & Wales,
1831.* Fiche reprint. 6 fiche. £7.50. Also
available by regions.
*Place names of Great Britain & Ireland,
1861.* Fiche reprint. 1 fiche. £1.50.
Compiled from census reports.
*Bartholomew's national gazetteer of Great
Britain and Ireland.* Fiche reprint of
c.1875 edition. Set £25.00.
 v.1. A to E. 10 fiche. £9.00.
 v.2. F to M. 10 fiche. £9.00.
 v.3. N to Z. 14 fiche. £12.50.
*Pharmaceutical Society of Great Britain
members and associates 1842.* Reprint.
1 fiche. £1.50.

Directories
Bedfordshire
Kelly's directory of Bedfordshire. Reprint.
3 fiche. £2.50.

Cambridgeshire
Pigot's directory of Cambridgeshire.
Reprint. 1 fiche. £1.50.

Cornwall
Kelly's directory of Cornwall, 1910. Reprint.
9 fiche. £8.75.

Cumberland
Slater's directory of Cumberland, 1848.
Reprint. 1 fiche. £1.50.

Derbyshire
Pigot's directory of Derbyshire, 1835.
Reprint. 1 fiche. £1.50.

Devon
Kelly's directory of Devonshire, 1910.
Reprint. 18 fiche. £15.00.

Durham

Slater's directory of Co. Durham, 1854.
Reprint. 1 fiche. £1.50.
Whellan's directory of Co. Durham, 1894.
Reprint. 23 fiche. £18.75. Also available
separately by ward.

Gloucestershire & Bristol

BEAVAN, ALFRED B. *Bristol lists, municipal
and miscellaneous.* Reprint, originally
published 1899. 2 fiche. £2.50.
*Matthew's new Bristol directory for the
year 1793/4.* Reprint. 1 fiche. £1.50.
Slater's Bristol directory, 1858/9. Reprint. 2
fiche. £2.50.
Post Office directory of Bristol 1861.
Reprint. 3 fiche. £3.75.
Slater's directory of Bristol 1881. Reprint. 2
fiche. £2.50. Trades and professions only.
*Wright's Bristol and Clifton directory,
1882.* Reprint. Fiche. £6.25.
*Kelly's directory of Gloucestershire
(excluding Bristol).* Reprint. 5 fiche.
£5.00.
Kelly's directory of Bristol, 1885. 4 fiche.
£3.75.
Wright's directory of Bristol 1911. 11 fiche.
£10.00.
*Stroud and mid-Gloucestershire directory,
1926.* 1 fiche. £1.50.

Hampshire

Pigot's Hampshire directory, 1835. Reprint
1 fiche. £1.50.
Slater's Hampshire directory, 1852. Reprint.
1 fiche. £1.50.
White's Hampshire directory, 1859.
Reprint. 3 fiche. £3.75.

Herefordshire

Pigot's Herefordshire directory, 1835.
Reprint. 1 fiche. £1.50.
Kelly's directory of Herefordshire, 1885.
Reprint. 3 fiche. £3.75.

Huntingdonshire

Kelly's directory of Huntingdonshire, 1894.
Reprint (fiche). Forthcoming.

Kent

Kelly's directory of Kent, 1905. Reprint. 13
fiche. £12.00. Also available in sections:
'places and inhabitants', 8 fiche £7.50;
'private residents and addresses', 2 fiche
£2.50; 'trades and professionals', 3 fiche
£3.75.

Lancashire

Gore's directory of Liverpool, 1816.
Forthcoming.
Baines' directory of Lancashire, 1824. Reprint.
v.1. A-K and Liverpool. 3 fiche. £3.75.
v.2. L-Z; with Stockport and
manufacturing villages in Cheshire.
3 fiche. £3.75.
*Pigot's Manchester & Salford directory,
1841.* Reprint.
Pt.1. 2 fiche. £2.50.
Pt.2. Towns & principal villages 12 miles
around Manchester. 2 fiche. £2.50.
Slater's Liverpool directory, 1858/9.
Reprint. 1 fiche. £1.50.
Slater's Liverpool directory, 1881. Reprint.
3 fiche. £2.50. Trades and professions
only.

Leicestershire & Rutland

*Pigot's Leicestershire and Rutland
directory, 1841.* Reprint. 1 fiche. £1.50.
*Kelly's directory of Leicestershire and
Rutland, 1916.* Reprint. Forthcoming.

Lincolnshire

Parson's Lincolnshire directory, 1826.
Reprint. 2 fiche. £1.75.
Pigot's directory of Lincolnshire, 1841.
Reprint. 2 fiche. £2.50.
*Ruddock's directory of Lincoln and
villages ten miles around.* Reprint. 2
fiche. £2.50.

London & Middlesex

Kent's London directory, 1817. Reprint. 2
fiche. £2.50.
Post Office directory of London, 1827.
Reprint. 2 fiche. £2.50.
Post Office directory of London, 1854.
Reprint. 39 fiche. £40.00.
Post Office directory of London, 1865.
Reprint. 42 fiche. £40.00.
Post Office directory of London, 1875.
Reprint. 43 fiche. £40.00.
N.B. The 1854, 1865 and 1875 directories are
also available in smaller sections.
*Collingridge's City of London directory,
1908.* Reprint. 16 fiche. £15.75. Also
available in sections.
*London County Council record of war
services 1914-1919.* 2 fiche. £2.50.
Westminster register of electors 1836.
Reprint. 2 fiche. £2.50.

M.M. Publications (*cont.*)

CANSICK, FREDERICK TEAGUE. *Monumental inscriptions of Highgate & St. Pancras cemeteries, vol. II.* 4 fiche. £3.75.
Kelly's directory of Harrow, Northwood, Pinner, Wembley, 1925. Reprint. Forthcoming.
Kelly's directory of Middlesex, 1926. Reprint. 9 fiche. £8.75.

Monmouthshire
Slater's Monmouthshire directory, 1858/9. Reprint. 1 fiche. £1.50.

Norfolk
Pigot's Norfolk directory, 1839. Reprint. 1 fiche. £1.50.
Kelly's directory of Norfolk, 1925. Reprint. 10 fiche. £9.25.

Northamptonshire
Pigot's Northamptonshire directory, 1841. Reprint. 1 fiche. £1.50.
Whellan's Northamptonshire directory, 1849. Reprint. 10 fiche. £9.25.
Kelly's directory of Northamptonshire, 1894. Forthcoming.

Northumberland
Slater's Northumberland directory, 1854. Reprint. 1 fiche. £1.50.

Nottinghamshire
Pigot's directory of Nottinghamshire, 1841. Reprint. 1 fiche. £1.50.

Shropshire
Kelly's directory of Shropshire, 1885. Reprint. 4 fiche. £3.75.

Somerset
Kelly's directory of Somerset, 1927. Reprint. 10 fiche. £9.25.

Staffordshire
Pigot's Staffordshire directory, 1835. Reprint. 1 fiche. £1.50.
Post Office directory of Staffordshire, 1854. Reprint. Forthcoming.

Suffolk
Pigot's Suffolk directory, 1839. Reprint. 1 fiche. £1.50.
Kelly's directory of Suffolk 1925. Reprint. 7 fiche. £6.50.

Surrey
Kelly's directory of Streatham, Norbury, Norwood and locality, 1925. Reprint. 3 fiche. £3.75.

Warwickshire
Post Office directory of Birmingham, 1854. Forthcoming.
Post Office directory of Birmingham, 1860. Forthcoming.

Westmorland
Pigot's directory of Westmorland, 1828/9. Reprint. 1 fiche. £1.50.

Yorkshire
Parson's directory of Hull, 1826. Reprint. 2 fiche. £2.50.
Pigot's Yorkshire directory, 1841. Reprint. 5 fiche. £5.00.

Scotland
1860 military review in Edinburgh. Muster list. Forthcoming.
Matthew's Dundee directory, 1874/5. Reprint. 2 fiche. £3.75.
Tait's Glasgow directory, 1783/4. Reprint. 1 fiche. £1.50.
Slater's Glasgow directory, 1881. 4 fiche. £3.75. Trades and professions only.
Linlithgow poll book, 1858. 1 fiche. £1.50. Includes voters in 1832, 1837 and 1838.
Linlithgow poll book, 1868. 1 fiche. £1.50.

Microformat Systems U.K. Ltd.
P.O. Box 5208, Southend, Reading, RG7 6YR
Phone: (0118) 9714087
Prices exclude V.A.T.

Cheshire
Broster's Chester guide, 1781. 1 fiche. £5.00.
Cowdroy's directory and guide for the city and county of Chester, 1789 1 fiche. £5.00.
BAGSHAW, SAMUEL. *History, gazetteer and directory of the County Palatine of Chester, 1850.* 6 fiche £15.00
Post Office directory of Cheshire 1857. 6 fiche. £15.00.
White's history, gazetteer and directory of Cheshire, 1860. 8 fiche. £20.00.
Morris's commercial directory & gazetteer of Cheshire, 1864. 6 fiche. £15.00.
Post Office directory of Cheshire, 1865. 7 fiche. £18.00.

Slater's directory of Cheshire and North Wales, 1869. 8 fiche. £20.00.
Morris's commercial directory & gazetteer of Cheshire & Stalybridge, 1874. 10 fiche. £25.00.
Slater's Royal national commercial directory of Cheshire, 1883. 10 fiche, £25.00.
Slater's directory of Cheshire, 1888. 9 fiche. £22.00.
Slater's directory of Cheshire, 1890. 11 fiche. £28.00.
Kelly's directory of Cheshire, 1892. 11 fiche. £28.00.
Kelly's directory of Cheshire, 1896. 12 fiche. £30.00.

Lancashire and Manchester

Kelly's directory of Lancashire with Manchester and Liverpool, 1895. 24 fiche. £49.00.
Slater's directory of Manchester, Salford & suburban, 1913. 40 fiche. £70.00.
Kelly's directory of Manchester, Salford & suburban, 1923. 29 fiche. £55.00.
Kelly's directory of Manchester, Salford & suburban, 1930. 37 fiche. £70.00.
Kelly's directory of Manchester, Salford & suburban, 1939. 38 fiche. £70.00.
Pigot's directory of Lancashire, 1834. 4 fiche. £10.00.
Slater's directory of Lancashire, 1869, pt.2. 12 fiche. £29.00.
Kelly's directory of Lancashire, 1887. 17 fiche. £39.00.
Kelly's directory of Lancashire, 1891. 17 fiche. £39.00.
Kelly's directory of Lancashire, 1898. 20 fiche. £45.00.
Kelly's directory of Lancashire, 1905. 23 fiche. £48.00.
Kelly's directory of Lancashire, 1913. 23 fiche. £48.00.
Kelly's directory of Lancashire, 1924. 23 fiche. £48.00.

North Wales

Pigot & Co's Denbighshire, Flintshire and Montgomeryshire directory, 1822. 1 fiche. £5.00.
Pigot & Co's North Wales directory, 1828-9. 1 fiche. £5.00.
Pigot & Co's North Wales directory, 1835. 1 fiche. £5.00.
Robson's commercial directory of North Wales 1840. 3 fiche. £10.00.

Slaters' North Wales directory, 1844. 2 fiche. £8.00.
Slaters' North Wales directory, 1850. 1 fiche. £5.00.
Slaters' North Wales directory, 1856. 2 fiche. £8.00.
Jones's Wrexham directory, 1859. 1 fiche. £5.00.
Slaters North Wales directory, 1868. 2 fiche. £8.00.
Worrall's Chester & North Wales directory, 1874. 5 fiche. £13.00.
Cassey's Chester & North Wales directory, 1876. 4 fiche. £11.00.
Croker's Wrexham area directory, 1881-2. 2 fiche. £8.00.
Slaters North Wales directory, 1883. 4 fiche. £11.00.
Porter's postal directory of Flintshire and Denbighshire, 1886. 7 fiche. £18.00.
Sutton's Chester & North Wales directory, 1889-90. 9 fiche. £22.00.
Slater's North Wales and Aberystwyth area directory, 1895. 10 fiche. £25.00.
Bennett's business directory of Chester and North Wales, 1913-14. 4 fiche. £11.00.
Bennett's business directory of Chester and North Wales, 1922. 3 fiche. £10.00.
Cope's standard directory of North Wales, 1932. 4 fiche. £11.00.
Bennetts business directory of Chester and North Wales, 1936. 3 fiche. £10.00.

Devon

Pigot's directory of Devon, 1822-3. 1 fiche. £5.00.
Pigot's directory of Devon, 1830. 2 fiche. £8.00.
Robson's directory of Devon, 1838. 4 fiche. £11.00.
Slater's directory of Devon, 1844. 4 fiche. £11.00.
White's directory of Devon, 1850. 13 fiche. £30.00.
Kelly's directory of Devon, 1856. 7 fiche. £18.00.
Billing's directory of Devon, 1857. 13 fiche. £30.00.
Kelly's directory of Devon, 1866. 13 fiche. £30.00.
Morris's directory of Devon, 1870. 18 fiche. £40.00.
Kelly's directory of Devon, 1873. 20 fiche. £20.00.

Microformat Systems (*cont.*)
Harrod's directory of Devon, 1878. 12 fiche. £29.00.
White's directory of Devon, 1890. 21 fiche. £46.00.
Kelly's directory of Devon, 1893. 18 fiche. £40.00.
Kelly's directory of Devon, 1897. 17 fiche. £39.00.
Kelly's directory of Devon, 1902. 22 fiche. £47.00.
Town and county directory of Devon, 1903-4. 13 fiche. £30.00.
Kelly's directory of Devon, 1906. 14 fiche. £31.00.
Town and county directory of Devon, 1906. 14 fiche. £31.00.
Kelly's directory of Devon, 1910. 19 fiche. £42.00.
Town and country directory of Devon, 1912-13. 15 fiche. £32.00.
Kelly's directory of Devon, 1914. 20 fiche. £45.00.
Town and country directory of Devon, 1915. 15 fiche. £32.00.
Kelly's directory of Devon, 1919. 19 fiche. £42.00.
Kelly's directory of Devon, 1923. 23 fiche. £48.00.
Town and country directory of Devon, 1926. 12 fiche. £29.00.
Kelly's directory of Devon, 1930-31. 20 fiche. £45.00.
Kelly's directory of Devon, 1939. 25 fiche. £50.00.
Wheaton's directory of Exeter, 1905. 4 fiche. £11.00.
Besley's directory of Exeter, 1941. 5 fiche. £13.00.
Eyre's directory of Plymouth, 1880. 8 fiche. £20.00.
Hill's Torquay directory, 1869. 6 fiche. £15.00

Wiltshire
Post Office directory of Wiltshire.
  1848. 3 fiche. £10.00.
  1855. 3 fiche. £10.00.
  1859. 3 fiche. £10.00.
  1867. 3 fiche. £10.00.
Kelly's directory of Wiltshire.
  1875. 4 fiche. £11.00.
  1880. 4 fiche. £11.00.
  1885. 4 fiche. £11.00.
  1889. 4 fiche. £11.00.

  1895. 5 fiche. £13.00.
  1899. 5 fiche. £13.00.
  1903. 6 fiche. £15.00.
  1907. 5 fiche. £13.00.
  1911. 5 fiche. £13.00.
  1915. 5 fiche. £13.00.
  1920. 6 fiche. £15.00.
  1923. 6 fiche. £15.00.
  1927. 5 fiche. £13.00.
  1931. 5 fiche. £13.00.
  1935. 6 fiche. £15.00.
  1939. 6 fiche. £15.00.

Home Counties, etc.
Post Office directory of Bedfordshire, 1847. (pp. 1707-58) 1 fiche. £5.00.
Post Office directory of Bedfordshire, Buckinghamshire, Huntingdonshire, Cambridgeshire, Norfolk, and Suffolk, 1854. 10 fiche. £25.00.
Post Office directory of Bedfordshire, 1866. (pp.289-994). 2 fiche. £8.00.
Post Office directory of Bedfordshire, 1969. (pp.309-440). 2 fiche. £8.00.
Post Office directory of Bedfordshire, Huntingdonshire, Northamptonshire, Berkshire, Buckinghamshire and Oxfordshire, 1877. 15 fiche. £32.00.
Pigot & Co's London and provincial directory, 1823. 10 fiche. £25.00.
Pigot & Co's directory of Bedfordshire 1839. (pp.9-40.) 1 fiche. £5.00.
Kelly's directory of Bedfordshire, 1890. 3 fiche. £10.00.
Kelly's directory of Bedfordshire, 1903. 3 fiche. £10.00.
Kelly's directory of Bedfordshire, Huntingdonshire and Northamptonshire, 1914. 10 fiche. £25.00.
Kelly's directory of Bedfordshire, Huntingdonshire and Northamptonshire, 1924. 11 fiche. £28.00.
Kelly's directory of Bedfordshire, 1931. 3 fiche. £10.00.
Kelly's directory of Bedfordshire, 1940. 3 fiche. £10.00.

Heather Morris & Barbara Hafslund

P.O.Box 257, Burpengary, Queensland 4505, Australia.

From here to there. Fiche or computer disk. 0646195239. 1994. New Zealand assisted passenger list, 1855-71.

North Fiche

c/o J.A. Readdie, 38, Archery Rise,
Durham, DH1 4LA.
http://btinternet.com/jwill

Parish register transcripts: Co. Durham.

Barnard Castle.
   CB 1719-1753. Fiche. £2.40.
   CB 1754-1753. Fiche. £2.40.
   CB 1754-1812. Fiche. £4.80.
   M 1719-1812. Fiche. £2.40.

Bishopwearmouth.
   CB 1729-1756 & M 1729-1754. Fiche.
   £2.40.
   C 1756-1778. Fiche. £1.20.
   C 1778-1812. Fiche. £3.60.
   B 1756-1778. Fiche. £1.20.
   B 1778-1795. Fiche. £1.20.
   B 1796-1812. Fiche. £1.20.

Boldon.
   CMB 1571-1812. Fiche. £3.60.

Brancepeth.
   C 1599-1699. Fiche. £2.40.
   C 1700-1812. Fiche. £3.60.
   B 1599-1812. Fiche. £2.40.
   M 1599-1812. Fiche. £2.40.

Chester-Le-Street.
   C 1582-1643. Fiche. £1.20.
   C 1652-1688. Fiche. £1.20.
   C 1668-1735. Fiche. £2.40.
   C 1735-1812. Fiche. £7.20.
   B 1582-1678. Fiche. £1.20.
   B 1708-1735. Fiche. £1.20.
   B 1735-1759. Fiche. £1.20.
   B 1759-1815. Fiche. £3.60.

Cockfield.
   CMB 1578-1812. Fiche. £2.40.

Durham St.Giles.
   C 1584-1812. Fiche. £2.40.
   M 1584-1814. Fiche. £1.20.
   B 1584-1812. Fiche. £2.40.

Durham St.Margaret.
   CB 1558-1720. Fiche. £3.60
   CB 1720-1812. Fiche. £3.60.

Durham St.Nicholas.
   C 1784-1812. Fiche. £3.60.
   B 1731-1812. Fiche. £4.80.

Easington.
   CMB 1570-1652. Fiche. £2.40.
   CMB 1653-1745. Fiche. £2.40.
   CMB 1745-1812. Fiche. £2.40.

Escomb.
   CMB 1543-1812. Fiche. £1.20.

Great Stainton
   CMB 1561-1812. Fiche. £1.20.

Heworth.
   CMB 1696-1768. Fiche. £3.60.
   CMB 1769-1812. Fiche. £6.00.

Houghton Le Spring.
   CMB 1563-1698. Fiche. £4.80.
   CMB 1696-1748. Fiche. £4.80.
   CB 1746-1812. Fiche. £4.80.
   M 1746-1812. Fiche. £2.40

Kirk Merrington.
   CMB 1579-1729. Fiche. £2.40.
   CMB 1729-1812. Fiche. £2.40.

Lanchester.
   C 1560-1602 & 1653-1778. Fiche. £2.40.
   C 1778-1831. Fiche. £2.40.
   C 1831-1848. Fiche. £1.20.
   B 1560-1847. Fiche. £3.60.

Monk Hesledon.
   CMB 1578-1812. Fiche. £3.60.

Pittington.
   CMB 1574-1812. Fiche. £3.60.

Redmarshall.
   CB 1559-1812 & M 1560-1812. Fiche.
   £2.40.

Ryton.
   C 1581-1748. Fiche. £4.80.
   C 1748-1812. Fiche. £4.80.
   B 1581-1701. Fiche. £2.40.
   B 1701-1771. Fiche. £2.40.
   B 1779-1812. Fiche. £2.40.

Sedgefield.
   CB 1766-1812 & M 1754-1812. Fiche.
   £3.60.

South Shields.
   C 1683-1737. Fiche. £2.40.
   C 1737-1774. Fiche. £2.40.
   C 1775-1809. Fiche. £4.80.
   C 1809-1812. Fiche. £1.20.
   B 1685-1717. Fiche. £1.20.
   B 1717-1797. Fiche. £4.80.
   B 1798-1812. Fiche. £2.40.

Staindrop.
   CMB 1635-1760. Fiche. £3.60.
   CMB 1760-1812. Fiche. £3.60.

Sunderland. (H.Trinity.)
   C 1754-1797. Fiche. £6.00.
   C 1798-1812. Fiche. £3.60.
   B 1770-1812. Fiche. £8.40.

Tanfield.
   CMB 1719-1812. Fiche. £4.80.

Trimdon.
   CMB 1720-1812. Fiche. £1.20.

Washington.
   CB 1600-1772. Fiche. £2.40.
   CB 1773-1812. Fiche. £2.40.

Parish register transcripts:
Northumberland.
Alwinton.
  CMB 1719-1812. Fiche. £3.60.
Alnwick.
  C 1645-1748. Fiche. £2.40.
  C 1749-1812. Fiche. £2.40.
Ancroft.
  CM 1742-1812 & B 1742-1840. Fiche. £1.20.
Bedlington.
  C 1653-1812. Fiche. £2.40.
  M 1653-1812. Fiche. £1.20.
  B 1653-1912. Fiche. £2.40.
Bolam.
  CMB 1661-1812. Fiche. £2.40.
Branxton.
  CMB 1739-1812. Fiche. £0.80.
Carham.
  CMB 1684-1812. Fiche. £1.20.
Cramlington.
  CMB 1665-1812. Fiche. £1.20.
Felton.
  CMB 1653-1745. Fiche. £3.60.
  CMB 1745-1812. Fiche. £3.60.
Ford.
  CMB 1684-1812. (indexed) Fiche. £4.80.
Hartburn.
  CMB 1672-1812. Fiche. £4.80.
Hexham.
  CB 1753-1800. Fiche. £3.60.
  CB 1801-1812. Fiche. £1.20.
Horton.
  CM 1753-1800 & B 1725-1812. Fiche. £2.40
Howick.
  CMB 1678-1812 & B 1725-1812. Fiche.
    £2.40.
Mitford.
  CMB 1665-1755. £2.40.
  CMB 1756-1812. £1.20.
Morpeth
  CMB 1583-1749. Fiche. £7.20.
  CB 1750-1777. Fiche. £2.40.
  CB 1778-1797. Fiche. £1.20.
  CB 1798-1812. Fiche. £2.40.
  M 1750-1812. Fiche. £1.20.
Netherwitton.
  CB 1696-1812 & M 1706-1812. Fiche.
    £2.40.
Newbiggin By The Sea.
  CMB 1659-1751. Fiche. £1.20.
Newburn.
  CMB 1659-1751. Fiche. £3.60.
  CB 1764-1812. Fiche. £4.80.

Norham.
  CMB 1653-1715. Fiche. £2.40.
  CB 1715-1801. Fiche. £2.40.
  CB 1802-1812. Fiche. £1.20.
  M 1714-1812. Fiche. £1.20.
Ponteland.
  CMB 1602-1728. Fiche. £2.40.
  CMB 1729-1812. Fiche. £3.60.
Rock & Rennington.
  Rock CB 1768-1812 and M 1771-80;
    Rennington CB 1768-1814 and M 1769-
    79. Fiche. £1.20.
Shilbottle.
  CMB 1684-1812. Fiche. £2.40.
Wallsend.
  CB 1773-1812. Fiche. £2.40.
  M 1754-1812. Fiche. £1.20.
Whitfield.
  CMB 1612-1812 (With tombstone
    inscriptions to 1911). (Indexed) Fiche.
    £7.20.
Widdrington.
  CMB 1698-1812. Fiche. £1.20.
Woodhorn.
  CMB 1605-1748. Fiche. £2.40.
  CB 1748-1812. Fiche. £1.20.
  M 1749-1812. Fiche. £1.20.
Wooler.
  CMB 1692-1812. Fiche. £2.40.
Newcastle All Saints.
  C 1600-1636. Fiche. £2.40.
  C 1637-1660. Fiche. £2.40.
  C 1660-1713. Fiche. £6.00.
  C 1714-1751. Fiche. £3.60.
  C 1751-1790. Fiche. £4.80.
  C 1791-1812. Fiche. £6.00.
  C 1813-1830. Fiche. £4.80.
  M 1600-1713. Fiche. £3.60.
  M 1713-1751. Fiche. £1.20.
  M 1751-1817. Fiche. £7.20.
  M 1817-1830. Fiche. £2.40.
  B 1600-1653. Fiche. £3.60.
  B 1653-1713. Fiche. £6.00.
  B 1713-1830. Fiche. £7.20.
Newcastle St. John.
  CMB 1587-1600. Fiche. £2.40.
  CMB 1600-1653. Fiche. £7.20.
  CMB 1653-1674. Fiche. £3.60.
  CMB 1675-1716. Fiche. £3.60.
  CMB 1717-1736. Fiche. £2.40.
  CMB 1737-1773. Fiche. £3.60.
  CMB 1773-1786. Fiche. £2.40.
  CMB 1786-1800. Fiche. £3.60.
  CMB 1801-1812. Fiche. £3.60.

Newcastle St. Andrew.
  CM 1656-1683 & B 1656-1687.
    Fiche. 4.80.
  CM 1683-1705 & B 1687-1705.
    Fiche. £4.80.
  CMB 1705-1725. Fiche. £4.80.
  CMB 1725-1741. Fiche. £3.60.
  CMB 1741-1797. Fiche. £8.40.
  C 1797-1810. Fiche. £4.80.
  B 1797-1812. Fiche. £3.60.
Newcastle St. Nicholas.
  CB 1558-1653. Fiche. £6.00.
  CB 1653-1678. Fiche. £2.40.
  CB 1678-1715. Fiche. £4.80.
  CB 1716-1755. Fiche. £4.80.
  CB 1756-1791. Fiche. £2.40.
  C 1791-1812. Fiche. £2.40.
  B 1791-1812. Fiche. £1.20.

Reprints of Printed Parish Registers.
County Durham.
Coniscliffe.
  CMB 1590-1812. £1.50
Dalton le Dale.
  CMB 1653-1812. £2.50.
Ebchester.
  CMB 1619-1812. £2.50.
Middleton St.George.
  C 1652-1812 & MB 1616-1812. £1.50.

Northumberland
Beadnell.
  CB 1766-1812 & M 1767-1781. £1.50.
Bothal.
  CMB 1678-1812. £2.50.
Chatton.
  CMB 1712-1812. £2.50.
Edlingham.
  CMB 1689-1812. £2.50.
Eglingham.
  CMB 1612-1812. £2.50.
Elsdon.
  CB 1672-1812 and M 1672-1780. £4.25.
Elsdon.
  M 1780-1812. (A modern MS transcript,
    indexed.) £1.50.
Hebron.
  CMB 1680-1812. £2.50.
Ilderton.
  CMB 1724-1812. £1.50.
Ingram.
  CMB 1682-1812. £1.50.
Lesbury.
  CMB 1689-1812. £3.20.

Longhoughton.
  CMB 1689-1812. £2.50.
Newcastle St.Nicholas.
  M 1574-1812. £5.20.
Whalton.
  CMB 1661-1812. £2.50.

Northumberland Record Office
catalogues and indexes
Schools. Fiche. £5.00.
Northumberland Quarter Sessions
  Indictments. Indexes. 2 vols. Fiche.
  1580-1630. £2.75.
  1771-1807. £2.75.
Hexham Apprentices Charity, applications
  1818-1906. Fiche. £2.50. Lists 1500
  applicants.
Parish chest material. 4 sets of fiche.
  (Listed by Parish.)
  A-C. £2.75 D-K. £2.75
  L-R. £2.75 S-W. £2.75.
Tithes. £4.95. Index to tithe
  apportionments.
Newcastle & Gosforth parish records.
  Fiche. £1.50. List only.
Roman Catholic parish records at
  Northumberland Record Office. Fiche.
  £1.50.
Index to reports of inquests in Alnwick
  Mercury, 1865-1880. Fiche. £2.25.
Manorial records in Northumberland
  Record Office. Fiche. £1.50. List.
W. Percy Hedley mss. Fiche. £1.50. Papers
  and notebook of a noted
  Northumberland genealogist; mentions
  over 850 families.
Wylam pitmens bonds, 1787-1867. Fiche.
  £2.75.
Poor Law records. Fiche. £1.50.
ROUNCE, W.E. Rounces marriage indexes.
  Fiche. (to 1837).
    County Durham
    Auckland St.Helen from 1593. £2.25.
    Aycliffe from 1566. £1.50.
    Barnard Castle from 1619. £2.50.
    Bishopwearmouth from 1568. £4.50.
    Brancepeth from 1599. £1.50.
    Chester Le Street from 1582. £3.00.
    Croxdale from 1732 with Whitworth
      from 1569. £1.25.
    Durham St.Giles from 1584. £1.50.
    Durham St.Margaret from 1588. £2.50.
    Durham St.Nicholas from 1540. £2.50.
    Easington from 1570, with Kelloe from
      1693. £1.50.

North Fiche (*cont.*)
 Gateshead from 1559. £4.00.
 Heighington from 1570. £1.50.
 Heworth from 1540.) £2.50.
 Houghton Le Spring from 1563.
   £3.50.
 Kirk Merrington from 1579. £1.50.
 Lamesley from 1603. £1.50.
 Lanchester from 1568. £2.50.
 Monk Hesledon from 1592, with
   Trimdon from 1721. £1.25.
 Ryton & Winlaton from 1581. £3.00.
 Seaham from 1652, with Dalton-le-Dale
   from 1653. £1.25.
 Sedgefield from 1581. £2.50.
 S. Shields St. Hilda, 1653-1812. £3.00.
 S. Shields St. Hilda, 1813-1837. £2.50.
 Stanhope from 1613, with St. John's
   Chapel from 1828. £2.50.
 Sunderland from 1713. £4.00.
 Usworth from 1835, with Washington
   from 1603. £1.50.
 Whickham from 1581. £3.00.
 Whitburn from 1579. £1.25.
 Witton-le-Wear from 1558. £1.50.
 Wolsingham from 1655. £1.50.

Northumberland
Bywell St. Andrew from 1685, with
   Bywell St. Peter from 1663. £1.50.
 Horton from 1665. £1.50.
 Newburn from 1659. £2.50.
 Newcastle St. Andrew from 1597.
   £3.50.
 Ovingham from 1679. £2.50.
 Whitfield from 1608, with Knaresdale
   from 1695, and with Lambley from
   1742. £1.50.
Memorials of Alnwick parish church.
   Fiche. £2.25.
Register of admissions to the Duke of
   Northumberland's School, Alnwick, 1811-
   1911. Fiche. £2.50.

Reprinted trade directories.
Whiteheads Newcastle directory, 1788.
   Reprint. Fiche £1.50.
Pigot's directory of Northumberland, 1828.
   Reprint. Fiche. £1.50.
Pigot's directory of Northumberland, 1834.
   Reprint. Fiche. £2.50.
Slater's directory of Northumberland, 1848.
   Reprint. Fiche. £2.50.
White's directory, 1847. Reprint. Fiche.
   £4.50.

Hagar's directory of County Durham, 1851.
   Reprint. Fiche. £5.00.
Whellan's directory of Northumberland,
   1855. Reprint. Fiche. £6.50.
Kelly's directory of Northumberland, 1879.
   Reprint. Fiche. £5.50.
Kelly's directory of County Durham, 1879.
   Reprint. Fiche. £5.50.
Bulmers Northumberland 1886/7. 3 pts.
   Reprints. Fiche. £13.25 the set.
   A. *Tindale (Hexham) and Coquetdale.*
     £6.00.
   B. *Tyneside.* £5.00.
   C. *Rest of County.* £5.00.
Kelly's directory of Co.Durham, 1897.
   Reprint. Fiche. £9.25.
Kelly's directory of Northumberland, 1897.
   Reprint. Fiche. £7.50.
Ward's directory of Tyneside & Wearside,
   1899 1900. Reprint. Fiche. 5pts. The set
   £11.95.
   A. North Shields / Tynemouth. £2.00.
   B. South Shields / Jarrow. £3.00.
   C. Sunderland and villages £3.50.
   D. Newcastle and villages. £4.50.
Wards' directory of Tyneside/Wearside,
   1915/16. Reprint. Fiche. 2 pts.
   A. North of the Tyne. £8.00.
   B. South of the Tyne. £8.00.

Voters lists.
Newcastle voters list 1836/37. Reprint.
   Fiche. £2.75.
Newcastle voters list 1858/59. Reprint.
   Fiche. £2.75.
Newcastle voters list 1877. Reprint. Fiche.
   £7.75.
Newcastle voters list 1886/87. Reprint.
   Fiche. £9.95.
Berwick Division. 1886/87. Reprint. Fiche.
   £9.95.
Hexham Division 1886/87. Reprint. Fiche.
   £10.95.
Wansbeck Division 1886/87. Reprint. Fiche.
   £6.75.

Northern Forebears
27, Piper Road, Ovingham, Northumberland.
Phone: (01661) 835103

Return of owners of land for Scotland 1873.
   Fiche. Pt.1. Six southern counties. Pt.2.
   The South West. Pt.3. The Lothians;
   Stirling; Fife. Pt.4. Eastern counties. Pt.5.
   Highlands and Islands. £2.50 per part, or
   £10.00 the set.

Webster's royal red book, or court &
fashionable register, January 1919.
9 fiche. £10.00. London directory.
The 1861 census index of Northumberland.
Fiche. Each part £3.00.
No.1. Bywell sub-district.
No.2. Hexham sub-district.
No.3. Stamfordham sub-district.
No.4. Chollerton sub-district.
Return of owners of land for
Northumberland, 1873. Fiche. £2.50.
Return of owners of land for County
Durham, 1873. Fiche. £2.50.
Return of owners of land for Cumberland
and Westmorland, 1873. Fiche. £2.50.
Whellan's directory for County Durham,
1856. 6 pts. £15.00 the set.
Pt.1. *Durham Ward.* £3.00.
Pt.2. *Darlington Ward* £4.00.
Pt.3. *Stockton Ward.* £3.00
Pt.4. *Easington Ward.* £3.50.
Pt.5. *Chester Ward.* £3.50.
Pt.6. *Newcastle upon Tyne* £3.00.
Bulmers 1886 directory for
Northumberland. (Hexham
Parliamentary Division). Fiche. £8.50.
Bulmers 1887 directory for
Northumberland (Tyneside, Wansbeck
and Berwick divisions). Reprint. Fiche.
4pts. Set £15.50.
Pt.1. Newcastle upon Tyne. £4.00.
Pt.2. Tynemouth and Tyneside. £3.50.
Pt.3. Wansbeck. £4.00.
Pt.4. Berwick £4.50. Set £15.50.
Ward's directory 1920 for Tyneside.
Reprint. Fiche. 2pts. Set £10.00.
Pt.1. Newcastle-on-Tyne; Bells Close;
Benton; Lemington; Newburn;
Gosforth; Coxlodge. £6.00.
Pt.2. Chirton; Cullercoats; Percy Main;
North Shields; Tynemouth; Whitley
Bay; Monkseaton; South Shields;
Monkton; Jarrow; Willington
(and Quay); Howdon; Wallsend. £5.00.
Berwick upon Tweed parish registers:
baptisms, 1574-1700. Fiche. £4.00.
Berwick upon Tweed parish registers:
marriages, 1572-1700. Fiche. £3.00.
Ebchester parish registers: baptisms,
marriages and burials, 1619-1812; banns
1760-1799. Fiche. £3.00.
Stanhope parish registers: marriages and
banns, 1613-1812. Fiche. £3.50.
Whellan's 1855 directory for
Northumberland. Fiche. Forthcoming.

Original Indexes

c/o George Bell, 113, East View,
Wideopen, Tyne and Wear, NE13 6EF.
Phone (0190) 2366416.
Email: george@original-
indexes.demon.co.uk

BELL, G. *Bell bap., mar., and bur.,*
Newcastle-upon-Tyne, 1813-1861. £4.00.
BELL, G. *(Former) Royal Navy seamen in*
receipt of parish relief, 1860. £2.25.
BELL, G. *North of England mining accident*
victims (Northumberland, Durham,
Cumberland, Westmoreland &
Cleveland.
1859-69. £2.25.
1870-79. £2.25.
1880-89. £4.00.
1890-99. £4.00.
BELL, G. *Northumberland and Durham*
Quarter Sessions & Assize courts;
newspaper index.
1782-1829. £4.00.
1830-1851. £5.50.
BELL, G. *Paupers in workhouses 1861.*
£7.75.
BELL, G. *Royal Navy invalids & pensioners,*
1866-1868. £4.00.
YELLOWLEY, C., & BELL, G. *Pre-1837*
Northumberland & Durham chapel
baptisms (includes Berwick, Walkergate,
Hamsterley, Middleton-in-Teesdale,
Newcastle - Berwick Street, Westgate
Street and Tuthill Stairs, North Shields,
Rowley, South Shields, Sunderland).
£2.25
Kelly's handbook to the titled, landed
and official classes. 12th ed. Fiche reprint
(originally published 1886). £21.25.
BELL, G. *Original indexes cornucopia*
volume 1. Trinity House (Deptford
Strand) petitioners 1835-36; Nentsbury
(Alston CUL) baptisms 1837-1900;
Bournmoor miscellany; Coanwood &
Redwing Chapel (Alston CUL) burials;
unknown register (tiny) of births
covering Wolsingham & Weardale;
S.O.F. births in Allerdale 1702-1707;
dissenters births in Alston 1704-1723;
Howdon Pans Ind. Chapel baptisms
1835-1837; Morpeth Ind. Chapel
baptisms 1829-1837; Newcastle Postern
Chapel baptisms 1784-1837; some
extracts from the 'Newcastle Courant'.
£2.25.

Original Indexes (*cont.*)
Original indexes cornucopia vol.II.
Newcastle Swedenborgians bap. 1808-
1837; Aberystwyth (WLS) Baptist chapel
bap. 1804-1837; Corham (NBL) dissenters
births 1801-1825; Sydenham (OXF)
Baptist Chapel bap. 1821-1837; Whitney
(OXF) Baptist Chapel bap. 1799-1819;
Chirbury (SAL) Baptist chapel bap. 1827-
1834; Instances of longevity (NBL &
DUR); Sunderland, Bishopwearmouth &
Monkwearmouth (DUR) bpt. 1901;
'Newcastle Courant' extracts. Fiche. 1998.
£2.25.

Berwickshire
BELL, G. *Coldstream Bridge marriages, 1793-*
1797. £2.25.
Lamberton Toll marriages, 1804-1816 &
1849-1855. £2.25.

Cumberland
YELLOWLEY, C., & BELL, G. *Alston & Garrigill*
bap. mar., & bur. 1813-1839. £5.50.

Co.Durham
YELLOWLEY, C., & BELL, G. *Durham*
marriages, 1798-1812. £6.75. Not in
Boyd's marriage index.
BELL, G. *Durham pre-1837 non-Anglican*
marriages. £1.00.
BELL, G., & YELLOWLEY, C. *Co.Durham*
burials 1813-1837 (Anglican). £24.75.
BELL, G., & YELLOWLEY, C. *Durham burials*
1813-1837 (non-Anglican). £1.00.
BELL, G. *Diocese of Durham marriage*
bonds, 1804-1808. 1998. £9.75.
BELL, G. *Diocese of Durham marriage*
bonds, 1809-1815. 1998. £6.75.

Bishopwearmouth
BELL, G., & YELLOWLEY, C. *Bishopwearmouth*
(Sunderland) bap., mar., & bur., 1813-
1839. £10.75.

Boldon
BELL, G., & YELLOWLEY, C. *Boldon bap., mar.,*
& bur., 1813-1839. £2.25.

Bournmoor
YELLOWLEY, C., & BELL, G. *Bournmoor bap.,*
mar., & bur., 1868-1901. (formerly in the
parish of Penshaw). £2.25.
BELL, G., & YELLOWLEY, C. *Bournmoor 1841 &*
1851 census returns. £2.25.
BELL, G., & YELLOWLEY, C. *Bournmoor 1861 &*
1871 census returns. £2.25.

BELL, G., & YELLOWLEY, C. *Bournmoor 1881 &*
1891 census returns. £2.25.

Chester-Le-Street
Chester-Le-Street Deanery burials; 1798-
1812 (Chester-Le-Street, Lamesley,
Tanfield and Washington.) £4.00.

Gateshead Fell
BELL, G. *Gateshead Fell bap., mar., and bur.*
1825-1839. £2.25.

Hamsterley
LAIDLER, K., YELLOWLEY, C., & BELL, G.
Hamsterley, Rowley, & Wolsingham
Baptist M.I's. £2.25.

Jarrow
BELL, G. *Jarrow bap., mar., & bur. 1813-1839.*
Fiche. £6.75.

Malings Rigg
YELLOWLEY, C., & BELL, G.. *Malings Rigg*
(Sunderland) Presbyterian baptisms,
1783-1879. £1.50.

Middleton in Teesdale
BELL, G., & YELLOWLEY, C. *Middleton in*
Teesdale & Egglestone bap., mar., & bur.
1813-1839. Fiche. 1998. £4.00.

Monkwearmouth
BELL, G. *Monkwearmouth (Sunderland)*
bap., mar., & bur., 1813-1839. £8.75.

Newbottle
YELLOWLEY, C., & LAIDLER, K. *Newbottle St.*
Mathews M.I's. £2.25.

Ryton
NICHOLSON, GEOFF. *Ryton bap., mar., & bur.,*
1813-1839. £5.50.

South Hylton
THORNTON, JEAN, YELLOWLEY, C., & BELL, G.
South Hylton bap., mar., & bur., 1821-
1851 together with M.I's. £2.25.
THORNTON, JEAN. *South Hylton*
(Bishopwearmouth) bap., mar & bur.,
1852-1891. £2.25.
BELL, G. *South Hylton and Ford 1851 census*
(part of Bishopwearmouth in Sunderland
P.R.O. HO/107/2395, ff.1-61). £2.25.

South Shields
BELL, G. *South Shields bap., mar., & bur.*
1813-1839. 1998. £12.75.
BELL, G. *South Shields Holy Trinity bap., &*
bur., 1834-1839. £2.25.

Stanhope Deanery

YELLOWLEY, C., & BELL, G. *Stanhope Deanery burials 1798-1812. (Edmundbyers, Hunstanworth, Muggleswick, St. Johns Chapel, Stanhope & Wolsingham).* £2.25.

Sunderland

YELLOWLEY, C. *A street index to the parishes of Sunderland, Bishopwearmouth & Monkwearmouth.* £2.25.

Whickham

NICHOLSON, GEOFF. *Whickham bap., mar., and bur., 1813-1839.* £5.50.

Whitburn

BELL., G, & YELLOWLEY, C. *Whitburn bap., mar., & bur., 1813-1839.* £2.25.

Winlaton

NICHOLSON, GEOFF. *Winlaton bap., mar., & bur., 1828-1839.* £2.25.

Witton le Wear

THORNTON, JEAN. *Witton-le-Wear bap., mar., & bur., 1754-1797.* Fiche. £2.25.

Northumberland

BELL, G. *Northumberland marriages 1798-1812 (those not on Boyd's marriage index).* Fiche. £5.50.

BELL, G., & YELLOWLEY, C. *Northumberland burials, 1813-1837. (Anglican).* 2nd ed. Fiche. £20.75.

BELL, G., & YELLOWLEY, C. *Northumberland burials, 1813-1837 (non-Anglican).* 2nd ed. Fiche. £7.75.

Northumberland burials 1813-1837 (Cemeteries) (Tynemouth General Cemetery, Newcastle General Cemetery, and Westgate Hill Cemetery, Newcastle). Fiche. £2.25.

BELL, G. *Northumberland pre-1837 non-Anglican marriages.* Fiche. £2.25.

BELL, G. *Marriages for the year 1841 extracted from the 'Newcastle Courant.'* Fiche. 1998. £2.25.

Alwinton

BELL, G. *Alwinton & Holystone bap., mar., & bur. 1813-1839.* Fiche. £2.25.

Ancroft

BELL, G. *Ancroft, Kyloe & Holy Island bap., mar., and bur. 1813-1839.* Fiche. £2.25.

Ballast Hills

Ballast Hills (Newcastle) burials, 1792-1801. £4.00. Includes notes from earlier inscriptions.

Belford

BELL, G., & GILROY, KEITH. *Belford bap., mar., & bur., 1813-1839.* Fiche. £2.25.

Bellingham Deanery

YELLOWLEY, C., & BELL, G. *Bellingham Deanery burials 1798-1812 (Bellingham, Birtley, Byrness, Chollerton, Elsdon, Falstone & Simonburn.* Fiche. £2.25.

Berwick on Tweed

BELL, G. *Berwick-upon-Tweed bap., mar., & bur., 1813-1839.* Fiche. £6.75.

Branxton

BELL, G. *Branxton, Carham, Ford & Lowick bap., mar., & bur., 1813-1839.* £4.00.

Byrness

YELLOWLEY, C, & BELL, G. *Byrness, Horsley & Otterburn bap., mar., & bur., 1840-1901.* Fiche. £2.25.

Bywell St.Andrew

YELLOWLEY, C., & BELL, G. *Bywell St.Andrew, Bywell St.Peter & Whittonstall bap., mar., & bur., 1813-1839.* £2.25.

YELLOWLEY, C., & BELL, G. *Bywell St. Andrew, Bywell St. Peter, Whittonstall, Henley & Newton Hall bap., mar., & bur., 1840-1901.* Fiche. £4.00.

Cullercoats

BELL, G. *Cullercoats St.Pauls (Whitley Bay) burials, 1864-1895 (formerly in the parish of Tynemouth).* Fiche. £2.25.

BELL, G. *Cullercoats St.Pauls' (Whitley Bay) burials, 1911-1962 (formerly in the parish of Tynemouth).* Fiche. £2.25.

Earsdon

WILKINSON, WINNIE. *Earsdon bap., mar., & bur., 1813-1839.* Fiche. £5.50.

Harbottle

CORNO, VALERIE. *Harbottle (Alwinton) Presbyterian Chapel: births/baptisms 1736-1805.* £2.25.

Longbenton

BELL, G. *Longbenton bap., mar., & bur., 1813-1839.* Fiche. £5.50.

Matfen
YELLOWLEY, C, &Bell, G.. *Matfen with Ryal bap., mar., & bur., 1844-1901 (formerly in the parish of Stamfordham).* Fiche. £2.25.

Newcastle
BELL, G. *Newcastle St.Andrews' M.I's.* Fiche. £4.00.
BELL, G. *Newcastle St.John's M.I's.* Fiche. £4.00.
BELL, G. *Newcastle St.Nicholas M.I's.* Fiche. £2.25.
BELL, G. *Newcastle St.Nicholas bap., mar., & bur., 1813-1839.* Fiche. £2.25.

Norham Deanery
YELLOWLEY, C, & BELL, G.. *Norham Deanery burials, 1798-1812.* 1998. Fiche. £4.00.
BELL, G. *Norham & Cornhill bap., mar., & bur., 1813-1839.* Fiche. £2.25.

Ovingham
BARKER, RIC. *Ovingham bap., mar., & bur., 1813-1839.* Fiche. £4.00.

Spittall
BELL, G. *Spittall (Tweedmouth) Presbyterian: bap. 1787-1837.* Fiche. £2.25.

Tweedmouth
BELL, G. *Tweedmouth bap., mar., & bur., 1813-1839.* Fiche. £4.00.

Walker
BELL, G. *Walker (Newcastle) bap., mar., & bur., 1848-1861.* Fiche. £4.00.
BELL, G. *Walker (Newcastle) 1841 census.* £2.25.
BELL, G. *Walker (Newcastle) 1891 census.* £5.50.

Woodhorn
ROSE, JOAN. *Woodhorn, Widdrington, Newbiggin, & Creswell bap., mar., & bur., 1813-1839.* £2.25.

Yorkshire
Barnard Castle
BELL, G. *Barnard Castle & Whorlton bap., mar., & bur. 1813-1839.* Fiche. £5.50.

Barningham
YELLOWLEY, C., & BELL, G. *Barningham, Brignall, Hutton Magna & Rokeby bap., mar., & bur., 1813-1839.* £2.25.

Bowes
BELL, G., & YELLOWLEY, C. *Bowes & Startforth bap., mar., & bur., 1813-1839.* Fiche. 1998. £2.25.

Cotherstone
YELLOWLEY, C., & BELL, G. *Cotherstone Particular Meeting. Quaker records (includes Lartington, Bowes and Barnard Castle) births 1588-1843; marriages 1847-1859; deaths 1657-1812; interments 1797-1896, and monumental inscriptions 1822-1922.* Fiche. £2.25.

Dufton
BELL, G., & YELLOWLEY, C. *Dufton bap., mar., & bur., 1789-1839.* Fiche. 1998. £2.25.

Laithkirk
BELL, G., & YELLOWLEY, C. *Laithkirk bap., mar., & bur., 1844-1911.* Fiche. 1998. £2.25.

Richmond Deanery
YELLOWLEY, C., & BELL, G. *Richmond Deanery (part) burials 1798-1812 (Barningham,. Bowes, Brignall, Gilling, Hutton Magna, Rokeby, Romaldkirk, Starforth & Wycliffe).* Fiche. £2.25.

Romaldkirk
BELL, G. *Romaldkirk bap., mar., & bur., 1813-1839.* £4.00.

P.B.N. Publications
22, Abbey Road, Eastbourne, E.Sussex, BN20 8TE.
WEBB, P., & WEIR, N., eds. *Sussex militia lists: Sussex, Hampshire, Surrey, & Kent (Officers 1804).* Fiche. £2.05.
WEBB, P., & WEIR, N., eds. *Eastbourne burials (St.Marys church) 1558-1837.* 2 fiche. £2.55.
WEBB, P., & WEIR, N., eds. *Hastings Union notices of marriage.* Fiche.
   1837-65. £3.95.
   1865-79. £3.95.
WEBB, P., & WEIR, N., eds. *Hastings ward lists of burgesses 1835-39.* Fiche. £2.80.
WEBB, P., & WEIR, N., eds. *Sussex census 1841.* Vol.1. Fiche. £3.30.
WEBB, P., & WEIR, N., eds. *Sussex directory, 1840.* Fiche. £2.80.
WEBB, P., & WEIR, N., eds. *Sussex poll for 1820.* 2 fiche. £2.80.

K.G. Saur

Postfach 70 16 20, D-8136 München, Germany.

BAILLIE, LAUREEN, ed. *British biographical archive.* 4 vols + 1236 fiche. 3-598-30479-X (silver halide); 3-598-30467-6 (diazo). 1984-9. DM22,800 (silver); DM20,800 (diazo). Brings together data from 324 biographical reference works dating from 1601 to 1929.

BAILLIE, LAUREEN. *British biographical index.* 4 vols. 2045pp. 0-86291-390-X. 1991. DM1,680. Indexes the *archive;* free with the *archive.*

BANK, DAVID, & ESPOSITO, ANTHONY, eds. *British biographical archive, series II.* 632 fiche. 3-598-33629-2 (silver halide); 3-598-33628-4 (diazo). 1991-4. DM22,480 (silver); DM20,800 (diazo). Includes data from a further 268 reference works, 19th-20th c.

British biographical index series II. 6 vols. 3-598-33630-6. 1998. DM1,680.

Peter Strutt

27, Jacob's Pool, Okehampton, Devon, EX20 1LJ

Phone: (01837) 82588

Fax: (01837) 55122

Email: 100064.1225@compuserve.com

1891 census on microfiche. £3.75 per fiche.

K. Willans

9, The Ridge Way, Kenton, Newcastle Upon Tyne, NE3 4LP

http://www.btinternet.com/~jwill/index/htm

1891 census surname index: Registration sub-district of Consett, Co. Durham.

1. *Benfieldside, Shotley Bridge, and Blackhill (part). Piece number RG12/4089.* 1996. £2.00 (inc. p&p).
2. *Conside and Knitsley (part). Piece number RG12/4090.* 1996. £2.00 (inc. p&p).
3. *Conside and Knitsley (part), Healeyfield, Castleside, Muggleswick, and Medomsley (part). Piece number RG12/4091.* £2.00 (inc. p&p).

World Microfilms

Microworld House, 2, North Wharf Road, London W2 1LA

Email: microworld@ndirect.co.uk

Catalogue of the Guildhall Library's major archive & manuscript holdings. 10 microfilm reels. £420.00.

Land tax commissioners for the City of London: Land tax assessments, vols 1-396, 1692-4; 1703-1831. 135 microfilm reels. £5750.00.

The Assembly order books at Sutton's Hospital, Charterhouse, 1613-1982. 9 microfilm reels. £375.00.

The Inner Temple archives 1547-1970. 55 reels. £2600.00.

The Shrewsbury papers at Lambeth Palace Library. 8 microfilm reels. £350.00.

Society of Friends Meetings for Sufferings archives: the great book of sufferings, 1659-1793. 29 reels. £1140.00.

Society of Friends' London two weeks meetings: minutes 1672-1789. 8 microfilm reels. £350.00. Records marriages of Friends.

Digest registers of births, marriages & burials for England & Wales, 17th c. - 1837. 32 microfilm reels. £1350.00. Register of the Society of Friends.

The Archives of the French Protestant church, 1560-1889. 37 microfilm reels. £1,850.00. Manuscripts of L'eglise Protestante Francaise de Londres.

Lloyds captains registers from the Guildhall Library, London (1851-1947). 63 microfilm reels. £4500.00.

Sun Insurance fire policy registers, 1775-87, together with the Royal Exchange Assurance records, 1775-87. 44 microfilm reels. £1995.00. Fiche index £130.00.

The Worshipful Society of Apothecaries records and accounts, 1606-1954. 60 microfilm reels. £2700.00.

The Worshipful Company of Barbers: archives, 1604-1890. 34 microfilm reels. £1500.00.

The Fellowship Porters & Tacklehouse & Ticket Porters: minute books, accounts & other records, 1566-1895. 13 microfilm reels. £570.00.

The Worshipful Company of Haberdashers: records, 1583-1970. 85 microfilm reels. £3400.00.

The Worshipful Company of Musicians: minutes, accounts and other records, 1712-1897. 4 microfilm reels. £150.00.

The Worshipful Company of Pewterers: records, registers and reports, 1451-1934. 32 microfilm reels. £1400.00.

The Shipwrights Company: constitutional records, minutes and accounts, 1428-1930. 8 microfilm reels. £375.00.

World Microfilms (*cont.*)

*The Watermen and Lightermens' Company:
minutes, accounts and other records,
1688-1971.* 84 microfilm reels. £3750.00.

*The Worshipful Company of Weavers:
records, 1681-1844.* 15 reels. £650.00.

PART 2
Societies

British Record Society

c/o Patric Dickinson, The College of
Arms, Queen Victoria Street, London
EC4V 4BT

Microfiche series

1. HULL, BRENDA L., ed. *Cornish probate records at the Cornwall Record Office, 1800-1857.* 4 fiche. £8.00.
2. FARADAY, M.L., & COLE, E.J.L., eds. *Calendars of probate and administration acts, 1407-1541, and abstracts of wills 1541-1581, in the court books of the Bishop of Hereford.* 7 fiche + booklet. £11.00.
3. *Gloucester wills and administrations, 1801-1858.* 2 fiche. £5.00.
4. WEBB, CLIFFORD. *Calendar of wills proved and letters of administration granted in the Diocese of Gloucester, 1801-1858.* 2 fiche + booklet. 1996.

Index Library reprints

Orders for microfiche reprints to:
Chadwyck-Healey Ltd., The Quorum,
Barnwell Road, Cambridge, CB5 8SW
Phone: (01223) 215512
Email: mail@chadwyck.co.uk
Http://www.chadwyck.co.uk

Many of these volumes are also available in hard copy; see *British genealogical books in print* for details.

1. PHILLIMORE, W.P.W., ed. *A calendar of wills relating to the counties of Northampton and Rutland proved in the court of the archdeacon of Northampton, 1510 to 1652.* 3 fiche. Reprint; originally published 1888. £21.00.
2. PHILLIMORE, W.P.W., ed. *A calendar of Chancery proceedings. Bills and answers filed in the reign of King Charles the First. Vol. I.* 3 fiche. Reprint; originally published 1889. £21.00.
3. PHILLIMORE, W.P.W., ed. *Index nominum to the royalist composition papers. First and second series. Vol. i: A to F.* 2 fiche. Reprint; originally published 1889. £14.00.

4. PHILLIMORE, W.P.W., ed. *An index to bills of privy signet, commonly called signet bills, 1584 to 1596 and 1603 to 1624, with a calendar of writs of privy seal, 1601 to 1603.* 3 fiche. Reprint; originally published 1890. £21.00.
5. PHILLIMORE, W.P.W., ed. *A calendar of Chancery proceedings. Bills and answers ... Vol. ii.* 3 fiche. Reprint; originally published 1890. £21.00.
6. PHILLIMORE, W.P.W., ed. *A calendar of Chancery proceedings. Bills and answers ... Vol. iii.* 3 fiche. Reprint; originally published 1890. £21.00.
7. PHILLIMORE, W.P.W., ed. *Calendars of wills and administrations in the consistory court of the bishop of Lichfield and Coventry, 1516 to 1652. Also those in the peculiars now deposited in the probate registries at Lichfield, Birmingham and Derby, 1529-1652, 1675-1790, 1753-1790.* 8 fiche. Reprint; originally published 1892. £56.00.
8. PHILLIMORE, W.P.W., ed. *Index to wills proved and administrations granted in the court of the archdeacon of Berks, 1508 to 1652.* 3 fiche. Reprint; originally published 1893. £21.00.
9. PHILLIMORE, W.P.W., & FRY, GEORGE S., eds. *Abstracts of Gloucestershire inquisitiones post mortem returned into the Court of Chancery in the reign of King Charles the First. Pt. i: 1-11 Charles I, 1625-1636.* 3 fiche. Reprint; originally published 1893. £21.00.
10. SMITH, J. CHALLENOR C., ed. *Index of wills proved in the Prerogative Court of Canterbury, 1383-1558, and now preserved in the Principal Probate Registry, Somerset House, London. Vol. 1.* 4 fiche. Reprint; originally published 1893. £28.00.
11. SMITH, J. CHALLENOR C., ed. *Index of wills proved in the Prerogative Court of Canterbury, 1383-1558 ... Vol. 2.* 5 fiche. Reprint; originally published 1895. £35.00.

British Record Society (cont.)

12. PHILLIMORE, W.P.W., & DUNCAN, LELAND L., eds. *A calendar of wills proved in the Consistory Court of the bishop of Gloucester, 1541-1650, with an appendix of dispersed wills and wills proved in the peculiar courts of Bibury and Bishop's Cleeve.* 4 fiche. Reprint; originally published 1895. £28.00.

13. PHILLIMORE, W.P.W., & FRY, GEORGE S., eds. *Abstracts of Gloucestershire inquisitiones post mortem ... Pt. ii: 12-18 Charles I, 1637-1642.* 3 fiche. Reprint; originally published 1895. £21.00.

14. FRY, EDWARD ALEXANDER, ed. *A calendar of Chancery proceedings. Bills and answers ... Vol. iv.* 3 fiche. Reprint; originally published 1896. £21.00.

15. FRY, GEORGE S., ed. *Abstracts of inquisitiones post mortem relating to the city of London returned into the Court of Chancery. Pt. i: 1 Henry VII to 3 Elizabeth, 1485-1561.* 3 fiche. Reprint; originally published 1896. £21.00.

16. GRANT, FRANCIS J., ed. *The commissariot record of Edinburgh: register of testaments. Pt. 1: vols 1 to 35, 1514-1600.* 4 fiche. Reprint; originally published 1897. £28.00.

17. FRY, EDWARD ALEXANDER, ed. *A calendar of wills proved in the Consistory Court (city and deanery of Bristol division) of the bishop of Bristol, 1572-1792. And also a calendar of wills in the Great Orphan Books preserved in the Council House, Bristol, 1379-1674.* 2 fiche. Reprint; originally published 1897. £14.00.

18. SMITH, S.A. *Index of wills proved in the Prerogative Court of Canterbury. Vol. iii: 1558-1583,* ed. Leland L. Duncan. 5 fiche. Reprint; originally published 1898. £35.00.

19. PHILLIMORE, W.P.W., ed. *Placita coram domino rege apud Westmonasterium de termino Sancte Trinitatis anno regni regis Edwardii filii regis Henrici vicesimo quinto. The pleas of the court of King's Bench, Trinity term, 25 Edward I, 1297.* 4 fiche. Reprint; originally published 1898. £28.00.

20. GRANT, FRANCIS J., ed. *The commissariot record of Inverness: register of testaments, 1630-1800.* Includes *The commissariot record of Hamilton and Campsie: register of testaments, 1564-1800.* 2 fiche. Reprint; originally published 1897-8. £14.00.

21. FRY, EDWARD ALEXANDER, ed. *Abstracts of Gloucestershire inquisitiones post mortem ... Pt. iii: Miscellaneous series, 1-18 Charles I, 1625-1642.* 2 fiche. Reprint; originally published 1899. £14.00.

22. FRY, EDWARD ALEXANDER, ed. *A calendar of wills and administrations relating to the county of Dorset proved in the Consistory Court (Dorsetshire division) of the late diocese of Bristol, 1681-1792, and in the Archdeaconry Court of Dorset 1568-1792, and in the several peculiars, 1660-1799, all now preserved in the probate registry, Blandford.* 3 fiche. Reprint; originally published 1900. £21.00.

23. FRY, GEORGE S., & FRY, EDWARD ALEXANDER, eds. *Abstracts of Wiltshire inquisitiones post mortem returned into the Court of Chancery in the reign of King Charles the First.* 6 fiche. Reprint; originally published 1901. £42.00.

24. HALL, WILLIAM HAMILTON, ed. *Calendar of wills and administrations in the Archdeaconry Court of Lewes in the Bishopric of Chichester, together with those in the Archbishop of Canterbury's peculiar jurisdiction of South Malling and the peculiar of the Deanery of Battle, comprising together the whole of the eastern division of the county of Sussex and the parish of Edburton in west Sussex. From the earliest extant instruments in the reign of Henry VIII to the Commonwealth.* 5 fiche. Reprint; originally published 1901. £35.00.

25. SMITH, S.A. *Index of wills proved in the Prerogative Court of Canterbury. Vol. iv: 1584-1604,* ed. Edward Alexander Fry. 7 fiche. Reprint; originally published 1901. £49.00.

26. MADGE, SIDNEY J., ed. *Abstracts of inquisitiones post mortem for the city of London returned into the Court of Chancery during the Tudor period. Pt. ii: 4-19 Elizabeth, 1561-1577.* 3 fiche. Reprint; originally published 1901. £28.00.

27. HARTOPP, HENRY, ed. *Calendars of wills and administrations relating to the county of Leicester proved in the Archdeaconry Court of Leicester, 1495-1649, and in the peculiars of St. Margaret, Leicester, Rothley, Groby, Evington, and the unproved wills, etc., previous to 1801, all now preserved in the probate registry at Leicester.* 4 fiche. Reprint; originally published 1902. £28.00.

28. FOSTER, C.W., ed. *Calendars of Lincoln wills. Vol. i: 1320-1600.* 4 fiche. Reprint; originally published 1902. £28.00.

29. FRY, EDWARD ALEXANDER, ed. *Index of Chancery proceedings (Reynardson's division) preserved in the Public Record Office, A.D. 1649-1714. Vol. i: A to K.* 3 fiche. Reprint; originally published 1903. £21.00.

30. MADGE, SIDNEY J., ed. *Abstracts of inquisitiones post mortem for Gloucestershire returned into the Court of Chancery during the Plantagenet period. Pt. iv: 20 Henry III to 29 Edward I, 1236-1300.* 3 fiche. Reprint; originally published 1903. £21.00.

31. FRY, EDWARD ALEXANDER, ed. *Calendar of wills and administrations in the Consistory Court of the Bishop of Worcester, 1451-1600. Also marriage licences and sequestrations now deposited in the probate registry at Worcester.* 6 fiche. Reprint; originally published 1904. £42.00.

32. FRY, EDWARD ALEXANDER, ed. *Index of Chancery proceedings (Reynardson's division) ... Vol. ii: L to Z.* 3 fiche. Reprint; originally published 1904. £21.00.

33. COKAYNE, GEORGE E., & FRY, EDWARD ALEXANDER, eds. *Calendar of marriage licences issued by the faculty office, 1632-1714.* 5 fiche. Reprint; originally published 1905. £35.00.

34. FRY, EDWARD ALEXANDER, & PHILLIMORE, W.P.W., eds. *A calendar of wills proved in the Consistory Court of the Bishop of Gloucester. Vol. ii: 1660 to 1800.* 5 fiche. Reprint; originally published 1907. £35.00.

35. FRY, EDWARD ALEXANDER, ed. *Calendars of wills and administrations relating to the counties of Devon and Cornwall, proved in the court of the Principal Registry of the Bishop of Exeter, 1559-1799, and of Devon only, proved in the court of the Archdeacon of Exeter, 1540-1799, all now preserved in the probate registry at Exeter.* 10 fiche. Reprint; originally published 1908. £70.00.

36. FRY, EDWARD ALEXANDER, ed. *Abstracts of inquisitiones post mortem for the city of London ... Pt. iii: 19-45 Elizabeth, 1577-1603.* 5 fiche. Reprint; originally published 1908. £35.00.

37. FRY, EDWARD ALEXANDER, ed. *Abstracts of Wiltshire inquisitiones post mortem returned into the Court of Chancery in the reigns of Henry III, Edward I, and Edward II, A.D. 1242-1326.* 6 fiche. Reprint; originally published 1908. £42.00.

38. HARTOPP, HENRY, ed. *Leicestershire marriage licences; being abstracts of the bonds and allegations for marriage licences preserved in the Leicester Archdeaconry registry, 1570-1729.* 6 fiche. Reprint; originally published 1910. £42.00.

39. FRY, EDWARD ALEXANDER, ed. *Calendar of wills and administrations in the Consistory Court of the Bishop of Worcester, 1601-1652. Also marriage licences and sequestrations now deposited in the probate registry at Worcester.* 3 fiche. Reprint; originally published 1910. £21.00.

40. FRY, EDWARD ALEXANDER, ed. *Abstracts of inquisitiones post mortem for Gloucestershire ... Pt. v: 30 Edward I to 32 Edward III, 1302-1358.* 5 fiche. Reprint; originally published 1910. £35.00.

41. *Calendars of Lincoln wills. Vol. ii: Consistory court wills, 1601-1652.* 3 fiche. Reprint; originally published 1910. £21.00.

42. NOBLE, W.M., ed. *Calendars of Huntingdonshire wills, 1479-1652.* 3 fiche. Reprint; originally published 1911. £21.00.

43. STOKES, ETHEL, ed. *Index of wills proved in the Prerogative Court of Canterbury. Vol. v: 1605-19.* 7 fiche. Reprint; originally published 1912. £49.00.

44. HILL, R.H. ERNEST, ed. *Index of wills proved in the Prerogative Court of Canterbury. Vol. vi: 1620-9.* 5 fiche. Reprint; originally published 1912. £35.00.

45. FRY, EDWARD ALEXANDER, ed. *Calendar of wills and administrations in the court of the Archdeacon of Taunton. Pts. 1 and 2: Wills only, 1537-1799.* 5 fiche. Reprint; originally published 1912. £35.00.

46. FRY, EDWARD ALEXANDER, ed. *Calendar of wills and administrations relating to the counties of Devon and Cornwall proved in the consistory court of the Bishop of Exeter, 1532-1800, now preserved in the probate registry at Exeter.* 4 fiche. Reprint; originally published 1914. £28.00.

British Record Society (cont.)

47. STOKES, ETHEL, ed. *Abstracts of inquisitiones post mortem for Gloucestershire ... Pt. vi: 33 Edward III to 14 Henry IV, 1359-1413.* 3 fiche. Reprint; originally published 1914. £21.00.

48. STOKES, ETHEL, ed. *Abstracts of Wiltshire inquisitiones post mortem returned into the Court of Chancery in the reign of King Edward III, A.D. 1327-1377.* 5 fiche. Reprint; originally published 1914. £35.00.

49. FRY, EDWARD ALEXANDER, ed. *Calendar of wills in the Consistory Court of the Bishop of Chichester, 1482-1800.* 5 fiche. Reprint; originally published 1915. £35.00.

50. PLOMER, HENRY R., ed. *Index of wills and administrations now preserved in the Probate Registry at Canterbury, 1396-1558 and 1640-1650.* 7 fiche. Reprint; originally published 1920. £49.00.

51. HARTOPP, HENRY, ed. *Index to the wills and administrations proved and granted in the Archdeaconry Court of Leicester, 1660-1750, and in the peculiars of St. Margaret, Leicester, and Rothley, and the Rutland peculiars of Caldecott, Ketton and Tixover, and Liddington prior to 1821, now preserved in the probate registry at Leicester.* 5 fiche. Reprint; originally published 1920. £35.00.

52. FOSTER, C.W., ed. *Calendars of administrations in the Consistory Court of Lincoln, A.D. 1540-1659.* 5 fiche. Reprint; originally published 1921. £35.00.

53. FRY, GEORGE S., ed. *Calendars of wills and administrations relating to the county of Dorset.* 4 fiche. Reprint; originally published 1922. £28.00.

54. BLAGG, THOMAS M., & MOIR, JOSEPHINE SKEATE, eds. *Index of wills proved in the Prerogative Court of Canterbury. Vol. vii: 1653-1656.* 9 fiche. Reprint; originally published 1925. £63.00.

55. FRY, E.A., & JENKINS, CLAUDE, eds. *Index to the act books of the archbishops of Canterbury, 1663-1859. Pt. i: A-K.* 7 fiche. Reprint; originally published 1929. £49.00.

56. GLENCROSS, R.M., ed. *Calendar of wills, administrations and accounts relating to the counties of Cornwall and Devon in the connotorial archidiaconal court of Cornwall (with which are included the records of the royal peculiar of St. Burian) now preserved in the district probate office at Bodmin. Pt. i: 1569-1699.* 4 fiche. Reprint; originally published 1929. £28.00.

57. FOSTER, C.W., ed. *Calendars of wills and administrations at Lincoln. Vol. iv: Archdeaconry of Stow, peculiar courts, and miscellaneous courts.* 6 fiche. Reprint; originally published 1930. £42.00.

58. BLAGG, THOMAS M., & WADSWORTH, F. ARTHUR, eds. *Abstracts of Nottinghamshire marriage licences. Vol. i: Archdeaconry court, 1577-1700; peculiar of Southwell, 1588-1754.* 8 fiche. Reprint; originally published 1930. £56.00.

59. GLENCROSS, R.M., ed. *Calendar of wills ... relating to the counties of Cornwall and Devon ... Pt. ii: 1700-1799.* 3 fiche. Reprint; originally published 1932. £21.00.

60. BLAGG, THOMAS M., & WADSWORTH, F. ARTHUR, eds. *Abstracts of Nottinghamshire marriage licences. Vol. ii: Archdeaconry court, 1701-1753; peculiar of Southwell, 1755-1853.* 8 fiche. Reprint; originally published 1935. £56.00.

61. BLAGG, THOMAS M., ed. *Index of wills proved in the Prerogative Court of Canterbury. Vol. viii: 1657-1660.* 10 fiche. Reprint; originally published 1936. £70.00.

62. GLENCROSS, REGINALD M., ed. *A calendar of the marriage licence allegations in the registry of the bishop of London. Vol. i: 1597 to 1648.* 5 fiche. Reprint; originally published 1937. £35.00.

63. JENKINS, CLAUDE, ed. *Index to the act books of the Archbishops of Canterbury, 1663-1859. Pt. ii: L-Z, with index locorum.* 7 fiche. Reprint; originally published 1938. £49.00.

64. FRY, EDWARD ALEXANDER, ed. *Calendar of administrations in the Consistory Court of the bishop of Chichester, 1555-1800; calendar of wills and administrations in the peculiar court of the Archbishop of Canterbury, 1520-1670; calendar of wills and administrations in the peculiar court of the dean of Chichester, 1577-1800.* 3 fiche. Reprint; originally published 1940. £21.00.

65. RIDGE, C. HAROLD, ed. *Index of wills and administrations now preserved in the Probate Registry at Canterbury. Vol. ii: Wills and administrations, 1558-1577, and administrations, 1539-1545.* 2 fiche. Reprint; originally published 1940. £14.00.

66. GLENCROSS, REGINALD M., ed. *A calendar of the marriage licence allegations in the registry of the Bishop of London. Vol. ii: 1660-1700.* 3 fiche. Reprint; originally published 1940. £21.00.

67. AINSWORTH, JOHN, ed. *Index of wills proved in the Prerogative Court of Canterbury. Vol. ix: 1671-1675.* 4 fiche. Reprint; originally published 1942. £28.00.

68. AINSWORTH, JOHN, ed. *Index to administrations in the Prerogative Court of Canterbury, and now preserved in the Principal Probate Registry, Somerset House, London. Vol. i: 1649-1654.* 6 fiche. Reprint; originally published 1944. £42.00.

69. FARROW, M.A., ed. *Index to wills proved in the Consistory Court of Norwich and now preserved in the district probate registry at Norwich, 1370-1550, and wills among the Norwich enrolled deeds, 1286-1508.* 5 fiche. Reprint; originally published 1945. £35.00.

70. DRUCKER, LUCY, ed. *Administrations in the Archdeaconry of Northampton, 1677-1710, now preserved in the District Probate Registry at Birmingham.* 3 fiche. Reprint; originally published 1947. £21.00.

71. RIDGE, C. HAROLD, ed. *Index to wills proved in the Prerogative Court of Canterbury. Vol. x: 1676-1685.* 6 fiche. Reprint; originally published 1948. £42.00.

72. RIDGE, C. HAROLD, ed. *Index to administrations in the Prerogative Court of Canterbury ... Vol. ii: 1655-1660, A-F.* 2 fiche. Reprint; originally published 1949. £14.00.

73. MILLICAN, PERCY, ed. *Index to wills proved in the consistory court of Norwich ... 1550-1603.* 2 fiche. Reprint; originally published 1950. £14.00.

74. RIDGE, C. HAROLD, ed. *Index to administrations in the Prerogative Court of Canterbury ... Vol. ii: 1655-1660, G-Q.* 2 fiche. Reprint; originally published 1952. £14.00.

75. RIDGE, C. HAROLD, ed. *Index to administrations in the Prerogative Court of Canterbury ... Vol. ii: 1655-1660, R-Z.* 2 fiche. Reprint; originally published 1953. £14.00.

76. RIDGE, C. HAR0LD, ed. *Index to administrations in the Prerogative Court of Canterbury ... Vol. iii: 1581-1596.* 2 fiche. Reprint; originally published 1954. £14.00.

77. RIDGE, C. HAROLD, ed. *Index to wills proved in the Prerogative Court of Canterbury. Vol. xi: 1686-1693.* 5 fiche. Reprint; originally published 1958. £35.00.

78. EMMISON, F.G., ed. *Index to wills at Chelmsford (Essex and East Hertfordshire). Vol. i: 1400-1619.* 6 fiche. Reprint; originally published 1958. £42.00.

79. EMMISON, F.G., ed. *Index to wills at Chelmsford (Essex and East Hertfordshire). Vol. ii: 1620-1720.* 5 fiche. Reprint; originally published 1961. £35.00.

80. FITCH, MARC, ed. *Index to wills proved in the Prerogative Court of Canterbury. Vol. xii: 1694-1700.* 6 fiche. Reprint; originally published 1960. £42.00.

81. FITCH, MARC, ed. *Index to administrations in the Prerogative Court of Canterbury. Vol. iv: 1596-1608.* 3 fiche. Reprint; originally published 1964. £21.00.

82. FITCH, MARC, ed. *Index to testamentary records in the Commissary Court of London (London division) now preserved in the Guildhall Library, London. Vol. i: 1374-1488.* 3 fiche. Reprint; originally published 1969. £21.00.

83. FITCH, MARC, ed. *Index to administrations in the Prerogative Court of Canterbury. Vol. v: 1609-1619.* 3 fiche. Reprint; originally published 1968. £21.00.

84. EMMISON, F.G., ed. *Index to wills at Chelmsford (Essex and East Hertfordshire). Vol. iii: 1721-1858.* 5 fiche. Reprint; originally published 1969. £35.00.

85. HOUSTON, JANE, ed. *Index of cases in the records of the Court of Arches at Lambeth Palace library, 1660-1913.* 7 fiche. Reprint; originally published 1972. £49.00.

86. *Index to testamentary records in the Commissary Court of London (London division). Vol. ii: 1489-1570.* 4 fiche. Reprint; originally published 1974. £28.00.

87. HOWSE, JASMINE S., ed. *Index of the probate records of the court of the Archdeaconry of Berkshire. Vol. ii: 1653-1710.* 2 fiche. Reprint; originally published 1975. £14.00.

88. THURLEY, CLIFFORD A., & THURLEY, DOROTHEA, eds. *Index of the probate records of the court of the Archdeacon of Ely, 1513-1857.* 3 fiche. Reprint; originally published 1976. £21.00.

Friends of the Public Record Office

Ashton Lodge, Church Road, Lyminge, Folkestone, Kent CT18 8JA

Index to Prerogative Court of Canterbury registered wills and administration acts for 1701-1749, compiled from PROB12/71-119. Fiche. £25.00 + p&p £1.00.

Huguenot Society of Great Britain and Ireland

Huguenot Library, University College, Gower Street, London WC1E 6BT
Phone: (0171) 3807094
Email: s.massil@ucl.ac.uk
Members are entitled to a substantial discount

Quarto Series 0509-8554. Fiche set vols 1-47. £150.00.

1. MOENS, WILLIAM JOHN CHARLES. *The Walloons and their church at Norwich: their history and registers, 1565-1832.* 2 parts. 1887-8. Baptisms 1595-1752, marriages 1599-1611, banns 1628-91. Fiche reprint, £5.00.

2. CHAMIER, ADRIEN CHARLES, ed. *Les actes de colloques des églises françaises et des synodes des églises étrangères réfugiées en Angleterre, 1581-1654.* 1890. Fiche reprint, £5.00.

4. GODFRAY, HUMPHREY MARETT, ed. *Registre des baptesmes, mariages et mortz, et jeusnes, et de léglise wallonne et des isles de Jersey, Guernesey, Serq, Origny, etc., établie a Southampton par patente du roy Edouard sixe et de la reine Elizabeth.* 1890. Registers begin 1567, baptisms end 1779, marriages 1753, deaths 1722. With professions of faith, 1567-1665 and 1722, and register of *jeunes*, 1568-1721. Fiche reprint, £5.00.

5. HOVENDEN, ROBERT, ed. *The registers of the Walloon church in Canterbury.* 3 vols. 1891-8. Baptisms 1581-1837, marriages 1590-1747, deaths 1581-1715, *etc.* Fiche reprint, £5.00.

8. PAGE, WILLIAM, ed. *Letters of denization and acts of naturalization for aliens in England, 1509-1603.* 1893. Fiche reprint, £5.00.

9. MOENS, WILLIAM JOHN CHARLES, ed. *The registers of the French church of Threadneedle Street, London. Part 1.* 1896. Marriages 1600-36; baptisms 1600-39. Fiche reprint, £5.00.

10. KIRK, R.E.G. & KIRK, ERNEST F., eds. *Returns of aliens dwelling in the city and suburbs of London, from the reign of Henry VIII to that of James I.* 4 vols. 1900-1908. Fiche reprint, £5.00.

11. MINET, WILLIAM & WALLER, WILLIAM CHAPMAN, eds. *Registers of the church known as La Patente in Spittlefields from 1689 to 1785.* 1898. Fiche reprint, £5.00.

12. MOENS, W. J. C., ed. *Register of baptisms in the Dutch church at Colchester from 1645 to 1728.* 1905. Fiche reprint, £5.00.

13. *The registers of the French church, Threadneedle Street, London. Vol. II.* 1899. Marriages 1637-85; baptisms 1640-85. Fiche reprint, £5.00.

15. CROSS, FRANCIS W. *History of the Walloon and Huguenot church at Canterbury.* 1898. Fiche reprint, £5.00.

16. COLYER-FERGUSSON, T.C., ed. *The registers of the French church, Threadneedle Street, London. Vol. III.* 1906. Marriages and baptisms 1686-1714. Fiche reprint, £5.00.

17. PEET, HENRY, ed. *Register of baptisms of the French protestant refugees settled at Thorney, Cambridgeshire, 1654-1727.* 1903. Fiche reprint, £5.00.

18. SHAW, WILLIAM A., ed. *Letters of denization and acts of naturalisation for aliens in England and Ireland, 1603-1700.* 1911. Fiche reprint, £5.00.

20. LART, CHARLES EDMUND, ed. *Registers of the French churches of Bristol, Stonehouse and Plymouth.* 1912. Includes WALLER, WILLIAM CHAPMAN, ed. *The register of the French church at Thorpe-le-Soken in Essex, 1684-1726.* Bristol: baptisms 1687-1762; marriages 1688-1744; burials 1688-1807. Stonehouse: baptisms 1692-1791; marriages 1693-1748; burials 1692-1788. Plymouth: baptisms 1733-1807; marriages 1734-40; burials 1733-4. Thorpe-le-Soken: baptisms 1684-1726; marriages 1684-1708; burials 1685-1718. Fiche reprint, £5.00.

21. MINET, WILLIAM, & MINET, SUSAN, eds. *Livre des tesmoignages de l'église de Threadneedle Street, 1669-1789.* 1909. Alphabetical list of newly admitted members of the congregation. Fiche reprint, £5.00.

23. *The registers of the French church, Threadneedle Street, London. Vol. IV.* 1916. Fiche reprint, £5.00. Marriages 1707-52; baptisms 1715-1840.

25. MINET, WILLIAM & MINET, SUSAN, eds. *Registers of the church of Le Carré and Berwick Street, 1690-1788.* 1921. Fiche reprint, £5.00.

26. MINET, WILLIAM & MINET, SUSAN, eds. *Registres des églises de la Savoye, de Spring Gardens, et des Grecs, 1684-1900.* 1922. Baptisms 1684-1900, marriages 1684-1753. Fiche reprint, £5.00.

27. SHAW, WILLIAM A., ed. *Letters of denization and acts of naturalisation for aliens in England and Ireland, 1701-1800.* 1923. Fiche reprint, £5.00.

28. MINET, WILLIAM, & MINET, SUSAN, eds. *Registres des églises de la chapelle royale de Saint James, 1700-1756, et de Swallow Street, 1690-1709.* 1924. Fiche reprint, £5.00.

29. MINET, WILLIAM, & MINET, SUSAN, eds. *Registers of the churches of the Tabernacle, Glasshouse Street and Leicester Fields, 1688-1783.* 1926. Marriages and baptisms 1688-1783. Fiche reprint, £5.00.

30. MINET, WILLIAM, & MINET, SUSAN, eds. *Register of the church of Rider Court, 1688-1738.* 1927. Fiche reprint, £5.00. Marriages, 1700-1738; baptisms, 1700-1747, *etc.*

31. MINET, WILLIAM, & MINET, SUSAN, eds. *Register of the church of Hungerford Market, later Castle Street.* 1928. Baptisms and marriages, 1688-1754, also *reconnaissances.* Fiche reprint, £5.00.

32. MINET, WILLIAM, & MINET, SUSAN, eds. *Registres des quatre églises du Petit Charenton, de West Street, de Pearl Street, et de Crispin Street.* 1929. Baptisms, marriages and *reconnaissances.* Petit Charenton: 1701-5. West Street: 1693-1743. Crispin Street: 1694-1716. Pearl Street: 1698-1701. Fiche reprint, £5.00.

33. WALLER, WILLIAM CHAPMAN, ed. *Extracts from the court books of the Weaver's Company of London, 1610-1730.* 1931. Fiche reprint, £5.00.

35. *A supplement to Dr W. A. Shaw's Letters of denization and acts of naturalisation which formed volumes 18 and 27 ...* 1932. Fiche reprint, £5.00.

37. MINET, WILLIAM & MINET, SUSAN, eds. *Register of the church of Saint Martin Orgars, with its history and that of Swallow Street.* 1938. Baptisms 1698-1762, marriages 1698-1751, *etc.* Fiche reprint, £5.00.

38. JOHNSON, ELSIE, ed. *Actes du consistoire de l'église française de Threadneedle Street, Londres. Vol. I. 1560-1565.* 1937. Fiche reprint, £5.00.

39. MINET, SUSAN, ed. *The register of the church of Saint Jean, Spitalfields.* 1938. Baptisms 1687-1823, marriages 1687-1751, *etc.* Fiche reprint, £5.00.

42. MINET, SUSAN, ed. *Register of the church of the Artillery, Spitalfields, 1691-1786.* 1948. Baptisms 1691-1786, marriages 1691-1754, with other entries. Fiche reprint, £5.00.

45. MINET, SUSAN, ed. *Registers of the churches of La Patente de Soho, Wheeler Street, Swanfields and Hoxton; also the Répertoire général.* 1956. Fiche reprint, £5.00.

Bedfordshire

Bedfordshire Historical Record Society

Orders for microfiche reprints to: Chadwyck-Healey Ltd., The Quorum, Barnwell Road, Cambridge, CB5 8SW
Phone: (01223) 215512
Email: mail@chadwyck.co.uk
Http://www.chadwyck.co.uk

6. FOWLER, G. HERBERT, ed. *A calendar of the feet of fines for Bedfordshire, preserved in the Public Record Office, of the reigns of Richard I, John, and Henry III.* 3 fiche. Reprint; originally published 1919. £21.00.

7. FOWLER, G. HERBERT, & HUGHES, MICHAEL W., ed. *A calendar of the pipe rolls of the reign of Richard I for Buckinghamshire and Bedfordshire, 1189-1199.* 3 fiche. Reprint; originally published 1923. £21.00.

10. FOWLER, G. HERBERT, ed. *A digest of the charters preserved in the cartulary of the priory of Dunstable.* 5 fiche. Reprint; originally published 1926. £35.00.

13. FOWLER, G. HERBERT, ed. *Cartulary of the abbey of Old Wardon.* 5 fiche. Reprint; originally published 1930. £35.00.

16. MARSHALL, LYDIA M., ed. *The rural population of Bedfordshire, 1671-1921, based on the hearth tax return of 1671 and the census returns of 1801 and 1921.* 3 fiche. Reprint; originally published 1934. £21.00.

Huguenot Society (cont.)

17. FOWLER, G. HERBERT, ed. *Records of Harrold Priory.* 3 fiche. Reprint; originally published 1935. £21.00.

20. EMMISON, F.G., ed. *Jacobean household inventories,* with WIFFIELD, W.M., ed. *Recusancy and nonconformity in Bedfordshire, illustrated by select documents between 1622 and 1842.* 3 fiche. Reprint; originally published 1938. £21.00.

21. FOWLER, G. HERBERT, ed. *Calendar of the roll of the justices on eyre, 1247.* 3 fiche. Reprint; originally published 1939. £21.00.

22. FOWLER, G. HERBERT, & GODBER, JOYCE, ed. *The cartulary of Bushmead Priory.* 4 fiche. Reprint; originally published 1945. £28.00.

26. PARSLOE, GUY, ed. *The minute book of Bedford corporation, 1647-1664.* 3 fiche. Reprint; originally published 1949. £21.00.

27. TIBBUTT, H.G., ed. *The life and letters of Sir Lewis Dyve, 1599-1699.* 2 fiche. Reprint; originally published 1948. £14.00.

28. DALE, MARIAN K., ed. *Court roll of Chalgrave manor, 1278-1313.* 2 fiche. Reprint; originally published 1950. £14.00.

29. BASSETT, MARGERY, ed. *Knights of the shire for Bedfordshire during the middle ages.* 2 fiche. Reprint; originally published 1949. £14.00.

30. LINNELL, C.D., ed. *The diary of Benjamin Rogers, rector of Carlton, 1720-71.* 2 fiche. Reprint; originally published 1950. £14.00.

31. POYNTER, F.N.L., & BISHOP, W.J. *A seventeenth century doctor and his patients: John Symcotts, 1592?-1662.* 2 fiche. Reprint; originally published 1951. £14.00.

33. FARMILOE, J.E., & NIXSEAMAN, ROSITA, eds. *Elizabethan churchwardens' accounts.* 2 fiche. Reprint; originally published 1953. £14.00.

36. *The Gostwicks of Willington, and other studies.* 2 fiche. Reprint; originally published 1956. £14.00.

37. CIRKET, A.F., ed. *English wills, 1498-1526,* with STITT, BETTE, ed. *Diana Astry's recipe book, c. 1700.* 3 fiche. Reprint; originally published 1957. £21.00.

39. GAYDON, A.T., ed. *The taxation of 1297. A translation of the local rolls of assessment for Barford, Biggleswade and Flitt Hundreds, and for Bedford, Dunstable, Leighton Buzzard and Luton.* 2 fiche. Reprint; originally published 1958. £14.00.

40. *Some Bedfordshire diaries.* 3 fiche. Reprint; originally published 1959. £21.00. 11 diaries + letters, 17-19th c.

41. HUNNISETT, R.F., ed. *Bedfordshire coroners' rolls.* 3 fiche. Reprint; originally published 1960. £21.00. Medieval.

42. TIBBUTT, H.G., ed. *The letter books of Sir Samuel Luke, 1644-45.* 8 fiche. Reprint; originally published 1963. £56.00. Parliamentary Governor of Newport Pagnell.

43. GODBER, JOYCE, ed. *The cartulary of Newnham Priory.* 6 fiche. Reprint; originally published 1963-4. £42.00.

44. GODBER, JOYCE, ed. *The Oakley Hunt.* 2 fiche. Reprint; originally published 1965. £14.00.

45. BELL, PATRICIA, ed. *Bedfordshire wills, 1480-1519.* 2 fiche. Reprint; originally published 1966. £14.00.

46. JACK, R.I., ed. *The Greys of Ruthin valor: the valor of the English lands of Edmund Grey, Earl of Kent, drawn up from the ministers' accounts of 1467-68.* 2 fiche. Reprint; originally published 1965. £14.00.

Quarto Series

1. FOWLER, G. HERBERT. *Bedfordshire in 1086. An analysis and synthesis of Domesday Book.* 2 fiche. Reprint; originally published 1922. £14.00.

3. FOWLER, G. HERBERT, ed. *Rolls from the office of the sheriff of Beds. and Bucks., 1332-1334.* 1 fiche. Reprint; originally published 1929. £7.00.

Buckinghamshire

Buckinghamshire Record Society

Orders for microfiche reprints to:
Chadwyck-Healey Ltd., The Quorum, Barnwell Road, Cambridge, CB5 8SW
Phone: (01223) 215512
Email: mail@chadwyck.co.uk
Http://www.chadwyck.co.uk

1. SNELL, BEATRICE SAXON SNELL, ed. *The minute book of the monthly meeting of the Society of Friends for the upperside of Buckinghamshire, 1669-1690.* 3 fiche. Reprint; originally published 1937. £21.00.

2. JENKINS, J.G., ed. *The cartulary of Missenden Abbey. Pt. I, containing royal and episcopal charters and charters relating to Missenden, Kingshill, the Lee, and Wendover.* 3 fiche. Reprint; originally published 1938. £21.00.

3. FOWLER, G. HERBERT, & JENKINS, J.G., ed. *Early Buckinghamshire charters.* 1 fiche. Reprint; originally published 1939. £7.00.
4. HUGHES, M.W., ed. *A calendar of the feet of fines for the county of Buckingham, 7 Richard I to 44 Henry III.* 2 fiche. Reprint; originally published 1940. £14.00.
5. *A calendar of deeds and other records preserved in the muniment room at the museum, Aylesbury.* 2 fiche. Reprint; originally published 1941. £14.00.
6. JENKINS, J.G., ed. *Calendar of the roll of the justices on eyre, 1227.* 2 fiche. Reprint; originally published 1945. £14.00.
7. BRINKWORTH, E.R.C., ed. *Episcopal visitation book for the Archdeaconry of Buckingham, 1662.* 2 fiche. Reprint; originally published 1947. £14.00.
8. CHIBNALL, A.C., & WOODMAN, A. VERE, ed. *Subsidy roll for the county of Buckingham, anno 1524.* 2 fiche. Reprint; originally published 1950. £14.00.
9. JENKINS, J.G., ed. *The cartulary of Snelshall priory.* 1 fiche. Reprint; originally published 1952. £7.00.
10. JENKINS, J.G., ed. *The Missenden cartulary. Part ii.* 3 fiche. Reprint; originally published 1955. £21.00.
11. GREAVES, R.W., ed. *The first ledger book of High Wycombe.* 4 fiche. Reprint; originally published 1956. £28.00.

Cheshire
See Lancashire

Devon & Cornwall
Devon and Cornwall Record Society
Orders for microfiche reprints to:
Chadwyck-Healey Ltd., The Quorum, Barnwell Road, Cambridge, CB5 8SW
Phone: (01223) 215512
Email: mail@chadwyck.co.uk
Http://www.chadwyck.co.uk

1. FRY, HENRY ALEXANDER, ed. *A calendar of inquisitiones post mortem for Cornwall and Devon, from Henry III to Charles I, 1216-1649.* 2 fiche. Reprint; originally published 1906. £14.00.
2. DREDGE, JOHN INGLE, ed. *The registers of Parkham.* 3 fiche. Reprint; originally published 1906. £21.00.

3. TAPLEY-SOPER, H., ed. *The register of baptisms, marriages and burials of the parish of Ottery St. Mary, Devon, 1601-1837.* 13 fiche. Reprint; originally published 1908-29. £91.00.
4. *Subsidy rolls, muster and hearth tax rolls, and probate calendars of the parish of St. Constantine (Kerrier), Cornwall.* 2 fiche. Reprint; originally published 1910. £14.00.
5. *The registers of baptisms, marriages and burials of the city of Exeter.* 12 fiche. Reprint; originally published 1910-33. £84.00.
6. *Devon feet of fines.* 11 fiche. Reprint; originally published 1912-39. £77.00.
7. TAPLEY-SOPER, H., & CHICK, ELIJAH, ed. *The register of baptisms, marriages and burials of the parish of Branscombe, Devon, 1539-1812.* 4 fiche. Reprint; originally published 1913. £28.00.
8. *Cornwall feet of fines.* 10 fiche. Reprint; originally published 1914-50. £70.00.
9. GAY, SUSAN ELIZABETH, & FOX, HOWARD, MRS, ed. *The register of baptisms, marriages and burials of the parish of Falmouth in the county of Cornwall, 1663-1812.* 13 fiche. Reprint; originally published 1914-15. £91.00.
10. SKINNER, A.J.P., ed. *The register of baptisms, marriages and burials of the parish of Parracombe, Devon, 1597-1836.* 2 fiche. Reprint; originally published 1917. £14.00.
11. HARTE, WALTER J., SCHOPP, J.W., & TAPLEY-SOPER, H., eds. *The description of the citie of Excester, by Iohn Vowell alias Hoker, gentleman and chamberlayne of the same.* 13 fiche. Reprint; originally published 1919-47. £91.00.
13. SKINNER, A.J.P., ed. *The register of baptisms, marriages and burials of the parish of Hemyock, Devon, 1635-1837, with the bishop's transcripts for the years 1602, 1606, 1609, 1611, 1617, 1625, 1626, 1633, 1636, and a list of the rectors and chaplain priests.* 3 fiche. Reprint; originally published 1923. £21.00.
12. JOHNSON, HERBERT, & TAPLEY-SOPER, H., ed. *The register of baptisms, marriages and burials of the parish of Lustleigh, Devon, 1631-1837, and extracts from the bishop's transcripts, 1608-1811.* 2 fiche. Reprint; originally published 1927-30. £14.00.

Devon and Cornwall Record Society (*cont.*)

14. SKINNER, A.J.P., ed. *The register of baptisms, marriages and burials of the parish of Colyton, Devon, 1538-1837.* 1 vol. in 2. 9 fiche. Reprint; originally published 1928. £63.00.

15. FURSDON, C.A.T., ed. *The register of baptisms, marriages and burials of the parish of Halberton, Devon, 1605-1837.* 5 fiche. Reprint; originally published 1930-1. £35.00.

16. DREDGE, JOHN INGLE, & CHOPE, R. PEARSE, ed. *The register of baptisms, marriages and burials of the parish of Hartland, Devon, 1558-1837.* 7 fiche. Reprint; originally published 1930-4. £49.00.

17. WOOD, E.C., & TAPLEY-SOPER, H., ed. *The register of marriages, baptisms and burials of the parish of Widecombe-in-the-Moor, Devon.* 4 fiche. Reprint; originally published 1938. £28.00.

18. TAPLEY-SOPER, H., ed. *Parish of Topsham, co. Devon. Marriages, baptisms and burials, A.D. 1600 to 1837, from the parochial register, the register of the independent meeting, the register of the Presbyterians, the register of the Quakers, together with copies of memorial inscriptions.* 10 fiche. Reprint; originally published 1938. £70.00.

19. HAY, EDGAR, ed. *The register of marriages, baptisms and burials of the parish of Plymtree, co. Devon, A.D. 1538 to 1837.* 3 fiche. Reprint; originally published 1940. £21.00.

20. GAY, SUSAN E., FOX, HOWARD, MRS, FOX, STELLA, & TAPLEY-SOPER, H., eds. *The register of marriages, baptisms and burials of the parish of St. Mary, Truro, co. Cornwall, A.D. 1597 to 1837.* 9 fiche. Reprint; originally published 1940. £63.00.

21. TAPLEY-SOPER, H., ed. *The register of marriages, baptisms and burials of the parish of Camborne, co. Cornwall, A.D. 1538-1837.* 11 fiche. Reprint; originally published 1945. £77.00.

23. DENSHAM, A.R., ed. *The register of baptisms, marriages and burials of the parish of Lapford, co. Devon, A.D. 1567-1850.* 3 fiche. Reprint; originally published 1954. £21.00.

24. CRUWYS, M.C.S., ed. *The register of the parish of St. Andrew's, Plymouth, co. Devon, A.D. 1581-1618, with baptisms, 1619-1633.* 7 fiche. Reprint; originally published 1954. £49.00.

New series

1. YOUINGS, JOYCE, ed. *Devon monastic lands: calendar of particulars for grants 1536-1558.* 3 fiche. Reprint; originally published 1955. £21.00.

2. HOSKINS, W.G. *Exeter in the seventeenth century: tax and rate assessments 1602-1699.* 2 fiche. Reprint; originally published 1957. £14.00.

3. COOK, MICHAEL, ed. *The Diocese of Exeter in 1821: Bishop Carey's replies to queries before visitation. Vol. 1. Cornwall.* 2 fiche. Reprint; originally published 1958. £14.00.

4. COOK, MICHAEL, ed. *The Diocese of Exeter in 1821: Bishop Carey's replies to queries before visitation. Vol. 2. Devon.* 3 fiche. Reprint; originally published 1960. £21.00.

5. HULL, P.L., ed. *The cartulary of St. Michael's Mount, Cornwall.* 2 fiche. Reprint; originally published 1965. £14.00.

6. BROCKETT, ALLAN, ed. *The Exeter Assembly: minutes of the assemblies of the United Brethren of Devon and Cornwall 1691-1717 as transcribed by the Rev. Isaac Gilling.* 2 fiche. Reprint; originally published 1963. £14.00.

7. DUNSTAN, G.R., ed. *The register of Edmund Lacy, Bishop of Exeter 1420-1455. Registrum commune. Vol. I: 1420-1436.* 4 fiche. Reprint; originally published 1963. £28.00.

8. LONDON, V.C.M., ed. *The cartulary of Canonsleigh Abbey, Devon. A calendar.* 3 fiche. Reprint; originally published 1965. £21.00.

10. DUNSTAN, G.R., ed. *The register of Edmund Lacy, Bishop of Exeter 1420-1455. Registrum commune. Vol. II: 1436-1448.* 5 fiche. Reprint; originally published 1966. £35.00.

11. CASH, MARGARET, ed. *Devon inventories of the sixteenth and seventeenth centuries.* 3 fiche. Reprint; originally published 1966. £21.00.

12. WELCH, EDWIN, ed. *Plymouth building accounts of the sixteenth and seventeenth centuries.* 2 fiche. Reprint; originally published 1967. £14.00.

13. DUNSTAN, G.R., ed. *The register of Edmund Lacy, Bishop of Exeter 1420-1455. Registrum commune. Vol. III: 1448-1455.* 5 fiche. Reprint; originally published 1968. £35.00.

14. ERSKINE, AUDREY M., ed. *The Devonshire lay subsidy of 1332.* 3 fiche. Reprint; originally published 1969. £21.00.

15. HANHAM, ALISON., ed. *Churchwardens' accounts of Ashburton, 1479-1580.* 3 fiche. Reprint; originally published 1970. £21.00.

Co.Durham
Surtees Society

Orders for microfiche reprints to:
Chadwyck-Healey Ltd., The Quorum, Barnwell Road, Cambridge, CB5 8SW
Phone: (01223) 215512
Email: mail@chadwyck.co.uk
Http://www.chadwyck.co.uk

2. RAINE, JAMES, ed. *Wills and inventories illustrative of the history, manners, language, statistics, etc., of the northern counties of England, from the eleventh century downwards. Part I, 11th c.-1581.* 5 fiche. Reprint; originally published 1835. £35.00. Mainly of Durham Diocese.

4. RAINE, JAMES, ed. *Testamenta Eboracensia; or wills registered at York illustrative of the history, manners, language, statistics, etc., of the province of York, from the year 1300 downwards. Part i, 1316-1430.* 5 fiche. Reprint; originally published 1836. £35.00.

6. RAINE, JAMES, ed. *The priory of Finchale. The charters of endowment, inventories, and account rolls, of the priory of Finchale, in the county of Durham.* 8 fiche. Reprint; originally published 1837. £56.00.

13. STEVENSON, JOSEPH, ed. *Liber vitae ecclesiae Dunelmensis; nec non obituaria duo eiusdem ecclesiae.* 2 fiche. Reprint; originally published 1841. £14.00. Register of benefactors.

21. RAINE, JAMES, ed. *Depositions and other ecclesiastical proceedings from the courts of Durham, extending from 1311 to the reign of Elizabeth.* 4 fiche. Reprint; originally published 1845. £28.00.

25. GREENWELL, WILLIAM, ed. *Boldon buke: a survey of the possessions of the see of Durham, made by order of Bishop Hugh Pudsey in the year 1183. With a translation, an appendix of original documents, and a glossary.* 2 fiche. Reprint; originally published 1852. £14.00.

26. RAINE, JAMES, ed. *Wills and inventories from the registry of the Archdeaconry of Richmond, extending over portions of the counties of York, Westmorland, Cumberland, and Lancaster (1442-1579).* 4 fiche. Reprint; originally published 1853. £28.00.

29. RAINE, JAMES, ed. *The inventories and account rolls of the Benedictine houses or cells of Jarrow and Monk-Wearmouth, in the county of Durham.* 4 fiche. Reprint; originally published 1854. £28.00.

30. RAINE, JAMES, ed. *Testamenta Eboracensia: a selection of wills from the registry at York. Part ii, 1429-67.* 4 fiche. Reprint; originally published 1855. £28.00.

31. RAINE, JAMES, ed. *The obituary roll of William Ebchester and John Burnby, priors of Durham, with notices of similar records preserved at Durham, from the year 1233 downwards, letters of fraternity, etc.* 2 fiche. Reprint; originally published 1856. £14.00.

32. GREENWELL, WILLIAM, ed. *Bishop Hatfield's survey. A record of the possessions of the see of Durham, made by order of Thomas de Hatfield, bishop of Durham.* 4 fiche. Reprint; originally published 1857. £28.00.

33. ROBINSON, C.B., ed. *Rural economy in Yorkshire in 1641; being the farming and account books of Henry Best, of Elmswell in the East Riding of the county of York.* 3 fiche. Reprint; originally published 1857. £21.00.

34. LONGSTAFF, W.H.D., ed. *The acts of the high commission court within the diocese of Durham.* 4 fiche. Reprint; originally published 1858. £28.00.

35. RAINE, JAMES, ed. *The fabric rolls of York minster; with an appendix of illustrative documents.* 5 fiche. Reprint; originally published 1859. £35.00.

36. DAVIES, ROBERT, ed. *The visitation of the county of Yorke, begun in 1665 and finished 1666, by William Dugdale, Norroy King of arms.* 5 fiche. Reprint; originally published 1859.

Surtees Society (*cont.*)

38. GREENWELL, WILLIAM, ed. *Wills and inventories from the registry at Durham. Part ii.* 5 fiche. Reprint; originally published 1860. £35.00.

40. RAINE, JAMES, ed. *Depositions from the castle of York, relating to offences committed in the northern counties in the seventeenth century.* 4 fiche. Reprint; originally published 1861. £28.00.

41. LONGSTAFFE, W.HYLTON DYER, ed. *Heraldic visitation of the northern counties in 1530, by Thomas Tonge, Norroy King of Arms; with an appendix of other heraldic documents relating to the north of England.* 3 fiche. Reprint; originally published 1863. £21.00.

42. WALBRAN, J.R., ed. *Memorials of the abbey of St. Mary of Fountains. Vol. 1.* 6 fiche. Reprint; originally published 1863. £42.00.

45. RAINE, JAMES, ed. *Testamenta Eboracensia: a selection of wills from the registry at York. Part iii, 1395-1491.* 5 fiche. Reprint; originally published 1865. £35.00.

46. *The priory of Hexham. Vol. 2: Its title deeds, black book, etc.* 4 fiche. Reprint; originally published 1865. £28.00.

49. SCAIFE, R.H., ed. *The survey of the county of York, taken by John de Kirkby, commonly called Kirkby's inquest. Also inquisitions of knights' fees, the nomina villarum for Yorkshire, and an appendix of illustrative documents.* 6 fiche. Reprint; originally published 1867. £42.00.

53. *Testamenta Eboracensia: a selection of wills from the registry at York. Part iv, 1420-1509.* 5 fiche. Reprint; originally published 1869. £35.00.

54. JACKSON, CHARLES, ed. *The diary of Abraham de la Pryme, the Yorkshire antiquary (c.1680-1704).* 5 fiche. Reprint; originally published 1870. £35.00.

56. RAINE, JAMES, ed. *The register, or rolls, of Walter Gray, lord archbishop of York; with appendices of illustrative documents.* 5 fiche. Reprint; originally published 1872. £35.00.

57. SCAIFE, R.H., ed. *The register of the guild of Corpus Christi in the city of York; with an appendix of illustrative documents, containing some account of the hospital of St. Thomas of Canterbury without Micklegate-bar, in the suburbs of the city.* 4 fiche. Reprint; originally published 1872. £28.00.

58. GREENWELL, WILLIAM, ed. *Feodarium prioratus Dunelmensis. A survey of the estates of the prior and convent of Durham, compiled in the fifteenth century, illustrated by the original grants and other evidences.* 5 fiche. Reprint; originally published 1872. £35.00.

62. JACKSON, CHARLES, ed. *The autobiography of Mrs Alice Thornton, of East Newton, co. York, died 1706.* 5 fiche. Reprint; originally published 1875. £35.00.

64. FOWLER, J.T., ed. *Acts of the chapter of the collegiate church of SS. Peter and Wilfrid, Ripon, A.D.1452 to A.D.1506.* 5 fiche. Reprint; originally published 1875. £35.00.

65. *Yorkshire diaries and autobiographies in the seventeenth and eighteenth centuries.* 6 fiche. Reprint; originally published 1877. £42.00.

66. FOWLER, J.T., ed. *Chartularium abbathiae de novo monasterio, ordinis Cisterciensis, fundatae anno MCXXXVII.* 4 fiche. Reprint; originally published 1878. £28.00. Newminster, Northumberland.

67. WALBRAN, J.R., & RAINE, JAMES, eds. *Memorials of the abbey of St.Mary of Fountains. Vol. 2, part 1.* 4 fiche. Reprint; originally published 1878. £28.00.

68. ORNSBY, GEORGE, ed. *Selections from the household books of the Lord William Howard of Naworth Castle, with an appendix containing some of his papers and letters, and other documents illustrative of his life and times.* 7 fiche. Reprint; originally published 1878. £49.00.

69. ATKINSON, J.C., ed. *Cartularium abbathiae de Whitby, ordinis S. Benedicti, fundatae anno 1078. Pt.2.* 5 fiche. Reprint; originally published 1879. £35.00.

72. ATKINSON, J.C., ed. *Cartularium abbathiae de Whitby. Pt. 2.* 6 fiche. Reprint; originally published 1881. £42.00.

73. LUKIS, W.C., ed. *The family memoirs of the Rev. William Stukeley, M.D., and the antiquarian and other correspondence of William Stukeley, Roger and Samuel Gale, etc. Vol. 1.* 6 fiche. Reprint; originally published 1882. £42.00.

76. LUKIS, W.C., ed. *The family memoirs of the Rev. William Stukeley ... Vol. 2.* 5 fiche. Reprint; originally published 1883. £35.00.

77. *Yorkshire diaries and autobiographies ... Vol. 2.* 2 fiche. Reprint; originally published 1886. £14.00.

78. *Memorials of the church of SS. Peter and Wilfrid, Ripon. Vol. 2.* 5 fiche. Reprint; originally published 1886. £35.00.

79. RAINE, JAMES, ed. *Testamenta Eboracensia: a selection of wills from the registry at York. Part v, 1509-31.* 4 fiche. Reprint; originally published 1884. £28.00.

80. LUKIS, W.C., ed. *The family memoirs of the Rev. William Stukeley ... Vol. 3.* 7 fiche. Reprint; originally published 1887. £49.00.

81. *Memorials of the church of SS. Peter and Wilfrid, Ripon. Vol. 3.* 5 fiche. Reprint; originally published 1888. £35.00.

82. LONGSTAFFE, W.H., & BOOTH, J., eds. *Halmota prioratus Dunelmensis. Containing extracts from the halmote court or manor rolls of the prior and convent of Durham, 1296-1384.* 4 fiche. Reprint; originally published 1889. £28.00.

83. ATKINSON, J.C., ed. *Cartularium abbathiae de Rievalle, ordinis Cisterciensis, fundatae anno 1132.* 7 fiche. Reprint; originally published 1889. £49.00.

84. BARMBY, J., ed. *Churchwardens' accounts of Pittington and other parishes in the diocese of Durham, from 1580 to 1700.* 5 fiche. Reprint; originally published 1888. £35.00.

86. BROWN, W., ed. *Cartularium prioratus de Gyseburne, Ebor. dioeceseos, ordinis S. Augustini, fundati A.D.MCXIX. Vol. 1.* 4 fiche. Reprint; originally published 1889. £28.00.

88. PAGE, WILLIAM, ed. *Three early assize rolls for the county of Northumberland, 13th century.* 6 fiche. Reprint; originally published 1891. £42.00.

89. BROWN, W., ed. *Cartularium prioratus de Gyseburne, Ebor. dioeceseos, ordinis S. Augustini, fundati A.D.MCXIX. Vol. 2.* 6 fiche. Reprint; originally published 1894. £42.00.

90. PAGE, WILLIAM, ed. *The chartulary of Brinkburn Priory.* 3 fiche. Reprint; originally published 1893. £21.00.

91. PAGE, WILLIAM, ed. *The certificates of the commissioners appointed to survey the chantries, guilds, hospitals, etc., in the county of York, 1546. Pt. 1.* 3 fiche. Reprint; originally published 1894. £21.00.

92. PAGE, WILLIAM, ed. *The certificates of the commissioners appointed to survey the chantries, guilds, hospitals, ect., in the county of York, 1546. Pt. 2.* 5 fiche. Reprint; originally published 1895. £35.00.

93. BOYLE, J.R., & DENDY, F.W., ed. *Extracts from the records of the Merchant Adventurers of Newcastle-upon-Tyne. Vol. i.* 4 fiche. Reprint; originally published 1895. £28.00.

94. BROWN, W., ed. *Pedes finium Ebor. regnante Johanne, A.D. MCXCIX - A.D. MCCDIV.* 3 fiche. Reprint; originally published 1897. £21.00.

95. BARMBY, J., ed. *Memorials of St. Giles's, Durham, being grassmen's accounts and other parish records, together with documents relating to the hospitals of Kepier and St. Mary Magdalene.* 4 fiche. Reprint; originally published 1896. £28.00. Includes parish register, 1584-1756.

96. COLLINS, FRANCIS, ed. *Register of the freemen of the city of York. Vol. i: 1272-1558.* 4 fiche. Reprint; originally published 1897. £28.00.

97. PAGE, WILLIAM, ed. *The inventories of church goods for the counties of York, Durham and Northumberland.* 3 fiche. Reprint; originally published 1897. £21.00.

98. LEACH, A.F., ed. *Memorials of Beverley minster. The chapter act-book of the collegiate church of St. John of Beverley, A.D. 1286-1347. Vol. i.* 6 fiche. Reprint; originally published 1898. £42.00.

99. FOWLER, J.T., ed. *Extracts from the account rolls of the abbey of Durham. Vol. 1.* 4 fiche. Reprint; originally published 1898. £28.00.

100. FOWLER, J.T., ed. *Extracts from the account rolls of the abbey of Durham. Vol. 2.* 4 fiche. Reprint; originally published 1899. £28.00.

101. DENDY, F.W., ed. *Extracts from the records of the Merchant Adventurers of Newcastle-upon-Tyne. Vol. ii.* 5 fiche. Reprint; originally published 1899. £35.00.

102. *Register of freemen of the city of York. Vol. ii: 1559-1759.* 4 fiche. Reprint; originally published 1900. £28.00.

Surtees Society (cont.)

103. FOWLER, J.T., ed. *Extracts from the account rolls of the abbey of Durham. Vol. 3.* 6 fiche. Reprint; originally published 1901. £42.00.

104. COLLINS, FRANCIS, ed. *Wills and administrations from the Knaresborough court rolls. Vol. i.* 4 fiche. Reprint; originally published 1902. £28.00. 1506-1606.

105. DENDY, F.W., ed. *Extracts from the records of the Company of Hostmen of Newcastle-upon-Tyne.* 5 fiche. Reprint; originally published 1901. £35.00.

106. CLAY, J.W., ed. *Testamenta Eboracensia: a selection of wills from the registry at York. Vol. vi.* 4 fiche. Reprint; originally published 1902. £28.00. 1516-51.

108. *Memorials of Beverley minster. The chapter act-book ... Vol. ii.* 6 fiche. Reprint; originally published 1903. £42.00. Medieval.

109. BROWN, WILLIAM, ed. *The register of Walter Giffard, lord archbishop of York, 1266-1279.* 5 fiche. Reprint; originally published 1904. £35.00.

110. *Wills and administrations from the Knaresborough court rolls. Vol. ii, with index to original wills, etc., at Somerset House.* 4 fiche. Reprint; originally published 1905. £28.00.

111. WELFORD, RICHARD, ed. *Records of the committees for compounding, etc., with delinquent royalists in Durham and Northumberland during the civil war, etc., 1643-1660.* 6 fiche. Reprint; originally published 1905. £42.00.

112. HODGSON, J.C., ed. *Wills and inventories from the registry at Durham. Pt. iii.* 3 fiche. Reprint; originally published 1906. £21.00. 1543-1602.

113. KITCHIN, G.W., ed. *The records of the northern convocation.* 6 fiche. Reprint; originally published 1907. £42.00.

114. BROWN, WILLIAM, ed. *The register of William Wickwane, lord archbishop of York, 1279-1285.* 5 fiche. Reprint; originally published 1907. £35.00.

115. FOWLER, J.T., ed. *Memorials of the church of SS. Peter and Wilfrid, Ripon. Vol. iv, consisting of the Ingilby ms.* 4 fiche. Reprint; originally published 1908. £28.00.

116. CLAY, J.W., ed. *North country wills, being abstracts of wills relating to the counties of York, Nottingham, Northumberland, Cumberland, and Westmorland at Somerset House and Lambeth Palace. Vol. i. 1383 to 1558.* 4 fiche. Reprint; originally published 1908. £28.00.

117. MARTIN, M.T., ed. *The Percy chartulary.* 6 fiche. Reprint; originally published 1911. £42.00.

118. HODGSON, J.C., ed. *Six north country diaries.* 4 fiche. Reprint; originally published 1910. £28.00.

119. KITCHIN, G.W., ed. *Richard d'Aungerville, of Bury. Fragments of his register, and other documents.* 4 fiche. Reprint; originally published 1910. £28.00.

120. SELLERS, MAUD, ed. *York memorandum book. Pt. i: 1376-1419.* 4 fiche. Reprint; originally published 1912. £28.00.

121. CLAY, J.W., ed. *North country wills ... Vol. ii: 1558 to 1604.* 3 fiche. Reprint; originally published 1912. £21.00.

122. DENDY, F.W., ed. *Visitations of the north, or some early heraldic visitations of, and collections of pedigrees relating to, the north of England. Pt. i.* 4 fiche. Reprint; originally published 1912. £28.00.

123. BROWN, WILLIAM, ed. *The register of John le Romeyn, lord archbishop of York, 1286-1296. Pt. i.* 5 fiche. Reprint; originally published 1913. £35.00.

124. HODGSON, J.C., ed. *North country diaries (second series).* 4 fiche. Reprint; originally published 1915. £28.00.

125. *York memorandum book. Pt. ii: 1388-1493.* 5 fiche. Reprint; originally published 1915. £35.00.

126. WILSON, JAMES, ed. *The register of the priory of St. Bees.* 8 fiche. Reprint; originally published 1915. £56.00.

128. BROWN, WILLIAM, ed. *The registers of John le Romeyn, lord archbishop of York, 1286-1296, pt. ii, and of Henry of Newark, lord archbishop of York, 1296-1299.* 5 fiche. Reprint; originally published 1917. £35.00.

129. SELLERS, MAUD, ed. *The York mercers and merchant adventurers, 1356-1917.* 5 fiche. Reprint; originally published 1918. £35.00.

130. FOWLER, J.T., ed. *Memorials of the abbey of St. Mary of Fountains. Vol. iii, consisting of bursars' books, 1456-1459, and memorandum book of Thomas Swynton, 1446-1458.* 4 fiche. Reprint; originally published 1918. £28.00.

131. HODGSON, J.C., ed. *Northumbrian documents of the seventeenth and eighteenth centuries, comprising the register of the estates of Roman Catholics in Northumberland and the correspondence of Miles Stapylton.* 4 fiche. Reprint; originally published 1918. £28.00.

133. *Visitations of the north ... Pt. ii.* 3 fiche. Reprint; originally published 1921. £21.00.

134. HODGSON, J.C., ed. *Percy bailiff's rolls of the fifteenth century.* 2 fiche. Reprint; originally published 1921. £14.00.

135. WOOD, H.M., ed. *Durham protestations, or the returns made to the House of Commons in 1641-2 for the maintenance of the protestant religion for the county palatine of Durham, for the borough of Berwick-upon-Tweed and the parish of Morpeth.* 3 fiche. Reprint; originally published 1922. £21.00.

137. OLIVER, A.M., ed. *Early deeds relating to Newcastle-upon-Tyne.* 3 fiche. Reprint; originally published 1924. £21.00.

138. BROWN, WILLIAM, ed. *The register of Thomas of Corbridge, lord archbishop of York, 1300-1304. Pt. i.* 4 fiche. Reprint; originally published 1925. £28.00.

139. BOUTFLOWER, D.S., ed. *Fasti Dunelmenses. A record of the beneficed clergy of the diocese of Durham down to the dissolution of the monastic and collegiate churches.* 3 fiche. Reprint; originally published 1927. £21.00.

141. THOMPSON, A. HAMILTON, ed. *The register of Thomas of Corbridge, lord archbishop of York, 1300-1304. Pt. ii.* 3 fiche. Reprint; originally published 1929. £21.00.

142. WOOD, H.M., ed. *Wills and inventories from the registry at Durham. Pt. iv.* 4 fiche. Reprint; originally published 1929. £28.00.

144. BLAIR, C.H. HUNTER, ed. *Visitations of the north. Pt. iii: A visitation of the north of England circa 1480-1500.* 3 fiche. Reprint; originally published 1930. £21.00.

145. THOMPSON, A. HAMILTON, ed. *The register of William Greenfield, lord archbishop of York, 1306-1315. Pt.i.* 4 fiche. Reprint; originally published 1931. £28.00.

146. BLAIR, C.H. HUNTER, ed. *Visitations of the north. Pt. iv: Visitations of Yorkshire and Northumberland in A.D. 1575, and a book of arms from Ashmole ms. no. 834.* 3 fiche. Reprint; originally published 1932. £21.00.

147. HOWDEN, MARJORIE PEERS, ed. *The register of Richard Fox, lord bishop of Durham, 1494-1501.* 3 fiche. Reprint; originally published 1932. £21.00.

149. THOMPSON, A. HAMILTON, ed. *The register of William Greenfield, lord archbishop of York, 1306-1315. Pt. ii.* 4 fiche. Reprint; originally published 1934. £28.00.

150. THOMPSON, A. HAMILTON, ed. *The Surtees Society, 1834-1934, including a catalogue of its publications, with notes on their sources and contents, and a list of the members of the society from its beginning to the present day.* 4 fiche. Reprint; originally published 1939. £28.00.

151. THOMPSON, A. HAMILTON, ed. *The register of William Greenfield, lord archbishop of York, 1306-1315. Pt. iii.* 4 fiche. Reprint; originally published 1936. £28.00.

152. THOMPSON, A. HAMILTON, ed. *The register of William Greenfield, lord archbishop of York, 1306-1315. Pt. iv.* 5 fiche. Reprint; originally published 1938. £35.00.

153. THOMPSON, A. HAMILTON, ed. *The register of William Greenfield, lord archbishop of York, 1306-1315. Pt. v.* 5 fiche. Reprint; originally published 1940. £35.00.

158. THOMPSON, A. HAMILTON, ed. *Northumbrian pleas from De Banco rolls 1-19 (1-5 Edward I.).* 2 fiche. Reprint; originally published 1950. £14.00.

159. THOMPSON, A. HAMILTON, ed. *Northumbrian pleas from De Banco rolls 20-37 (5-8 Edward I.).* 2 fiche. Reprint; originally published 1950. £14.00.

160. WHITING, C.E., ed. *Durham civic memorials.* 3 fiche. Reprint; originally published 1952. £21.00.

Surtees Society (*cont.*)

161. HINDE, GLADYS, ed. *The registers of Cuthbert Tunstall, bishop of Durham, 1530-59, and James Pilkington, bishop of Durham, 1561-76.* 3 fiche. Reprint; originally published 1952. £21.00.

162. FRASER, C.M., ed. *Records of Antony Bek, bishop and patriarch, 1283-1311.* 3 fiche. Reprint; originally published 1953. £21.00.

163. JAMES, M.E., ed. *Estate accounts of the Earls of Northumberland, 1562-1637.* 4 fiche. Reprint; originally published 1955. £28.00.

164. STOREY, R.L., ed. *The register of Thomas Langley, bishop of Durham, 1406-1437. Vol. i.* 3 fiche. Reprint; originally published 1956. £21.00.

165. HUGHES, EDWARD, ed. *Letters of Spencer Cowper, dean of Durham, 1746-74.* 3 fiche. Reprint; originally published 1956. £21.00.

166. STOREY, R.L., ed. *The register of Thomas Langley, bishop of Durham, 1406-1437. Vol. ii.* 3 fiche. Reprint; originally published 1957. £21.00.

168. HUDLESTON, C. ROY, ed. *Naworth estate and household accounts, 1648-1660.* 3 fiche. Reprint; originally published 1958. £21.00.

169. STOREY, R.L., ed. *The register of Thomas Langley, bishop of Durham, 1406-1437. Vol. iii.* 3 fiche. Reprint; originally published 1959. £21.00.

170. STOREY, R.L., ed. *The register of Thomas Langley, bishop of Durham, 1406-1437. Vol. iv.* 3 fiche. Reprint; originally published 1961. £21.00.

172. DICKENS, A.G., ed. *Clifford letters of the sixteenth century.* 2 fiche. Reprint; originally published 1962. £14.00.

173. HUDLESTON, C. ROY, ed. *Durham recusants' estates, 1717-1778.* 3 fiche. Reprint; originally published 1962. £21.00.

175. *Miscellanea. Vol. iii.* 3 fiche. Reprint; originally published 1965. £21.00.

176. FRASER, C.M., ed. *Ancient petitions relating to Northumberland.* 3 fiche. Reprint; originally published 1966. £21.00.

177. *The register of Thomas Langley, bishop of Durham, 1406-1437. Vol.v.* 3 fiche. Reprint; originally published 1966. £21.00.

178. DICKINSON, H.T., ed. *The correspondence of Sir James Clavering.* 3 fiche. Reprint; originally published 1967. £21.00.

179. OFFLER, H.S., ed. *Durham episcopal charters, 1071-1152.* 3 fiche. Reprint; originally published 1968. £21.00.

180. FORSTER, ANN M.C., ed. *Selections from the disbursements book, 1691-1709, of Sir Thomas Haggerston, Bart.* 2 fiche. Reprint; originally published 1969. £14.00. Of Haggerston, Northumberland.

181. ROWE, D.J., ed. *The records of the Company of Shipwrights of Newcastle upon Tyne, 1622-1967.* 3 fiche. Reprint; originally published 1970-1971. £21.00.

Gloucestershire & Bristol

Bristol Record Society
Orders for microfiche reprints to:
Chadwyck-Healey Ltd., The Quorum, Barnwell Road, Cambridge, CB5 8SW
Phone: (01223) 215512
Email: mail@chadwyck.co.uk
Http://www.chadwyck.co.uk

1. HARDING, N. DERMOTT, ed. *Bristol charters, 1155-1373.* 3 fiche. Reprint; originally published 1930. £21.00.

2. VEALE, E.W.W., ed. *The great red book of Bristol. Introduction, pt. 1: Burgage tenure in mediaeval Bristol.* 4 fiche. Reprint; originally published 1931. £28.00.

3. BUTCHER, EMILY E., ed. *Bristol corporation of the poor. Selected records, 1696-1834.* 3 fiche. Reprint; originally published 1932. £21.00.

4. VEALE, E.W.W., ed. *The great red book of Bristol. Text, pt. i.* 4 fiche. Reprint; originally published 1933. £28.00.

5. RICH, E.E., ed. *The staple court books of Bristol.* 4 fiche. Reprint; originally published 1934. £28.00.

6. NOTT, H.E., ed. *The deposition books of Bristol. Vol. i: 1643-1647.* 4 fiche. Reprint; originally published 1935. £28.00.

7. CARUS-WILSON, ELEONORA M., ed. *The overseas trade of Bristol in the later middle ages.* 4 fiche. Reprint; originally published 1937. £28.00.

8. VEALE, E.W.W., ed. *The great red book of Bristol. Text, pt. ii.* 3 fiche. Reprint; originally published 1938. £21.00.

9. BEACHCROFT, GWEN, & SABIN, ARTHUR, ed. *Two compotus rolls of St. Augustine's abbey, Bristol, for 1491-2 and 1511-12.* 4 fiche. Reprint; originally published 1938. £28.00.

10. MATTHEWS, HAROLD EVANS, ed. *Proceedings, minutes and enrolments of the Company of Soapmakers, 1562-1642.* 3 fiche. Reprint; originally published 1940. £21.00.

11. CRONNE, H.A., ed. *Bristol charters, 1378-1499.* 3 fiche. Reprint; originally published 1946. £21.00.

12. LATHAM, R.C., ed. *Bristol charters, 1509-1899.* 3 fiche. Reprint; originally published 1947. £21.00.

13. NOTT, H.E., & RALPH, ELIZABETH, ed. *The deposition books of Bristol. Vol. ii: 1650-54.* 3 fiche. Reprint; originally published 1948. £21.00.

14. HOLLIS, D., ed. *Calendar of the Bristol apprentice book, 1532-1565. Pt. 1: 1532-1542.* 3 fiche. Reprint; originally published 1949. £21.00.

15. FARR, GRAHAME E., ed. *Records of Bristol ships, 1800-1838. Vessels over 150 tons.* 4 fiche. Reprint; originally published 1950. £28.00.

16. VEALE, E.W.W., ed. *The great red book of Bristol. Text, pt. iii.* 3 fiche. Reprint; originally published 1951. £21.00.

17. MCGRATH, PATRICK, ed. *Records relating to the Society of Merchant Venturers of the city of Bristol in the seventeenth century.* 4 fiche. Reprint; originally published 1952. £28.00.

18. VEALE, E.W.W., ed. *The great red book of Bristol. Text, pt. iv.* 2 fiche. Reprint; originally published 1953. £14.00.

19. MCGRATH, PATRICK, ed. *Merchants and merchandise in seventeenth century Bristol.* 4 fiche. Reprint; originally published 1955.

Hampshire
Hampshire Record Society

Orders for microfiche reprints to:
Chadwyck-Healey Ltd., The Quorum, Barnwell Road, Cambridge, CB5 8SW
Phone: (01223) 215512
Email: mail@chadwyck.co.uk
Http://www.chadwyck.co.uk

1. KITCHIN, G.W., & MADGE, F.T., ed. *Documents relating to the foundation of the chapter of Winchester, A.D. 1541-1547.* 3 fiche. Reprint; originally published 1889. £21.00.

3. BAIGENT, FRANCIS JOSEPH, ed. *A collection of records and documents relating to the hundred and manor of Crondal in the county of Southampton. Pt. i: Historical and manorial.* 6 fiche. Reprint; originally published 1891. £42.00.

4. MACRAY, W. DUNN, ed. *Calendar of charters and documents relating to Selborne and its priory preserved in the muniment room of Magdalen College, Oxford.* 2 fiche. Reprint; originally published 1896. £14.00.

7. KITCHIN, G.W., ed. *Compotus rolls of the obedientiaries of St. Swithun's Priory, Winchester, from the Winchester cathedral archives.* 6 fiche. Reprint; originally published 1892. £42.00.

8. BAIGENT, FRANCIS JOSEPH, ed. *The registers of John de Sandale and Rigaud de Asserio, bishops of Winchester, A.D. 1316-1323, with an appendix of contemporaneous and other illustrative documents.* 10 fiche. Reprint; originally published 1897. £70.00.

9. *Calendar of charters and documents relating to the possessions of Selborne ... Second series.* 2 fiche. Reprint; originally published 1894. £14.00.

10. KITCHIN, G.W., ed. *The manor of Manydown, Hampshire.* 3 fiche. Reprint; originally published 1895. £21.00.

11. KIRBY, T.F., ed. *Wykeham's register.* 12 fiche. Reprint; originally published 1896-9. £84.00.

12. STEPHENS, W.R.W., & MADGE, F.W., ed. *Documents relating to the history of the cathedral church of Winchester in the seventeenth century.* 3 fiche. Reprint; originally published 1897. £21.00.

Southampton Record Society

Orders for microfiche reprints to:
Chadwyck-Healey Ltd., The Quorum, Barnwell Road, Cambridge, CB5 8SW
Phone: (01223) 215512
Email: mail@chadwyck.co.uk
Http://www.chadwyck.co.uk

1. HEARNSHAW, F.J.C., & HEARNSHAW, D.M., ed. *Southampton court leet records.* 10 fiche. Reprint; originally published 1905-8. £70.00.

2. ROGERS, W.H., ed. *Maps and plans of old Southampton.* 1 fiche. Reprint; originally published 1907. £7.00.

Southamton Record Society *(cont.)*

3. HEARNSHAW, F.J.C., ed. *Leet jurisdiction in England, especially as illustrated by the records of the court leet of Southampton.* 5 fiche. Reprint; originally published 1908. £35.00.
4. GIDDEN, H.W., ed. *The charters of the borough of Southampton.* 5 fiche. Reprint; originally published 1909-10. £35.00.
5. AUBREY, ELINOR R., ed. *The history and antiquity of Southampton, with some conjectures concerning the Roman Clausentum, by John Speed, written about the year 1770.* 3 fiche. Reprint; originally published 1909. £21.00. Includes many documents.
6. STUDER, P., ed. *The oak book of Southampton, of c.A.D. 1300.* 7 fiche. Reprint; originally published 1910-11. £49.00.
7. CHAPMAN, A.B. WALLIS, ed. *The black book of Southampton.* 7 fiche. Reprint; originally published 1912-15. £49.00.
8. STUDER, PAUL, ed. *The port books of Southampton, or Anglo-French accounts of Robert Florys, water-bailiff and receiver of petty customs, A.D. 1427-1430.* 3 fiche. Reprint; originally published 1913. £21.00.
9. HAMILTON, GERTRUDE H., ed. *Books of examinations and depositions, 1570-1594.* 3 fiche. Reprint; originally published £21.00.
10. GIDDEN, HARRY W., ed. *The sign manuals and the letters patent of Southampton to 1422.* 4 fiche. Reprint; originally published 1916-19. £28.00.
11. HORROCKS, J.W., ed. *The assembly books of Southampton.* 7 fiche. Reprint; originally published 1917-25. £49.00.
12. ANDERSON, R.C., ed. *Letters of the fifteenth and sixteenth centuries from the archives of Southampton.* 3 fiche. Reprint; originally published 1921. £21.00.
13. ANDERSON, R.C., ed. *The assize of bread book, 1477-1517.* 1 fiche. Reprint; originally published 1923. £7.00.
14. ANDERSON, R.C., ed. *The book of examinations, 1601-1602, with a list of ships belonging to Southampton in the year 1570-1603.* 2 fiche. Reprint; originally published 1926. £14.00.
15. GIDDEN, H.W., ed. *The book of remembrance of Southampton.* 5 fiche. Reprint; originally published 1927-30. £35.00. 1440-1563.

16. ANDERSON, R.C., ed. *The book of examinations and depositions, 1622-1644.* 6 fiche. Reprint; originally published 1929-36. £42.00.
17. RUTHERFORD, J., ed. *The miscellaneous papers of Captain Thomas Stockwell, 1590-1611.* 3 fiche. Reprint; originally published 1932-3. £21.00. Records of Sir Oliver Lambton's Southampton estates.
18. GIDDEN, H.W., ed. *The stewards' books of Southampton, from 1428.* 4 fiche. Reprint; originally published 1935-9. £28.00.
19. QUINN, D.B., ed. *The port books or local customs accounts of Southampton for the reign of Edward IV.* 4 fiche. Reprint; originally published 1937-8. £28.00.
20. BUNYARD, BARBARA D.M., ed. *The brokage book of Southampton, from 1439-40.* 3 fiche. Reprint; originally published 1941. £21.00.

Southampton Record Series

Orders for microfiche reprints to:
Chadwyck-Healey Ltd., The Quorum,
Barnwell Road, Cambridge, CB5 8SW
Phone: (01223) 215512
Email: mail@chadwyck.co.uk
Http://www.chadwyck.co.uk

1. RUDDOCK, ALWYN A., ed. *Italian merchants and shipping in Southampton, 1270-1600.* 4 fiche. Reprint; originally published 1951. £28.00.
2. MERSON, A.L., ed. *The third book of remembrance of Southampton, 1514-1602. Vol. i: 1514-1540.* 2 fiche. Reprint; originally published 1952. £14.00.
3. MERSON, A.L., ed. *The third book of remembrance of Southampton, 1514-1602. Vol. ii: 1540-1573.* 3 fiche. Reprint; originally published 1955. £21.00.
4. COLEMAN, OLIVE, ed. *The brokage book of Southampton, 1443-1444. Vol. 1.* 2 fiche. Reprint; originally published 1960. £14.00.
5. COBB, HENRY S., ed. *The local port book of Southampton for 1439-40.* 3 fiche. Reprint; originally published 1961. £21.00.
6. COLEMAN, OLIVE, ed. *The brokage book of Southampton, 1443-1444. Vol. 2.* 3 fiche. Reprint; originally published 1961. £21.00.
7. FOSTER, BRIAN, ed. *The local port book of Southampton for 1435-36.* 2 fiche. Reprint; originally published 1963. £14.00.

8. MERSON, A.L., ed. *The third book of remembrance of Southampton, 1514-1602. Vol. iii: 1573-1589.* 2 fiche. Reprint; originally published 1965. £14.00.

Herefordshire
Cantilupe Society
Orders for microfiche reprints to:
Chadwyck-Healey Ltd., The Quorum, Barnwell Road, Cambridge, CB5 8SW
Phone: (01223) 215512
Email: mail@chadwyck.co.uk
Http://www.chadwyck.co.uk

1. CAPES, WILLIAM W., ed. *Charters and records of Hereford Cathedral.* 4 fiche. Reprint; originally published 1908. £28.00.
2. BANNISTER, A.T., ed. *Diocese of Hereford. Institutions, etc., A.D. 1539-1900.* 3 fiche. Reprint; originally published 1923. £21.00.
3. DEW, E.N., ed. *Index to the registers of the diocese of Hereford, 1275-1535.* 1 fiche. Reprint; originally published 1925. £7.00.
4. DEW, E.N., ed. *Extracts from the Cathedral registers, 1275-1535.* 2 fiche. Reprint; originally published 1932. £14.00.

Kent
Kent Archaeological Society, Records Branch
Orders for microfiche reprints to:
Chadwyck-Healey Ltd., The Quorum, Barnwell Road, Cambridge, CB5 8SW
Phone: (01223) 215512
Email: mail@chadwyck.co.uk
Http://www.chadwyck.co.uk

1. BUCKLAND, W.E., ed. *The parish registers and records in the diocese of Rochester: a summary of information collected by the ecclesiastical records committee of the Rochester diocesan conference.* 2 fiche. Reprint; originally published 1912. £14.00.
2. CHURCHILL, IRENE JOSEPHINE, ed. *A handbook to Kent records, containing a summary account of the principal classes of historical documents relating to the county, and a guide to their chief places of deposit.* 3 fiche. Reprint; originally published 1914. £21.00.

3. WOODRUFF, C. EVELEIGH, ed. *Sede vacante wills. A calendar of wills proved before the commissary of the prior and chapter of Christ Church, Canterbury, during vacancies in the primacy, with an appendix containing transcripts of archiepiscopal and other wills of importance.* 2 fiche. Reprint; originally published 1914. £14.00.
4. JOHNSON, CHARLES, ed. *Registrum Hamonis Hethe, diocesis Roffensis, 1319-1352.* 14 fiche. Reprint; originally published 1915-1948. £98.00.
5. PLOMER, HENRY R., ed. *The churchwardens' accounts of St. Nicholas, Strood. Pt. 1: 1555-1600; pt. 2: 1603-1662,* with MERCER, FRANCIS R., ed. *Churchwardens' accounts of Betrysden, 1515-1573.* 5 fiche. Reprint; originally published 1927-8. £35.00.
7. CHURCHILL, IRENE JOSEPHINE, ed. *East Kent records. A calendar of some unpublished deeds and court rolls in the library of Lambeth Palace, with appendices referring especially to the manors of Knowlton, Sandown, South Court, and North Court.* 3 fiche. Reprint; originally published 1922. £21.00.
8. WOODRUFF, C. EVELEIGH, ed. *Calendar of institutions by the chapter of Canterbury sede vacante.* 3 fiche. Reprint; originally published 1923. £21.00.
9. DUNCAN, LELAND L., ed. *Index of wills proved in the Rochester consistory court between 1440 and 1561.* 3 fiche. Reprint; originally published 1924. £21.00.
10. THOMSON, GLADYS SCOTT, ed. *The Twysden lieutenancy papers, 1583-1668.* 2 fiche. Reprint; originally published 1926. £14.00.
11. COTTON, CHARLES, ed. *A Kentish cartulary of the order of St. John of Jerusalem.* 3 fiche. Reprint; originally published 1930. £21.00.
12. HUSSEY, ARTHUR, ed. *Kent chantries.* 5 fiche. Reprint; originally published 1936. £35.00.
13. PUTNAM, BRENDA HAVEN, ed. *Kent keepers of the peace, 1316-1317.* 3 fiche. Reprint; originally published 1933. £21.00.
14. HUSSEY, ARTHUR, ed. *Kent obit and lamp rents.* 2 fiche. Reprint; originally published 1936. £14.00.

Kent Archaeological Society (cont.)

15. CHURCHILL, IRENE J., GRIFFIN, RALPH, & HARDMAN, F.W., ed. *Calendar of Kent feet of fines to the end of Henry III's reign.* 7 fiche. Reprint; originally published 1956. £49.00.

16. MURRAY, K.M. ELISABETH, ed. *Register of Daniel Rough, common clerk of Romney, 1352-1380.* 5 fiche. Reprint; originally published 1945. £35.00

18. DU BOULAY, F.R., ed. *Documents illustrative of medieval Kentish society.* 5 fiche. Reprint; originally published 1964. £35.00. Includes lay subsidy, 1334/5, and Canterbury freemens' rolls, 1298-1363, *etc.*

19. HULL, FELIX, ed. *A calendar of the white and black books of the Cinque ports, 1432-1955.* 10 fiche. Reprint; originally published 1966. £70.00.

DUNCAN, LELAND L., ed. *Kentish monumental inscriptions. Inscriptions at Tenterden.* 1 fiche. Reprint; originally published 1919. £7.00.

FINN, ARTHUR, ed. *Monumental inscriptions in the churchyard and church of All Saints, Lydd, Kent.* 1 fiche. Reprint; originally published 1927. £7.00.

COTTON, CHARLES, ed. *The Canterbury chantries and hospitals, together with some others in the neighbourhood, in 1546.* 12 fiche. Reprint; originally published 1934. £84.00.

Lancashire
Lancashire and Cheshire Record Society

Orders for microfiche reprints to:
Chadwyck-Healey Ltd., The Quorum, Barnwell Road, Cambridge, CB5 8SW

Phone: (01223) 215512
Email: mail@chadwyck.co.uk
Http://www.chadwyck.co.uk

1. FISHWICK, HENRY, ed. *Lancashire and Cheshire church surveys, 1649-1655. Pt. 1: Parochial surveys of Lancashire. Pt. 2: Surveys of the lands, etc., of the bishop and dean and chapter of Chester, and of the warden and fellows of the collegiate church of Manchester.* 4 fiche. Reprint; originally published 1879. £28.00.

2. EARWAKER, J.P., ed. *An index to the wills and inventories now preserved in the court of probate at Chester, from A.D. 1545 to 1620; together with (1) a list of the transcripts of early wills, preserved in the consistory court, Chester; (2) a list of the wills printed by the Chetham Society; (3) a list of the wills seen and noted by the Revs. J. & G.J. Piccope, and not now to be found at Chester; (4) a list of the wills preserved in Harl. ms. 1991 in the British Museum.* 3 fiche. Reprint; originally published 1879. £21.00.

3. RYLANDS, J. PAUL, ed. *Lancashire inquisitions returned into the chancery of the Duchy of Lancaster and now existing in the Public Record Office, London. Stuart period, pt. i: 1 to 11 James I.* 4 fiche. Reprint; originally published 1880. £28.00.

4. *An index to the wills and inventories now preserved in the Court of Probate at Chester, from A.D. 1621 to 1650; with two appendices: (1) a list of the Lancashire and Cheshire wills proved in the Prerogative Court of Canterbury, 1650-1660; (2) a list of the Lancashire and Cheshire administrations granted in the Prerogative Court of Canterbury, 1650-1660.* 4 fiche. Reprint; originally published 1881. £28.00.

5. CROSTON, JAMES, ed. *The register book of christenings, weddings, and burials, within the parish of Prestbury, in the county of Chester, 1560-1635.* 4 fiche. Reprint; originally published 1881. £28.00.

6. RYLANDS, JOHN PAUL, ed. *Cheshire and Lancashire funeral certificates, A.D. 1600 to 1678.* 3 fiche. Reprint; originally published 1882. £21.00.

7. SELBY, WALFORD D., ed. *Lancashire and Cheshire records preserved in the Public Record Office, London. Pt. 1.* 3 fiche. Reprint; originally published 1882. £21.00.

8. SELBY, WALFORD D., ed. *Lancashire and Cheshire records preserved in the Public Record Office, London. Pt. 2.* 5 fiche. Reprint; originally published 1883. £35.00.

9. ABRAM, W. ALEXANDER, ed. *The rolls of burgesses at the guilds merchant of the borough of Preston, co. Lancaster, 1397-1682.* 4 fiche. Reprint; originally published 1884. £28.00.

10. FISHWICK, HENRY, ed. *A list of the Lancashire wills proved within the Archdeaconry of Richmond, preserved in Somerset House, London, from A.D. 1457 to 1680; and of abstracts of Lancashire wills, belonging to the same archdeaconry, in the British Museum, from A.D. 1531 to 1652.* 4 fiche. Reprint; originally published 1884. £28.00.

11. FISHWICK, CAROLINE, ed. *A calendar of Lancashire and Cheshire exchequer depositions by commission, from 1558 to 1702.* 3 fiche. Reprint; originally published 1885. £21.00.

12. *Miscellanies relating to Lancashire and Cheshire. Vol. i.* 4 fiche. Reprint; originally published 1885. £28.00.

13. FISHWICK, HENRY, ed. *A list of the Lancashire wills proved within the Archdeaconry of Richmond and now preserved in Somerset House, London, from A.D. 1681 to 1748.* 4 fiche. Reprint; originally published 1886. £28.00.

15. *An index to the wills and inventories now preserved in the Court of Probate at Chester, from A.D. 1660 to 1680; with an appendix containing the list of the 'infra' wills (or those in which the personalty was under £40), between the same years.* 5 fiche. Reprint; originally published 1887. £35.00.

16. RYLANDS, J.PAUL, ed. *Lancashire inquisitions ... Stuart period, pt. 2: 12 to 19 James I.* 4 fiche. Reprint; originally published 1887. £28.00.

17. RYLANDS, J.PAUL, ed. *Lancashire inquisitions ... Stuart period, pt. 3: 20 to 23 James I.* 3 fiche. Reprint; originally published 1888. £21.00.

18. *An index to the wills and inventories now preserved in the Court of Probate at Chester, from A.D. 1681 to 1700; with an appendix containing the list of the 'infra wills' ...* 4 fiche. Reprint; originally published 1888. £28.00.

20. *An index to the wills and inventories now preserved in the Court of Probate at Chester, from A.D. 1701 to 1720; with an appendix containing the list of the 'infra wills' ...* 3 fiche. Reprint; originally published 1889. £21.00.

21. WHITE, WALTER STUART, ed. *The register book of christenings, weddings, and burials, within the parish of Leyland in the county of Lancaster, 1653 to 1710, with a few earlier 'transcripts', 1622-1641.* 4 fiche. Reprint; originally published 1890. £28.00.

22. *An index to the wills and inventories now preserved in the Court of Probate at Chester, from A.D. 1721 to 1740; with an appendix containing the list of the 'infra wills' ...* 4 fiche. Reprint; originally published 1890. £28.00.

23. *A list of the Lancashire wills proved within the Archdeaconry of Richmond and now preserved in the Court of Probate at Lancaster, from 1748 to 1792; also a list of wills proved in the peculiar of Halton, from A.D. 1615 to 1792.* 2 fiche. Reprint; originally published 1891. £14.00.

24. STANNING, J.H., ed. *The royalist composition papers; being the proceedings of the Committee for Compounding, A.D. 1643-1660, so far as they relate to the county of Lancaster, extracted from the records preserved in the Public Record Office, London. Vol. i: A-B.* 3 fiche. Reprint; originally published 1891. £21.00.

25. *An index to the wills and inventories now preserved in the Court of Probate at Chester, from A.D. 1741 to 1760; with an appendix containing the list of the 'infra wills' ...* 4 fiche. Reprint; originally published 1892. £28.00.

26. STANNING, J.H., ed. *The royalist composition papers; being the proceedings of the committee for compounding, A.D. 1643-1660, so far as they relate to the county of Lancaster, extracted from the records preserved in the Public Record Office, London. Vol. ii: C-F.* 4 fiche. Reprint; originally published 1892. £28.00.

27. VINCENT, JOHN A.C., ed. *Lancashire lay subsidies; being an examination of the lay subsidy rolls remaining in the Public Record Office, London, from Henry III to Charles II. Vol. i: Henry III to Edward I, 1216-1307.* 4 fiche. Reprint; originally published 1893. £28.00.

Lancashire and Cheshire Record Society
(cont.)

28. SHAW, W.A., ed. *Minutes of the committee for the relief of plundered ministers, and of the trustees for the maintenance of ministers, relating to Lancashire and Cheshire, 1643-1660. Pt. i: 1643-1654.* 4 fiche. Reprint; originally published 1893. £28.00.

29. STANNING, J.H., ed. *The royalist composition papers; being the proceedings of the Committee for Compounding, A.D. 1643-1660, so far as they relate to the county of Lancaster, extracted from the records preserved in the Public Record Office, London. Vol. iii: G-H.* 4 fiche. Reprint; originally published 1896. £28.00.

30. IRVINE, WM. FERGUSSON, ed. *A collection of Lancashire and Cheshire wills not now to be found in any probate registry, 1301-1752.* 3 fiche. Reprint; originally published 1896. £21.00.

32. FISHWICK, HENRY, ed. *Pleadings and depositions in the Duchy court of Lancaster, time of Henry VII and Henry VIII.* 3 fiche. Reprint; originally published 1896. £21.00.

33. *Miscellanies relating to Lancashire and Cheshire. Vol. iii.* 3 fiche. Reprint; originally published 1896. £21.00. Includes index to wills, *etc.,* in testamentary suits, 1487-1620, *etc.*

34. SHAW, W.A., ed. *Minutes of the committee for the relief of plundered ministers, and of the trustees for the maintainance of ministers relating to Lancashire and Cheshire, 1643-1660. Pt. ii: 1650-60.* 4 fiche. Reprint; originally published 1896. £28.00.

35. FISHWICK, HENRY, ed. *Pleadings and depositions in the duchy court of Lancaster, time of Henry VIII.* 3 fiche. Reprint; originally published 1897. £21.00.

36. STANNING, J.H., ed. *The royalist composition papers; being the proceedings of the Committee for Compounding, A.D. 1643-1660, so far as they relate to the county of Lancaster, extracted from the records preserved in the Public Record Office, London. Vol. iv: I-O.* 3 fiche. Reprint; originally published 1898. £21.00.

37. IRVINE, WM. FERGUSSON, ed. *An index to the wills and inventories now preserved in the probate registry at Chester; from A.D. 1761 to 1780. Vol. i: A-M.* 3 fiche. Reprint; originally published 1898. £21.00.

38. IRVINE, WM. FERGUSSON, ed. *An index to the wills and inventories now preserved in the probate registry at Chester; from A.D. 1761 to 1780. Vol. ii: N-Z.* 2 fiche. Reprint; originally published 1899. £14.00.

39. FARRER, WILLIAM, ed. *Final concords of the county of Lancaster, from the original chirographs, or feet of fines, preserved in the Public Record Office, London. Pt. i: 7 Richard I to 35 Edward I, A.D. 1196 to A.D. 1307.* 3 fiche. Reprint; originally published 1899. £21.00.

40. FISHWICK, HENRY, ed. *Pleadings and depositions in the Duchy court of Lancaster, time of Edward VI and Philip and Mary.* 4 fiche. Reprint; originally published 1899. £28.00.

41. FARRER, WILLIAM, ed. *Some court rolls of the lordships, wapentakes, and demesne manors of Thomas, Earl of Lancaster, in the county of Lancaster, for the 17th and 18th years of Edward II, A.D. 1323-4.* 3 fiche. Reprint; originally published 1901. £21.00.

43. *Miscellanies relating to Lancashire and Cheshire. Vol. iv.* 3 fiche. Reprint; originally published 1902. £21.00. Includes index to wills in testamentary suits, 1621-1700.

44. *An index to the wills and inventories now preserved in the Probate Registry at Chester, from A.D. 1781 to 1790; with an appendix containing the list of the 'infra' wills ...* 2 fiche. Reprint; originally published 1902. £14.00.

45. *An index to the wills and inventories now preserved in the Probate Registry at Chester, from A.D. 1791 to 1800; with an appendix containing the list of the 'infra' wills ...* 3 fiche. Reprint; originally published 1902. £21.00.

46. FARRER, WILLIAM, ed. *Final concords of the county of Lancaster, from the original chirographs, or feet of fines, preserved in the Public Record Office, London. Pt. ii: Edward II and Edward III, A.D. 1307 to A.D. 1377.* 3 fiche. Reprint; originally published 1903. £21.00.

47. PARKER, JOHN, ed. *A calendar of the Lancashire assize rolls preserved in the Public Record Office, London. Pt. 1.* 3 fiche. Reprint; originally published 1904. £21.00. 1241-81.

64

48. FARRER, WILLIAM, ed. *Lancashire inquests, extents, and feudal aids. Pt. i: A.D. 1205-A.D. 1307.* 5 fiche. Reprint; originally published 1903. £35.00.

49. PARKER, JOHN, ed. *A calendar of the Lancashire assize rolls preserved in the Public Record Office, London. Pt. 2.* 3 fiche. Reprint; originally published 1905. £21.00. 1284-5.

50. FARRER, WILLIAM, ed. *Final concords of the county of Lancaster, from the original chirographs, or feet of fines, preserved in the Public Record Office, London. Pt. iii: John Duke of Lancaster, to Henry VII, A.D. 1377-1509.* 3 fiche. Reprint; originally published 1905. £21.00.

51. BENNETT, J.H.E., ed. *The rolls of the freemen of the city of Chester. Pt. 1: 1392-1700.* 3 fiche. Reprint; originally published 1906. £21.00.

52. *Miscellanies relating to Lancashire and Cheshire. Vol. v.* 3 fiche. Reprint; originally published 1906. £21.00. Includes indexes to wills, and Chester hearth tax, 1664/5.

53. IRVINE, WM. FERGUSSON, ed. *Marriage licences granted within the Archdeaconry of Chester in the diocese of Chester. Vol. i: 1606-1616.* 3 fiche. Reprint; originally published 1907. £21.00.

54. FARRER, WILLIAM, ed. *Lancashire inquests, extents, and feudal aids. Pt. ii: A.D. 1310-A.D. 1333.* 4 fiche. Reprint; originally published 1907. £28.00.

55. BENNETT, J.H.E., ed. *The rolls of the freemen of the city of Chester. Pt. 2: 1700-1805.* 4 fiche. Reprint; originally published 1908. £28.00.

56. IRVINE, WM. FERGUSSON, ed. *Marriage licences granted within the Archdeaconry of Chester in the diocese of Chester. Vol. ii: 1616-1624.* 3 fiche. Reprint; originally published 1908. £21.00.

57. IRVINE, WM. FERGUSSON, ed. *Marriage licences granted within the Archdeaconry of Chester in the diocese of Chester. Vol. iii: 1624-1632.* 4 fiche. Reprint; originally published 1909. £28.00.

59. STEWART-BROWN, RONALD, ed. *Accounts of the chamberlains and other officers of the county of Chester, 1301-1360.* 4 fiche. Reprint; originally published 1910. £28.00.

60. FARRER, WILLIAM, ed. *Final concords of the county of Lancaster, from the original chirographs, or feet of fines, preserved in the Public Record Office, London. Pt. iv: Henry VIII to Philip and Mary, A.D. 1510-1558.* 3 fiche. Reprint; originally published 1910. £21.00.

61. IRVINE, WM. FERGUSSON, ed. *Marriage licences granted within the Archdeaconry of Chester in the diocese of Chester. Vol. iv: 1639-1644.* 2 fiche. Reprint; originally published 1911. £14.00.

62. STEWART-BROWN, R., ed. *An index to the wills and administrations, including the 'infra' wills, now preserved in the probate registry at Chester, for the year 1801-1810, both inclusive. Pt. i: A to L.* 3 fiche. Reprint; originally published 1911. £21.00.

63. STEWART-BROWN, R., ed. *An index to the wills and administrations now preserved in the probate registry at Chester for the years 1801-1810, both inclusive. Pt. ii: M-Z.* 3 fiche. Reprint; originally published 1912. £21.00.

65. IRVINE, WM. FERGUSSON, ed. *Marriage licences granted within the Archdeaconry of Chester in the diocese of Chester. Vol. v: 1661-1667.* 4 fiche. Reprint; originally published 1912. £28.00.

66. *A list of the Lancashire wills proved within the Archdeaconry of Richmond, and now preserved in the Probate Court at Lancaster, from 1793 to 1812; also a list of the wills proved in the peculiar of Halton, from 1793 to 1812.* 2 fiche. Reprint; originally published 1913. £14.00.

67. BROWNBILL, J., ed. *A calendar of that part of the collection of deeds and papers of the Moore family, of Bankhall, co. Lanc., now in the Liverpool Public Library.* 4 fiche. Reprint; originally published 1913. £28.00.

68. BROWNBILL, JOHN, ed. *The ledger book of Vale Royal Abbey.* 3 fiche. Reprint; originally published 1914. £21.00.

69. IRVINE, WM. FERGUSSON, ed. *Marriage licences granted within the Archdeaconry of Chester in the diocese of Chester. Vol. vi: 1667-1680.* 4 fiche. Reprint; originally published 1914. £28.00.

70. FARRER, WILLIAM, ed. *Lancashire inquests, extents, and feudal aids. Pt. iii: A.D. 1313- A.D. 1355.* 3 fiche. Reprint; originally published 1915. £21.00.

Lancashire and Cheshire Record Society
(*cont.*)

71. STEWART-BROWN, R., ed. *Lancashire and Cheshire cases in the Court of Star Chamber. Pt. i.* 3 fiche. Reprint; originally published 1916. £21.00.

72. BROWNBILL, JOHN, ed. *The royalist composition papers; being the proceedings of the Committee for Compounding, A.D. 1643-1660, so far as they relate to the county of Lancaster, extracted from the records preserved in the Public Record Office, London. Vol. v: P-R.* 3 fiche. Reprint; originally published 1917. £21.00.

73. IRVINE, WM. FERGUSSON, ed. *Marriage licences granted within the Archdeaconry of Chester in the diocese of Chester. Vol. vii: 1680-1691.* 3 fiche. Reprint; originally published 1918. £21.00.

74. BROWNBILL, JOHN, ed. *Marriage bonds for the deaneries of Lonsdale, Kendal, Furness and Copeland, part of the Archdeaconry of Richmond, now preserved at Lancaster. Pt. i: 1648-1710.* 5 fiche. Reprint; originally published 1920. £35.00.

75. STEWART-BROWN, R., ed. *Marriage bonds for the deaneries of the Archdeaconry of Richmond, now preserved at Lancaster. Pt. ii: 1711-1722.* 4 fiche. Reprint; originally published 1921. £28.00.

76. BEAZLEY, F.C., ed. *Calendar of persons commemorated in monumental inscriptions, and of abstracts of wills, administrations, etc., contained in books relating to Lancashire and Cheshire.* 3 fiche. Reprint; originally published 1922. £21.00.

77. *Marriage licences ... Vol. viii: 1691-1700.* 5 fiche. Reprint; originally published 1924. £35.00.

78. TONGE, WM. ASHETON, ed. *An index to the wills and administrations, including the 'infra' wills preserved in the probate registry at Chester, for the years 1811-1820, both inclusive. Pt. i: A to L.* 4 fiche. Reprint; originally published 1928. £28.00.

79. TONGE, WM. ASHETON, ed. *An index to the wills and administrations preserved in the probate registry at Chester, for the years 1811-1820, both inclusive. Pt. ii: M-Z.* 3 fiche. Reprint; originally published 1928. £21.00.

80. IRVINE, WM. FERGUSSON, ed. *Marriage bonds for the Deaneries of Lonsdale, Kendal, Furness, Copeland and Amounderness, part of the Archdeaconry of Richmond, now preserved at Lancaster. Pt. iv: 1729-1734.* 3 fiche. Reprint; originally published 1932. £21.00.

81. IRVINE, WM. FERGUSSON, ed. *Marriage bonds for the Deaneries of Lonsdale, Kendal, Furness, Copeland and Amounderness, part of the Archdeaconry of Richmond, now preserved at Lancaster. Pt. iv: 1729-1734.* 3 fiche. Reprint; originally published 1932. £21.00.

82. TONGE, WM. ASHETON, ed. *Marriage bonds of the ancient Archdeaconry of Chester now preserved at Chester. Pt. i: 1700-1706/7.* 4 fiche. Reprint; originally published 1933. £28.00.

83. IRVINE, WM. FERGUSSON, ed. *Marriage bonds for the Deaneries of Lonsdale, Kendal, Furness, Copeland and Amounderness, part of the Archdeaconry of Richmond, now preserved at Lancaster. Pt. v: 1734-1738.* 3 fiche. Reprint; originally published 1933. £21.00.

84. STEWART-BROWN, R., ed. *Cheshire inquisitions post mortem, Stuart period, 1603-1660. Vol. i: A-D.* 3 fiche. Reprint; originally published 1934. £21.00.

85. IRVINE, WM. FERGUSSON, ed. *Marriage bonds of the ancient Archdeaconry of Chester, now preserved at Chester. Pt. ii: 1707-1711.* 4 fiche. Reprint; originally published 1935. £28.00.

86. STEWART-BROWN, R., ed. *Cheshire inquisitions post mortem, Stuart period, 1603-1660. Vol. ii: E-O.* 3 fiche. Reprint; originally published 1935. £21.00.

87. KENDALL, W.B., & HUGHES, T. CANN, ed. *The rolls of the freemen of the borough of Lancaster, 1688 to 1840. Pt. 1: A-L.* 3 fiche. Reprint; originally published 1935. £21.00.

88. LUMBY, J.H., ed. *A calendar of the deeds and papers in the possession of Sir James de Hoghton, Bart., of Hoghton Tower, Lancashire.* 5 fiche. Reprint; originally published 1936. £35.00. 12-17th c.

89. BAILEY, F.A., ed. *A selection from the Prescot court leet and other records, 1447-1600.* 4 fiche. Reprint; originally published 1937. £28.00.

90. KENDALL, W.B., & HUGHES, T. CANN, ed. *The rolls of the freemen of the borough of Lancaster, 1688 to 1840. Pt. 2: M-Z.* 3 fiche. Reprint; originally published 1938. £21.00.

91. STEWART-BROWN, R., ed. STEWART-BROWN, R., ed. *Cheshire inquisitions post mortem, Stuart period, 1603-1660. Vol. iii: P-Y.* 3 fiche. Reprint; originally published 1938. £21.00.

92. STEWART-BROWN, R., ed. *Cheshire in the pipe rolls, 1158-1301.* 4 fiche. Reprint; originally published 1938. £28.00.

93. LUMBY, J.H., ed. *A calendar of the Norris deeds (Lancashire), 12th to 15th century, from the originals in the British Museum, the University of Liverpool, and the Liverpool Free Public Library.* 4 fiche. Reprint; originally published 1939. £28.00.

94. BENNETT, J.H.E., & DEWHURST, J.C., ed. *Quarter sessions records, with other records of the justices of the peace for the county palatine of Chester, 1559-1760, together with a few earlier miscellaneous records deposited with Cheshire County Council.* 3 fiche. Reprint; originally published 1940. £21.00.

95. BROWNBILL, JOHN, ed. *The royalist composition papers; being the proceedings of the Committee for Compounding, A.D. 1643-1660, so far as they relate to the county of Lancaster, extracted from the records preserved in the Public Record Office, London. Vol. vi, pt. 1: S-We.* 4 fiche. Reprint; originally published 1941. £28.00.

96. BROWNBILL, JOHN, ed. *The royalist composition papers; being the proceedings of the Committee for Compounding, A.D. 1643-1660, so far as they relate to the county of Lancaster, extracted from the records preserved in the Public Record Office, London. Vol. vi, pt. 2: We-Y.* 2 fiche. Reprint; originally published 1942. £14.00.

97. LAWSON, P.H., ed. *Marriage bonds of the ancient Archdeaconry of Chester now preserved at Chester. Pt. iii: 1711-1715.* 4 fiche. Reprint; originally published 1942. £28.00.

98. FRANCE, R. SHARPE, ed. *The registers of estates of Lancashire papists, 1717-1788. Vol. i: 1717.* 4 fiche. Reprint; originally published 1945. £28.00.

99. DICKINSON, R., ed. *A list of the Lancashire wills proved within the Archdeaconry of Richmond and now preserved at the probate court, Lancaster, from 1813 to 1837.* 2 fiche. Reprint; originally published 1947. £14.00.

100. DICKINSON, R., ed. *Marriage bonds for the Deaneries of Lonsdale, Kendal, Furness, Copeland and Amounderness, part of the Archdeaconry of Richmond, now preserved at Lancaster. Pt. vi: 1739-1745.* 3 fiche. Reprint; originally published 1938. £21.00.

101. LAWSON, P.H., ed. *Marriage bonds of the ancient Archdeaconry of Chester now preserved at Chester. Pt. iv: 1715-1719.* 4 fiche. Reprint; originally published 1949. £28.00.

102. FRANCE, R. SHARPE, ed. *The Thieveley lead mines, 1629-1635.* 3 fiche. Reprint; originally published 1951. £21.00. Includes numerous accounts.

103. BARKER, ERIC E., ed. *Talbot deeds, 1200-1682.* 2 fiche. Reprint; originally published 1953. £14.00.

104. BAILEY, F.A., ed. *The churchwardens' accounts of Prescot, Lancashire, 1523-1607.* 2 fiche. Reprint; originally published 1953. £14.00.

105. DICKINSON, ROBERT, ed. *A list of the Lancashire wills proved within the Archdeaconry of Richmond, and now preserved in the Probate Court of Lancaster, from 1838 to 1858; to which is appended a list of Lancashire wills not recorded in the printed indexes of either Chester or Richmond and which are now among the records deposited in the Lancashire Record Office, from 1359 to 1858.* 2 fiche. Reprint; originally published 1953. £14.00.

106. GROOMBRIDGE, MARGARET J., ed. *Calendar of Chester city council minutes, 1603-1642.* 4 fiche. Reprint; originally published 1956. £28.00.

107. DICKINSON, ROBERT, ed. *An index to the wills and administrations formerly preserved in the probate registry at Chester for the years 1821-1825, both inclusive.* 3 fiche. Reprint; originally published 1961. £21.00.

108. FRANCE, R.SHARPE,, ed. *The registers of estates of Lancashire papists, 1717-1788. Vol. ii: 1717.* 3 fiche. Reprint; originally published 1960. £21.00.

Chetham Society

Orders for microfiche reprints to:
Chadwyck-Healey Ltd., The Quorum,
Barnwell Road, Cambridge, CB5 8SW
Phone: (01223) 215512
Email: mail@chadwyck.co.uk
Http://www.chadwyck.co.uk

9. HEYWOOD, THOMAS, ed. *The Norris papers*. 3 fiche. Reprint; originally published 1846. £21.00. Of Speke.

10. HULTON, W.A., ed. *The coucher book or chartulary of Whalley Abbey. Vol. 1*. 4 fiche. Reprint; originally published 1847. £28.00.

11. HULTON, W.A., ed. *The coucher book or chartulary of Whalley Abbey. Vol. 2*. 4 fiche. Reprint; originally published 1847. £28.00.

12. HEYWOOD, THOMAS, ed. *The Moore rental*. 3 fiche. Reprint; originally published 1847. £21.00. Liverpool and district rental.

13. CROSSLEY, JAMES, ed. *The diary and correspondence of Dr. John Worthington, master of Jesus College, Cambridge, vice-chancellor of the University of Cambridge, etc., etc. Vol. i.* 5 fiche. Reprint; originally published 1847. £35.00.

14. RAINES, F.R., ed. *The journal of Nicholas Assheton of Downham, in the county of Lancaster, esq., for part of the year 1617, and part of the year following, interspersed with notes from the life of his contemporary, John Bruen of Bruen Stapelford, in the county of Chester, esq.* 3 fiche. Reprint; originally published 1848. £21.00.

16. HULTON, W.A., ed. *The coucher book or chartulary of Whalley Abbey. Vol. 3*. 4 fiche. Reprint; originally published 1848. £28.00.

17. BEAMONT, WILLIAM, ed. *Warrington in 1465 as described in a contemporary rent roll of the Legh family.* 3 fiche. Reprint; originally published 1849. £21.00.

18. HEYWOOD, THOMAS, ed. *The diary of the Rev. Henry Newcome, from September 30, 1661, to September 29, 1663*. 3 fiche. Reprint; originally published 1849. £21.00.

20. HULTON, W.A., ed. *The coucher book or chartulary of Whalley Abbey. Vol. 4*. 5 fiche. Reprint; originally published 1849. £35.00.

24. *Chetham miscellanies. Vol. i.* 3 fiche. Reprint; originally published 1851. £21.00.

26. PARKINSON, RICHARD, ed. *The autobiography of Henry Newcome, M.A. Vol. 1.* 3 fiche. Reprint; originally published 1852. £21.00.

27. PARKINSON, RICHARD, ed. *The autobiography of Henry Newcome, M.A. Vol. 2.* 3 fiche. Reprint; originally published 1852. £21.00.

28. BEAMONT, WILLIAM, ed. *The Jacobite trials at Manchester in 1694.* 3 fiche. Reprint; originally published 1853. £21.00.

29. HEYWOOD, THOMAS, ed. *The Stanley papers, pt. i. The Earls of Derby and the verse writers and poets of the sixteenth and seventeenth centuries.* 1 fiche. Reprint; originally published 1853. £7.00.

30. HULTON, W.A., ed. *Documents relating to the priory of Penwortham and other possessions in Lancashire of the abbey of Evesham.* 3 fiche. Reprint; originally published 1853. £21.00.

31. RAINES, F.R., ed. *The Stanley papers, pt. ii. The Derby household books; comprising an account of the household regulations and expenses of Edward and Henry, third and fourth Earls of Derby; together with a diary containing the names of the guests who visited the latter Earl at his houses in Lancashire, by William Ffarington, esquire, the comptroller.* 4 fiche. Reprint; originally published 1853. £28.00.

33. PICCOPE, G.J., ed. *Lancashire and Cheshire wills and inventories from the ecclesiastical court, Chester. Vol. i.* 3 fiche. Reprint; originally published 1857. £21.00. Transcripts.

35. HARLAND, JOHN, ed. *The house and farm accounts of the Shuttleworths of Gawthorpe Hall, in the county of Lancaster, at Smithils and Gawthorpe, from September 1582 to October 1621. Pt. 1.* 3 fiche. Reprint; originally published 1856. £21.00.

36. CROSSLEY, JAMES, ed. *The diary and correspondence of Dr. John Worthington, master of Jesus College, Cambridge, vice-chancellor of the University of Cambridge, etc., etc. Vol.ii, pt. 1.* 3 fiche. Reprint; originally published 1855. £21.00.

39. FFARINGTON, SUSAN MARIA, ed. *The Farington papers. The shrievalty of William Ffarington, esq., A.D. 1636: documents relating to the civil war; and an appendix containing a collection of letters taken from the Ffarington correspondence between the years 1547 and 1688.* 3 fiche. Reprint; originally published 1856. £21.00.

41. HARLAND, JOHN, ed. *The house and farm accounts of the Shuttleworths of Gawthorpe Hall, in the county of Lancaster, at Smithils and Gawthorpe, from September 1582 to October 1621. Pt. 2.* 3 fiche. Reprint; originally published 1856. £21.00.

43. HARLAND, JOHN, ed. *The house and farm accounts of the Shuttleworths of Gawthorpe Hall, in the county of Lancaster, at Smithils and Gawthorpe, from September 1582 to October 1621. Pt. 3.* 4 fiche. Reprint; originally published 1857. £28.00.

46. *The house and farm accounts of the Shuttleworths of Gawthorpe Hall, in the county of Lancaster, at Smithils and Gawthorpe, from September 1582 to October 1621. Pt. 4.* 5 fiche. Reprint; originally published 1858. £35.00.

49. HARLAND, JOHN, ed. *The Lancashire lieutenancy under the Tudors and Stuarts. The civil and military government of the county, as illustrated by a series of royal and other letters; orders of the privy council, the lord lieutenant, and other authorities; etc., etc., chiefly derived from the Shuttleworth mss. at Gawthorpe Hall, Lancashire. Pt. 1.* 3 fiche. Reprint; originally published 1859. £21.00.

50. HARLAND, JOHN, ed. *The Lancashire lieutenancy under the Tudors and Stuarts. The civil and military government of the county, as illustrated by a series of royal and other letters; orders of the privy council, the lord lieutenant, and other authorities; etc., etc., chiefly derived from the Shuttleworth mss. at Gawthorpe Hall, Lancashire. Pt. 2.* 3 fiche. Reprint; originally published 1859. £21.00.

51. PICCOPE, G.J., ed. *Lancashire and Cheshire wills and inventories from the ecclesiastical court, Chester. Vol. ii.* 4 fiche. Reprint; originally published 1860. £28.00. Transcripts.

54. PICCOPE, G.J., ed. *Lancashire and Cheshire wills and inventories from the ecclesiastical court, Chester. Vol. iii.* 3 fiche. Reprint; originally published 1861. £21.00. Transcripts.

59. RAINES, F.R., ed. *A history of the chantries within the county palatine of Lancaster, being the reports of the royal commissioners of Henry VIII, Edward VI, and Queen Mary. Vol. 1.* 3 fiche. Reprint; originally published 1862. £21.00.

60. RAINES, F.R., ed. *A history of the chantries within the county palatine of Lancaster, being the reports of the royal commissioners of Henry VIII, Edward VI, and Queen Mary. Vol. 2.* 2 fiche. Reprint; originally published 1862. £14.00.

63. HARLAND, JOHN, ed. *A volume of court leet records of the manor of Manchester in the sixteenth century.* 3 fiche. Reprint; originally published 1865. £21.00.

65. HARLAND, JOHN, ed. *Continuation of the court leet records of the manor of Manchester, A.D. 1586-1602.* 2 fiche. Reprint; originally published 1865. £14.00.

69. SMITH, JEREMIAH FINCH, ed. *The admission register of the Manchester school, with some notices of the more distinguished scholars. Vol. i: From A.D. 1730 to A.D. 1775.* 3 fiche. Reprint; originally published 1866. £21.00.

72. *Collectanea relating to Manchester and its neighbourhood at various periods. Vol. ii.* 3 fiche. Reprint; originally published 1867. £21.00.

73. SMITH, JEREMIAH FINCH, ed. *The admission register of the Manchester school, with some notices of the more distinguished scholars. Vol. ii: From A.D. 1776 to A.D. 1807.* 4 fiche. Reprint; originally published 1868. £28.00.

74. HARLAND, JOHN, ed. *Three Lancashire documents of the fourteenth and fifteenth centuries, comprising I: The great de Lacy inquisition, Feb. 16, 1311. II: The survey of 1320-1346. III: Custom roll and rental of the manor of Ashton-under-Lyne, November 11, 1422.* 2 fiche. Reprint; originally published 1868. £14.00.

75. KING, THOMAS WILLIAM, ed. *Lancashire funeral certificates.* 2 fiche. Reprint; originally published 1869. £14.00.

Chetham Society (*cont.*)

78-80. BEAMONT, WILLIAM, ed. *Tracts written in the controversy respecting the legitimacy of Amicia, daughter of Hugh Cyveliok, Earl of Chester, A.D. 1673-1679, by Sir Peter Leycester, bart., and Sir Thomas Mainwaring, bart.* Reprinted from the collection at Peover. Reprint; originally published 1869. 3 pts. Pt. 1. 3 fiche. £21.00. Pt. 2. 3 fiche. £21.00. Pt. 3. 3 fiche. £21.00.

81. RAINES, F.R., ed. *The visitation of the county palatine of Lancaster, made in the year 1567, by William Flower, esq., Norroy king of arms.* 2 fiche. Reprint; originally published 1870. £14.00.

82. RAINES, F.R., ed. *The visitation of the county palatine of Lancaster, made in the year 1613, by Richard St. George, esq., Norroy king of arms.* 2 fiche. Reprint; originally published 1871. £14.00.

84. RAINES, F.R., ed. *The visitation of the county palatine of Lancaster, made in the year 1664-5, by Sir William Dugdale, knight, Norroy king of arms. Pt. 1.* 2 fiche. Reprint; originally published 1872. £14.00.

85. RAINES, F.R., ed. *The visitation of the county palatine of Lancaster, made in the year 1664-5, by Sir William Dugdale, knight, Norroy king of arms. Pt. 2.* 2 fiche. Reprint; originally published 1872. £14.00.

86. BEAMONT, WILLIAM, ed. *Annals of the lords of Warrington for the first five centuries after the Conquest, with historical notices of the place and neighbourhood. Pt. 1.* 4 fiche. Reprint; originally published 1872. £28.00.

87. BEAMONT, WILLIAM, ed. *Annals of the lords of Warrington for the first five centuries after the Conquest, with historical notices of the place and neighbourhood. Pt. 2.* 4 fiche. Reprint; originally published 1873. £28.00.

88. RAINES, F.R., ed. *The visitation of the county palatine of Lancaster, made in the year 1664-5, by Sir William Dugdale, knight, Norroy king of arms. Pt. 3.* 2 fiche. Reprint; originally published 1873. £14.00.

93. SMITH, JEREMIAH FINCH, ed. *The admission register of the Manchester school, with some notices of the more distinguished scholars. Vol. iii: From May A.D. 1807 to September A.D. 1837, pt. 1.* 3 fiche. Reprint; originally published 1874. £21.00.

94. SMITH, JEREMIAH FINCH, ed. *The admission register of the Manchester school, with some notices of the more distinguished scholars. Vol. iii: From May A.D. 1807 to September A.D. 1837, pt. 2.* 3 fiche. Reprint; originally published 1874. £21.00.

95. LANGTON, WILLIAM, ed. *Abstracts of inquisitions post mortem made by Christopher Towneley and Roger Dodsworth. Vol. i.* 3 fiche. Reprint; originally published 1875. £21.00.

98. LANGTON, WILLIAM, ed. *The visitation of Lancashire and a part of Cheshire, made in the twenty-fourth year of the reign of King Henry the Eighth, A.D. 1533, by special commission of Thomas Benalt, Clarencieux. Pt. 1.* 2 fiche. Reprint; originally published 1876. £14.00.

99. LANGTON, WILLIAM, ed. *Abstracts of inquisitions post mortem made by Christopher Towneley and Roger Dodsworth. Vol. ii.* 3 fiche. Reprint; originally published 1876. £21.00.

107. BAILEY, JOHN EGLINGTON, ed. *Inventories of goods in the churches and chapels of Lancashire, taken in the year A.D. 1552. Pt. 1: Salford hundred.* 1 fiche. Reprint; originally published 1879. £7.00.

110. LANGTON, WILLIAM, ed. *The visitation of Lancashire and a part of Cheshire, made in the twenty-fourth year of the reign of King Henry the Eighth, A.D. 1533, by special commission of Thomas Benalt, Clarencieux. Pt. 2.* 2 fiche. Reprint; originally published 1882. £14.00.

112. LYONS, P.A., ed. *Two compoti of the Lancashire and Cheshire manors of Henry de Lacy, Earl of Lincoln, 24 and 33 Edward I.* 3 fiche. Reprint; originally published 1884. £21.00.

113. BAILEY, JOHN EGLINGTON, ed. *Inventories of goods in the churches and chapels of Lancashire, taken in the year A.D. 1552. Pt. 2: West Derby, Blackburn, and Leyland hundreds.* 2 fiche. Reprint; originally published 1888. £14.00.

114. CHRISTIE, RICHARD COPLEY, ed *The diary and correspondence of Dr. John Worthington, master of Jesus College, Cambridge, vice-chancellor of the University of Cambridge, etc., etc. Vol. ii, pt. 2.* 2 fiche. Reprint; originally published 1886. £14.00.

General index to the remains historical and literary published by the Chetham Society, vols. 1-30. 3 fiche. Reprint; originally published 1863. £21.00.
General index to the remains historical and literary published by the Chetham Society, vols 31-114. 4 fiche. Reprint; originally published 1893, £28.00.

New Series

1. RAINES, F.R., ed. *The vicars of Rochdale. Pt. 1,* ed. Henry Howorth. 3 fiche. Reprint; originally published 1883. £21.00.
2. RAINES, F.R., ed. *The vicars of Rochdale. Pt. 2,* ed. Henry Howorth. 3 fiche. Reprint; originally published 1883. £21.00.
3. EARWAKER, J.P., ed. *Lancashire and Cheshire wills and inventories at Chester, with an appendix of abstracts of wills now lost or destroyed.* 3 fiche. Reprint; originally published 1884. £21.00.
5. RAINES, F.R. *The rectors of Manchester and the wardens of the collegiate church of that town. Pt. 1.* 2 fiche. Reprint; originally published 1885. £14.00.
6. RAINES, F.R. *The rectors of Manchester and the wardens of the collegiate church of that town. Pt. 2.* 2 fiche. Reprint; originally published 1885. £14.00.
8. FISHWICK, HENRY, ed. *The history of the parish of Poulton-le-Fylde, in the county of Lancaster.* 3 fiche. Reprint; originally published 1885. £21.00. Includes extracts from parish registers, wills, *tc.*
9. ATKINSON, J.C., ed. *The coucher book of Furness Abbey. Vol. i, pt. 1.* 3 fiche. Reprint; originally published 1886. £21.00.
10. FISHWICK, HENRY. *The history of the parish of Bispham, in the county of Lancaster.* 2 fiche. Reprint; originally published 1887. £14.00. Includes extracts from parish registers, wills, *etc.*
11. ATKINSON, J.C., ed. *The coucher book of Furness Abbey. Vol. i, pt. 2.* 3 fiche. Reprint; originally published 1887. £21.00.

12. GIBSON, THOMAS ELLISON, ed. *Crosby records: a chapter of Lancashire recusancy. Containing a relation of troubles and persecutions sustained by William Blundell, of Crosby Hall, Lancashire, esq. (1560-1638), and an account of an ancient burial ground for recusants, called the Harkirke, and of coins discovered there.* 2 fiche. Reprint; originally published 1887. £14.00.
14. ATKINSON, J.C., ed. *The coucher book of Furness Abbey. Vol. i, pt. 3.* 3 fiche. Reprint; originally published 1887. £21.00.
20. SHAW, WILLIAM A., ed. *Minutes of the Manchester presbyterian classis. Pt. 1.* 3 fiche. Reprint; originally published 1890. £21.00.
21. RAINES, F.R. *The fellows of the collegiate church of Manchester. Pt. 1.* 3 fiche. Reprint; originally published 1891. £21.00.
22. SHAW, WILLIAM A., ed. *Minutes of the Manchester presbyterian classis, 1646-1660. Pt. 2.* 3 fiche. Reprint; originally published 1891. £21.00.
23. RAINES, F.R. *The fellows of the collegiate church of Manchester. Pt. 2.* 3 fiche. Reprint; originally published 1891. £21.00.
24. SHAW, WILLIAM A., ed. *Minutes of the Manchester presbyterian classis, 1646-1660. Pt. 3.* 2 fiche. Reprint; originally published 1891. £14.00.
28. EARWAKER, J.P., ed. *Lancashire and Cheshire wills and inventories, 1572 to 1696, now preserved at Chester, with an appendix of Lancashire and Cheshire wills and inventories proved at York or Richmond, 1542 to 1649.* 3 fiche. Reprint; originally published 1893. £21.00.
33. FISHER, HENRY, ed. *The note book of the Rev. Thomas Jolly, A.D. 1671-1693, extracts from the church book of Altham and Wymondhouses, A.D. 1649-1725, and an account of the Jolly family of Standish, Gorton, and Altham.* 3 fiche. Reprint; originally published 1894. £21.00.
36. SHAW, WILLIAM A., ed. *Minutes of the Bury presbyterian classis, 1647-1657. Pt. 1.* 2 fiche. Reprint; originally published 1896. £14.00.
37. RYLANDS, J. PAUL, ed. *Lancashire and Cheshire wills and inventories, 1563 to 1807, now preserved at Chester.* 2 fiche. Reprint; originally published 1897. £14.00.

Chetham Society (cont.)
38-40, 43, 56-7, 64. FARRER, WILLIAM, ed. *The chartulary of Cockersand Abbey of the Premonstratensian order.* Reprint; originally published 1898-1909.
Pt. 1. 2 fiche. £14.00.
Pt. 2. 2 fiche. £14.00.
Pt. 3. 3 fiche. £21.00.
Pt. 4. 3 fiche. £21.00.
Pt. 5. 2 fiche. £14.00.
Pt. 6. 3 fiche. £21.00.
Pt. 7. 4 fiche. £28.00.
41. SHAW, WILLIAM A., ed. *Minutes of the Bury presbyterian classis, 1647-1657. Pt. 2.* 2 fiche. £14.00.
44. COOKE, ALICE M., ed. *Act book of the ecclesiastical court of Whalley, 1510-1538.* 3 fiche. Reprint; originally published 1901. £21.00.
46, 48. MANDLEY, J.G. DE T., ed. *The portmote or court leet records of the borough or town and royal manor of Salford from the year 1597 to the year 1669 inclusive.* 2 vols. Reprint; originally published 1902. Vol.1. 3 fiche. £21.00. Vol.2. 4 fiche. £28.00.
49-50. RAINES, FRANCIS ROBERT, & SUTTON, CHARLES W., ed. *Life of Humphrey Chetham, founder of the Chetham Hospital and Library, Manchester.* 2 vols, 3 fiche per vol. Reprint; originally published 1903. £21.00 per vol.
66-8. STOCKS, GEORGE ALFRED, ed. *The records of Blackburn Grammar School.* 3 vols. 2 fiche per vol. Reprint; originally published 1909. £14.00 per part.
69. SPARKE, ARCHIBALD, ed. *The township booke of Halliwell.* 3 fiche. Reprint; originally published 1910. £21.00. Accounts.
71. FISHWICK, HENRY, ed. *The survey of the manor of Rochdale in the county of Lancaster, parcel of the possessions of the Rt. Worshipful Sir Robert Heath, knt., His Majesty's attorney-general, made in 1626.* 4 fiche. Reprint; originally published 1913. £28.00.
74. BROWNBILL, JOHN, ed. *The coucher book of Furness Abbey. Vol. ii, pt. 1.* 4 fiche. Reprint; originally published 1915. £28.00.
75. TAIT, JAMES, ed. *The domesday survey of Cheshire.* 3 fiche. Reprint; originally published 1916. £21.00.
76. BROWNBILL, JOHN, ed. *The coucher book of Furness Abbey. Vol. ii, pt. 2.* 4 fiche. Reprint; originally published 1916. £28.00.

77. TAIT, JAMES, ed. *Lancashire quarter sessions records. Vol. i: Quarter sessions rolls, 1590-1606.* 4 fiche. Reprint; originally published 1917. £28.00.
78. BROWNBILL, JOHN, ed. *The coucher book of Furness Abbey. Vol. ii, pt. 3.* 4 fiche. Reprint; originally published 1919. £28.00.
79, 82. TAIT, JAMES, ed. *The chartulary or register of the abbey of St. Werburgh, Chester.* 2 vols. Reprint; originally published 1920. Vol.1. 4 fiche. £28.00. Vol.2. 3 fiche. £21.00.
83. TAIT, JAMES, ed. *Taxation in Salford Hundred, 1524-1802.* 3 fiche. Reprint; originally published 1924. £21.00.
84. STEWART-BROWN, R., ed. *Calendar of county court, city court, and eyre rolls of Chester, 1259-1297, with an inquest of military service, 1288.* 4 fiche. Reprint; originally published 1925. £28.00.
87. PARKER, JOHN, ed. *Plea rolls of the county palatine of Lancaster. Roll I.* 2 fiche. Reprint; originally published 1928. £14.00.
89. TRAPPES-LOMAX, RICHARD, ed. *The diary and letter book of the Rev. Thomas Brockbank, 1671-1709.* 5 fiche. Reprint; originally published 1930. £35.00.
91. PARKER, JOHN, ed. *Lancashire deeds. Vol. i: Shuttleworth deeds, pt. 1.* 2 fiche. Reprint; originally published 1934. £14.00. Relating to Eccleshill, Barton, and High Whitaker, 13-17th c.
92. STOKES, C.W., ed. *Queen Mary's Grammar School, Clitheroe. Pt. 1: The sixteenth and seventeenth centuries.* 3 fiche. Reprint; originally published 1934. £21.00.
93. HORNYOLD-STRICKLAND, HENRY. *Biographical sketches of the members of parliament of Lancashire, 1290-1550.* 2 fiche. Reprint; originally published 1935. £14.00.
96. ROSKELL, JOHN S. *The knights of the shire for the county palatine of Lancaster, 1377-1460.* 3 fiche. Reprint; originally published 1937. £21.00.
97. AXON, ERNEST, ed. *Oliver Heywood's life of John Angier of Denton, together with Angier's diary, and extracts from his An helpe to better hearts; also Samuel Angier's diary.* 2 fiche. Reprint; originally published 1937. £14.00.

98. CANTLE, A., ed. *The pleas of quo warranto for the county of Lancaster.* 3 fiche. Reprint; originally published 1937. £21.00.

102. CHIPPINDALL, W.H., ed. *A sixteenth-century survey and year's account of the estates of Hornby Castle, Lancashire, with an introduction on the owners of the castle.* 2 fiche. Reprint; originally published 1939. £14.00.

105, 108. VARLEY, JOAN, ed. *A Middlewich chartulary compiled by William Vernon in the seventeenth century.* 2 vols. Reprint; originally published 1941-4. 3 fiche, £21.00 per vol.

110. LEATHERBARROW, J. STANLEY, ed. *The Lancashire Elizabethan recusants.* 2 fiche. Reprint; originally published 1947. £14.00.

Third Series

1. TUPLING, G.H., ed. *South Lancashire in the reign of Edward II as illustrated by the pleas at Wigan recorded in Coram Rege roll no. 254.* 3 fiche. Reprint; originally published 1949. £21.00.

2. HOPKINS, A., ed. *Selected rolls of the Chester city courts, late thirteenth and early fourteenth centuries.* 3 fiche. Reprint; originally published 1950. £21.00.

9. HIGHET, T.P. *The early history of the Davenports of Davenport.* 2 fiche. Reprint; originally published 1960. £14.00.

14. MARSHALL, J.D., ed. *The autobiography of William Stout of Lancaster, 1665-1752.* 4 fiche. Reprint; originally published 1967. £28.00.

15. CRAIG, ROBERT, & JARVIS, RUPERT, ed. *Liverpool registry of merchant ships.* 3 fiche. Reprint; originally published 1967. £21.00.

16. BROCKBANK, W., & KENWORTHY, REV. F., ed. *The diary of Richard Kay, 1716-1751, of Baldingstone, near Bury, a Lancashire doctor.* 3 fiche. Reprint; originally published 1968. £21.00.

18. WEBB, A.N., ed. *An edition of the Cartulary of Burscough Priory.* 4 fiche. Reprint; originally published 1970. £28.00.

Lincolnshire
Lincoln Record Society

Orders for microfiche reprints to:
Chadwyck-Healey Ltd., The Quorum,
Barnwell Road, Cambridge, CB5 8SW
Phone: (01223) 215512
Email: mail@chadwyck.co.uk
Http://www.chadwyck.co.uk

1. COLE, R.E.G., ed. *Lincolnshire church notes, made by Gervase Holles, A.D. 1634 to A.D. 1642.* 4 fiche. Reprint; originally published 1911. £28.00. Includes monumental inscriptions.

2. FOSTER, C.W., ed. *Lincoln episcopal records, in the time of Thomas Cooper, S.T.P., bishop of Lincoln, A.D. 1571-1584.* 6 fiche. Reprint; originally published 1912. £42.00.

3, 6, 9. PHILLIMORE, W.P.W., ed. *Rotuli Hugonis de Welles, episcopi Lincolniensis, 1209-1235.* 3 vols. Reprint; originally published 1912-14. Vol.1. 4 fiche. £28.00. Vol.2. 4 fiche. £28.00. Vol.3. 3 fiche. £21.00.

4. COLE, R.E.G., ed. *Speculum dioeceseos Lincolniensis sub epicopis Gul. Wake et Edm. Gibson, A.D. 1705-1723. Pt. i: Archdeaconries of Lincoln and Stow.* 3 fiche. Reprint; originally published 1913. £21.00.

5. FOSTER, C.W., ed. *Lincoln wills registered in the district probate registry at Lincoln. Vol. i: A.D. 1271 to A.D. 1526.* 3 fiche. Reprint; originally published 1914. £21.00.

7. THOMPSON, A.H., ed. *Visitations of religious houses in the Diocese of Lincoln. Vol.1. Injunctions and other documents from the registers of Richard Flemyng and William Gray, bishops of Lincoln, A.D. 1420-1436.* 6 fiche. Reprint; originally published 1914. £42.00.

8. GREEN, EVERARD, ed. *The visitation of the county of Lincoln made by Sir Edward Bysshe, knight, Clarenceux king of arms, in the year of our Lord 1666.* 2 fiche. Reprint; originally published 1917. £14.00.

10. FOSTER, C.W., ed. *Lincoln wills registered in the district probate registry at Lincoln. Vol. ii: A.D. 1505 to May 1530.* 4 fiche. Reprint; originally published 1918. £28.00.

Lincoln Record Society (cont.)

11. DAVIS, F.N., ed. *Rotuli Roberti Grosseteste, episcopi Lincolniensis, A.D. MCCXXXV-MCCLIII.* 7 fiche. Reprint; originally published 1914. £49.00.

12. COLE, R.E.G., ed. *Chapter acts of the cathedral church of St. Mary of Lincoln, A.D. 1520-1536.* 3 fiche. Reprint; originally published 1915. £21.00.

13. COLE, R.E.G., ed. *Chapter acts of the cathedral church of St. Mary of Lincoln, A.D. 1536-1547.* 3 fiche. Reprint; originally published 1917. £21.00.

14. THOMPSON, A.H., ed.*Visitations of religious houses. Vol.ii. Records of visitations held by William Alnwick, Bishop of Lincoln, A.D. 1436-1449, part 1.* 6 fiche. Reprint; originally published 1918. £42.00.

15. COLE, R.E.G., ed. *Chapter acts of the cathedral church of St. Mary of Lincoln, A.D. 1547-1559.* 3 fiche. Reprint; originally published 1920. £21.00.

16. FOSTER, C.W., ed. *Calendars of administrations in the Consistory Court of Lincoln, 1540-1659.* 5 fiche. Reprint; originally published 1921. £35.00.

17. FOSTER, C.W., ed. *Final concords of the county of Lincoln from the feet of fines preserved in the Public Record Office, A.D. 1244-1272, with additions from various sources, A.D. 1176-1250. Vol. ii.* 6 fiche. Reprint; originally published 1920. £42.00.

18. STENTON, F.M., ed. *Transcripts of charters relating to the Gilbertine houses of Sixle, Ormsby, Catley, Bullington, and Alvingham. Memoranda rolls nos. 183,185, and 187.* 4 fiche. Reprint; originally published 1922. £28.00.

19. FOSTER, C.W., & LONGLEY, THOMAS, ed. *The Lincolnshire domesday and the Lindsey survey.* 5 fiche. Reprint; originally published 1924. £35.00.

20. DAVIS, F.N., ed. *Rotuli Ricardi Gravesend, episcopi Lincolniensis.* 5 fiche. Reprint; originally published 1925. £35.00. 1258-1279.

21. THOMPSON, A.H., ed. *Visitations of religious houses. Vol. iii. Records of visitations held by William Alnwick, Bishop of Lincoln, A.D. 1436-1449, part 2.* 5 fiche. Reprint; originally published 1929. £35.00.

22. STENTON, DORIS M., ed. *The earliest Lincolnshire assize rolls, A.D. 1202-1209.* 5 fiche. Reprint; originally published 1926. £35.00.

23. FOSTER, C.W., ed. *The state of the church in the reigns of Elizabeth and James I as illustrated by documents relating to the diocese of Lincoln. Vol. i.* 8 fiche. Reprint; originally published 1926. £56.00.

24. FOSTER, C.W., ed. *Lincoln wills registered in the district probate registry at Lincoln. Vol. iii: A.D. 1530 to 1532.* 4 fiche. Reprint; originally published 1930. £28.00.

25-6. PEYTON, S.A., ed. *Minutes of proceedings in quarter sessions held for the parts of Kesteven in the county of Lincoln, 1674-1695.* 2 vols. Reprint; originally published 1931. vol.1. 4 fiche. £28.00.Vol.2. 5 fiche. £35.00.

27-9, 32, 34, 41, 46. FOSTER, C.W., et al, eds. *The Registrum antiquissimum of the Cathedral Church of Lincoln.* 7 vols. 6 fiche. Reprint; originally published 1931-. Vol.1. 6 fiche. £42.00. Vol.2. 6 fiche. £42.00. Vol.3. 6 fiche. £42.00. Vol.4. 5 fiche. £35.00. Vol.5. 3 fiche. £21.00. Vol.6. 3 fiche. £21.00. Vol.7. 4 fiche. £28.00. Further volumes are not available on fiche. See also **42** below.

30. SILLEM, ROSAMOND, ed. *Records of some Sessions of the Peace in Lincolnshire, 1360-1375.* 5 fiche. Reprint; originally published 1936. £35.00.

31. MONSON, JOHN, LORD, ed. *Lincolnshire church notes made by William John Monson, F.S.A., afterwards sixth Lord Monson of Burton, 1828-1840.* 6 fiche. Reprint; originally published 1936. £42.00. Mainly monumental inscriptions.

33. THOMPSON, A. HAMILTON, ed. *Visitations in the Diocese of Lincoln, 1517-1531. Vol. I: Visitations of rural deaneries by William Atwater, bishop of Lincoln, and his commissaries, 1517-1520.* 4 fiche. Reprint; originally published 1940. £28.00.

35. THOMPSON, A. HAMILTON, ed. *Visitations in the Diocese of Lincoln, 1517-1531. Vol. ii: Visitations of rural deaneries by John Longland, bishop of Lincoln, and of religious houses by Bishops Atwater and Longland, and by his and their commissaries, 1517-1531.* 5 fiche. Reprint; originally published 1944. £35.00.

36. THOMSON, WALTER SINCLAIR, ed. *A Lincolnshire assize roll for 1298 (P.R.O. Assize roll no. 505).* 3 fiche. Reprint; originally published 1944. £21.00.

37. THOMPSON, A. HAMILTON, ed. *Visitations in the diocese of Lincoln, 1517-1531. Vol. iii: Visitations of religious houses (concluded) by bishops Atwater and Longland and by their commissaries, 1517-1531.* 4 fiche. Reprint; originally published 1947. £28.00.

38. BRACE, HAROLD W., ed. *The first minute book of the Gainsborough monthly meeting of the Society of Friends, 1699-1719. Vol. i: 1669-1689.* 2 fiche. Reprint; originally published 1948. £14.00.

39. HILL, ROSALIND M.T., ed. *The rolls and register of Bishop Oliver Sutton, 1280-1299. Vol. i: Institutions to benefices and confirmations of heads of religious houses in the Archdeaconry of Lincoln.* 4 fiche. Reprint; originally published 1948. £28.00.

40. BRACE, H.W., ed. *The first minute book of Gainsborough monthly meeting of the Society of Friends. Vol. ii: 1689-1709.* 3 fiche. Reprint; originally published 1949. £21.00.

42. *The Registrum antiquissimum of the Cathedral Church of Lincoln. Facsimiles of charters in vols. v and vi.* 1 fiche. Reprint; originally published 1950. £7.00.

43. HILL, ROSALIND M.T., ed. *The rolls and register of Bishop Oliver Sutton, 1280-1299. Vol. ii: Institutions to benefices and confirmations of heads of religious houses in the Archdeaconry of Northampton.* 3 fiche. Reprint; originally published 1950. £21.00.

44. BRACE, H.W., ed. *The first minute book of the Gainsborough monthly meeting of the Society of Friends. Vol. iii: 1709-1719.* 3 fiche. Reprint; originally published 1951. £21.00.

45. HILL, J.W.F. *The letters and papers of the Banks family of Revesby Abbey, 1704-1760.* 4 fiche. Reprint; originally published 1952. £28.00.

48. HILL, ROSALIND M.T., ed. *The rolls and register of Bishop Oliver Sutton, 1280-1299. Vol. iii: Memoranda, May 19, 1290-May 18, 1292.* 4 fiche. Reprint; originally published 1954. £28.00.

49. KIMBALL, ELIZABETH G., ed. *Records of some Sessions of the Peace in Lincolnshire, 1381-1396. Vol. i: The parts of Kesteven and the parts of Holland.* 2 fiche. Reprint; originally published 1955. £14.00.

50. HINTON, R.W.K., ed. *The port books of Boston, 1601-1640.* 5 fiche. Reprint; originally published 1956. £35.00.

Middlesex
Middlesex County Record Society

Orders for microfiche reprints to:
Chadwyck-Healey Ltd., The Quorum, Barnwell Road, Cambridge, CB5 8SW
Phone: (01223) 215512
Email: mail@chadwyck.co.uk
Http://www.chadwyck.co.uk

1. JEAFFRESON, JOHN CORDY, ed. *Middlesex county records.* 23 fiche. Reprint; originally published 1886-1892. £161.00.

Norfolk
Norfolk Record Society

Orders for microfiche reprints to:
Chadwyck-Healey Ltd., The Quorum, Barnwell Road, Cambridge, CB5 8SW
Phone: (01223) 215512
Email: mail@chadwyck.co.uk
Http://www.chadwyck.co.uk

1. *Calendar of such of the Frere mss. as relate to the hundred of Holt. Muster roll for the hundred of North Greenhoe, circa 1523. Norwich subscriptions to the voluntary gift of 1662.* 2 fiche. Reprint; originally published 1931. £14.00.

2. WEST, J.R., ed. *St. Benet of Holme, 1020-1210. The eleventh and twelfth century sections of Cott. ms. Galba E.ii, the register of the abbey of St. Benet of Holme.* 2 vols. 3 fiche. Reprint; originally published 1932. Vol.1. 3 fiche. £21.00. Vol.2. 2 fiche. £14.00. Chartulary.

4-5. CLARKE, A.W.HUGHES, & CAMPLING, ARTHUR, eds.*The visitation of Norfolk anno domini 1664, made by Sir Edward Bysshe, knt., Clarenceus king of arms.* 2 vols. Reprint; originally published 1934. Vol.1. 2 fiche. £14.00. Vol.2. 3 fiche. £21.00.

6-7. BRADFER-LAWRENCE, H.L., ed. *The musters returns for divers hundreds in the county of Norfolk. 1569, 1572, 1574 and 1577.* 2 vols. 2 fiche per vol. Reprint; originally published 1935. £14.00 per vol.

Norfolk Record Society *(cont.)*

8. *Norfolk sessions of the peace: rolls of mainpernors and pledges, 1394-1397. The maritime trade of the port of Blakeney, which included Cley and Wiveton, 1587 to 1590. Election for two knights of the shire for Norfolk, 1702: votes polled for Sir Edward Ward, bart.* 2 fiche. Reprint; originally published 1936. £14.00.

9. GRACE, MARY, ed. *Records of the gild of St. George in Norwich, 1389-1547.* 2 fiche. Reprint; originally published 1937. £14.00.

10. STONE, E.D., ed. *Norwich Consistory Court depositions, 1499-1512 and 1518-1530.* 2 fiche. Reprint; originally published 1938. £14.00.

11. SAUNDERS, H.W., ed. *The first register of Norwich Cathedral Priory.* 2 fiche. Reprint; originally published 1939. £14.00.

12. BULLOCK, J.H., ed. *The Norfolk portion of the chartulary of the priory of St. Pancras of Lewes.* 2 fiche. Reprint; originally published 1939. £14.00.

13. CAMPLING, ARTHUR, ed. *East Anglian pedigrees.* 4 fiche. Reprint; originally published 1940. £28.00.

14. HUGHEY, RUTH, ed. *The correspondence of Lady Katherine Paston, 1603-1627.* 2 fiche. Reprint; originally published 1941. £14.00.

15. SACHSE, WILLIAM L., ed. *Minutes of the Norwich court of mayoralty, 1630-1631.* 3 fiche. Reprint; originally published 1942. £21.00.

16. FARROW, M.A. *Index of wills proved in the Consistory Court of Norwich and now preserved in the district probate registry at Norwich, 1370-1550, and wills among the Norwich enrolled deeds, 1298-1508.* 1 vol. in 3. 6 fiche. Reprint; originally published 1943-5. £42.00.

18. WILLIAMS, J.F., ed. *Diocese of Norwich: Bishop Redman's visitation, 1597. Presentments in the archdeaconries of Norwich, Norfolk, and Suffolk.* 3 fiche. Reprint; originally published 1946. £21.00.

19. WATKIN, AELRED, ed. *Archdeaconry of Norwich: inventory of church goods, temp. Edward III.* 5 fiche. Reprint; originally published 1947-8. £35.00.

20. SCHOFIELD, BERTRAM, ed. *The Knyvett letters, 1620-1644.* 3 fiche. Reprint; originally published 1949. £21.00.

21. FARROW, M.A. *Index to wills proved in the Consistory court of Norwich ... 1550-1603.* 3 fiche. Reprint; originally published 1950. £21.00.

22. *A miscellany.* 2 fiche. Reprint; originally published 1951. £14.00. Includes Old Meeting House, Norwich, baptisms, 1657-1781, Great Yarmouth Independent church baptisms and deaths, 1643-1705, etc.

23. *The freemen of Norwich, 1714-1752.* 2 fiche. Reprint; originally published 1952. £14.00.

24. WILLIAMS, J.F., & COZENS-HARDY, J.F., ed. *Extracts from the two earliest minute books of the dean and chapter of Norwich, 1566-1649.* 2 fiche. Reprint; originally published 1953. £14.00.

25. JEWSON, CHARLES BOARDMAN, ed. *Transcript of three registers of passengers from Great Yarmouth to Holland and New England, 1637-1639.* 2 fiche. Reprint; originally published 1954. £14.00.

26. JAMES, D.E. HOWELL, ed. *Norfolk quarter sessions order book, 1650-1657.* 2 fiche. Reprint; originally published 1955. £14.00.

28. FARROW, M.A., & BARTON, T.F., ed. *Index of wills proved in the consistory court of Norwich and now preserved in the district probate registry at Norwich, 1604-1686.* 3 fiche. Reprint; originally published 1958. £21.00.

29. RISING, WINIFRED M., & MILLICAN, PERCY, ed. *An index of indentures of Norwich apprentices enrolled with the Norwich Assembly, Henry VII - George II.* 3 fiche. Reprint; originally published 1961. £21.00.

30. COZENS-HARDY, B., ed. *Norfolk lieutenancy journal, 1676-1701.* 2 fiche. Reprint; originally published 1959. £14.00.

31. ROBINSON, J.A., ed. *The Ames correspondence. Letters to Mary: a selection from letters written by members of the Ames family of Lakenham, Norwich, 1837-1847.* 2 fiche. Reprint; originally published 1962. £14.00.

32. BARTON, T.F., ed. *The Registrum vagum of Anthony Harison.* 2 vols. Reprint; originally published 1963-4. £21.00. Vol.1. 3 fiche. £21.00. Vol.2. 2 fiche. £14.00.

34. BARTON, THOMAS F., & FARROW, M.A., ed. *Index of wills proved in the Consistory Court of Norwich, 1687-1750, and now preserved in the Norfolk and Norwich Record Office.* 3 fiche. Reprint; originally published 1965. £21.00.

35. BEDINGFELD, A.L., ed. *A cartulary of Creake Abbey.* 2 fiche. Reprint; originally published 1966. £14.00.

36. SACHSE, WILLIAM L., ed. *Minutes of the Norwich court of mayoralty, 1632-1635.* 3 fiche. Reprint; originally published 1967. £21.00.

37. COZENS-HARDY, B., ed. *Mary Hardy's diary.* 2 fiche. Reprint; originally published 1968. £14.00.

38. BARTON, THOMAS F., FARROW, M.A., & BEDINGFELD, A.L., ed. *Index of wills proved in the consistory court of Norwich, 1751-1818 and now preserved in the Norfolk and Norwich Record Office.* 3 fiche. Reprint; originally published 1969. £21.00.

39. RUTLEDGE, P., ed. *Great Yarmouth assembly minutes, 1538-1545,* and RICHWOOD, D.L., ed. *The Norwich accounts for the customs on strangers' goods and merchandise, 1582-1610.* 2 fiche. Reprint; originally published 1970. £14.00.

Northumberland
See also Durham

Newcastle upon Tyne Records Committee Publications
Orders for microfiche reprints to:
Chadwyck-Healey Ltd., The Quorum, Barnwell Road, Cambridge, CB5 8SW
Phone: (01223) 215512
Email: mail@chadwyck.co.uk
Http://www.chadwyck.co.uk

1. DODDS, MADELEINE HOPE, ed. *Extracts from the Newcastle upon Tyne council minute book, 1639-1656.* 3 fiche. Reprint; originally published 1920. £21.00.

2. THOMPSON, A. HAMILTON, ed. *Northumberland pleas from the curia regis and assize rolls, 1198-1272.* 5 fiche. Reprint; originally published 1923. £35.00.

3. DODDS, MADELEINE HOPE, ed. *The register of freemen of Newcastle upon Tyne. From the corporation guild and admission books, chiefly of the seventeenth century.* 3 fiche. Reprint; originally published 1923. £21.00.

4. BLAIR, C.H. HUNTER, ed. *Northumbrian monuments, or, the shields of arms, effigies, and inscriptions in the churches, castles, and halls of Northumberland.* 3 fiche. Reprint; originally published 1924. £21.00.

5. BLAIR, C.H. HUNTER, ed. *Durham monuments, or, the shields of arms, effigies, and inscriptions in the churches, castles, and halls of the county of Durham.* 4 fiche. Reprint; originally published 1925. £28.00.

6. OLIVER, A.M., ed. *The register of freemen of Newcastle upon Tyne. From the corporation guild and admission books, chiefly of the eighteenth century.* 4 fiche. Reprint; originally published 1926. £28.00.

7. OLIVER, A.M., ed. *Northumberland and Durham deeds from the Dodsworth mss. in Bodley's library, Oxford.* 4 fiche. Reprint; originally published 1929. £28.00.

8. WOOD, H.M., ed. *Index of wills, etc., in the probate registry, Durham, and from other sources, 140-1599.* 3 fiche. Reprint; originally published 1928. £21.00.

10. OLIVER, A.M., & JOHNSON, CHARLES, ed. *Feet of fines, Northumberland and Durham.* 2 fiche. Reprint; originally published 1931. £14.00. 1196-1228.

11. JOHNSON, CHARLES, ed. *Feet of fines, Northumberland, A.D. 1273-A.D. 1346.* 2 fiche. Reprint; originally published 1932. £14.00.

12. BLAIR, C.H. HUNTER, ed. *The renaissance heraldry of the county palatine of Durham, from A.D. 1666 to A.D. 1800.* 2 fiche. Reprint; originally published 1933. £14.00.

Nottinghamshire
Thoroton Society Record Series
Orders for microfiche reprints to:
Chadwyck-Healey Ltd., The Quorum, Barnwell Road, Cambridge, CB5 8SW
Phone: (01223) 215512
Email: mail@chadwyck.co.uk
Http://www.chadwyck.co.uk

1. BLAGG, T.M., ed. *Seventeenth century parish register transcripts belonging to the peculiar of Southwell.* 2 fiche. Reprint; originally published 1903. £14.00.

2. LEADAM, I.S., ed. *The domesday of inclosures for Nottinghamshire. From the returns to the Inclosure Commissioners of 1517, in the Public Record Office.* 2 fiche. Reprint; originally published 1904. £14.00.

Thoroton Society (cont.)

3. PHILLIMORE, W.P.W., ed. *Abstracts of the inquisitiones post mortem relating to Nottinghamshire. Vol. i: Henry VII and Henry VIII, 1485 to 1546.* 4 fiche. Reprint; originally published 1905. £28.00.

4. STANDISH, JOHN, ed. *Abstracts of the inquisitiones post mortem relating to Nottinghamshire. Vol. ii: Edward I and Edward II, 1279 to 1321.* 4 fiche. Reprint; originally published 1914. £28.00.

5. TATE, WILLIAM EDWARD, ed. *Parliamentary land enclosures in the county of Nottingham during the 18th and 19th centuries (1743-1868).* 3 fiche. Reprint; originally published 1935. £21.00.

6. BLAGG, THOMAS M., ed. *Abstracts of the inquisitiones post mortem and other inquisitions relating to Nottinghamshire. Vol. iii: Edward II and Edward III, 1321 to 1350.* 3 fiche. Reprint; originally published 1939. £21.00.

7. HODGKINSON, R.F.B., ed. *The account books of the gilds of St. George and of St. Mary in the church of St. Peter, Nottingham.* 2 fiche. Reprint; originally published 1939. £14.00.

8. GRAY, DUNCAN, ed. *Newstead Priory cartulary, 1344, and other archives.* 3 fiche. Reprint; originally published 1940. £21.00.

10. BLAGG, THOMAS M., ed. *Abstracts of the bonds and allegations for marriage licences in the Archdeaconry court of Nottingham, 1754-1770.* 4 fiche. Reprint; originally published 1947. £28.00.

11. BLAGG, THOMAS M., ed. *A miscellany of Notts. records.* 3 fiche. Reprint; originally published 1945. £21.00.

12. TRAIN, K.S.S., ed. *Abstracts of the inquisitiones post mortem relating to Nottinghamshire, 1350-1436.* 3 fiche. Reprint; originally published 1952. £21.00.

13. TRAIN, K.S.S., ed. *Nottinghamshire visitation, 1662-1664.* 2 fiche. Reprint; originally published 1950. £14.00. Pedigrees.

14. TRAIN, K.S.S., ed. *A second miscellany of Nottinghamshire records.* 1 fiche. Reprint; originally published 1951. £7.00.

15. TRAIN, K.S.S., ed. *Lists of the clergy of central Nottinghamshire.* 3 fiche. Reprint; originally published 1953-5. £21.00.

16. BARLEY, M.W., ed. *Documents relating to the manor and soke of Newark-on-Trent.* 2 fiche. Reprint; originally published 1956. £14.00.

17. RENSHAW, MARY A., ed. *Inquisitiones post mortem relating to Nottinghamshire, 1437-1485.* 2 fiche. Reprint; originally published 1956. £14.00.

Oxfordshire

Oxfordshire Record Society

Orders for microfiche reprints to:
Chadwyck-Healey Ltd., The Quorum, Barnwell Road, Cambridge, CB5 8SW
Phone: (01223) 215512
Email: mail@chadwyck.co.uk
Http://www.chadwyck.co.uk

Oxfordshire Record Series

1. GRAHAM, ROSE, ed. *The chantry certificates ... and the Edwardian inventories of church goods.* 2 fiche. Reprint; originally published 1919. £14.00.

2, 4, 11. DAVIS, F.N., ed. *Parochial collections ... made by Anthony à Wood and Richard Rawlinson.* 3 vols. 2 fiche per vol. Reprint; originally published 1920-29. £14.00 per vol.

3. SALTER, H.E., ed. *Newington Longeville charters.* 2 fiche. Reprint; originally published 1921. £14.00.

5. BARNETT, HERBERT, ed. *Glympton. The history of an Oxfordshire manor.* 2 fiche. Reprint; originally published 1923. £14.00.

6. WEAVER, F.W., & CLARK, G.N., ed. *Churchwardens' accounts of Marston, Spelsbury, Pyrton.* 2 fiche. Reprint; originally published 1925. £14.00.

7. COOKE, A.H., ed. *The early history of Mapledurham.* 3 fiche. Reprint; originally published 1925. £21.00.

8. HOBSON, T.F., ed. *Adderbury 'rectoria'. The manor at Adderbury belonging to New College, Oxford; the building of the chancel, 1408-18; account rolls, deeds and court rolls.* 2 fiche. Reprint; originally published 1926. £14.00.

9. JEFFERY, REGINALD W., ed. *The manors and advowsons of Great Rollright.* 3 fiche. Reprint; originally published 1927. £21.00.

10. PEYTON, SIDNEY A., ed. *The churchwardens' presentments in the Oxfordshire peculiars of Dorchester, Thame and Banbury.* 5 fiche. Reprint; originally published 1928. £35.00.

12. SALTER, H.E., ed. *The feet of fines for Oxfordshire, 1195-1291.* 4 fiche. Reprint; originally published 1930. £28.00.
13. GAMBIER-PARRY, T.R., ed. *A collection of charters relating to Goring, Streatley, and the neighbourhood, 1181-1546, preserved in the Bodleian Library, with a supplement.* Reprint; originally published 1931-2. Vol.1. 3 fiche. £21.00. Vol.2. 2 fiche. £14.00.
16. GRETTON, MARY STURGE, ed. *Oxfordshire Justices of the Peace in the seventeenth century.* 3 fiche. Reprint; originally published 1934. £21.00.
19, 22. LEYS, AGNES M., ed. *The Sandford cartulary.* 2 vols. 2 fiche per vol. Reprint; originally published 1937-41. £14.00 per vol.
20. LEGG, L.G. WICKHAM, ed. *Tusmore papers.* 2 fiche. Reprint; originally published 1939. £14.00.
21. WEINSTOCK, MAUREEN M.B., ed. *Hearth tax returns, Oxfordshire, 1665.* 3 fiche. Reprint; originally published 1940. £21.00.
23-4. BRINKWORTH, E.R., ed. *The Archdeacon's court: liber actorum, 1584.* 2 vols. 2 fiche per vol. Reprint; originally published 1942. £14.00 per vol.
25-6. SALTER, H.E., ed. *The Thame cartulary.* 2 vols. 2 fiche per vol. Reprint; originally published 1947-8. £14.00 per vol.
27. RICKARD, R.L., ed. *The progress notes of Warden Woodward round the Oxfordshire estates of New College, Oxford, 1659-1675.* 2 fiche. Reprint; originally published 1949. £14.00.
35. BAKER, E.P., ed. *Bishop Wilberforce's visitation returns for the Archdeaconry of Oxford in the year 1854.* 2 fiche. Reprint; originally published 1954. £14.00.
37. HASSALL, W.O., ed. *Wheatley records, 956-1956.* 3 fiche. Reprint; originally published 1956. £21.00.

Staffordshire
Staffordshire Record Society
Orders for microfiche reprints to:
Chadwyck-Healey Ltd., The Quorum, Barnwell Road, Cambridge, CB5 8SW
Phone: (01223) 215512
Email: mail@chadwyck.co.uk
Http://www.chadwyck.co.uk
Many volumes of miscellanea not listed here are also available.

First series
5(2) GRAZEBROOK, H. SYDNEY, ed. *The heraldic visitations of Staffordshire made by Sir Richard St. George, Norroy, in 1614, and by Sir William Dugdale, Norroy, in the years 1663 and 1664.* 5 fiche. Reprint; originally published 1885. £35.00.
6(2) COX, J. CHARLES, ed. *Catalogue of the muniments and manuscript books pertaining to the Dean and Chapter of Lichfield; analysis of the Magnum registrum album: catalogue of the muniments of the Lichfield vicars.* 3 fiche. Reprint; originally published 1886. £21.00.
7(1-2). WROTTESLEY, GEORGE, ed. *Pt. 1: Extracts from the plea rolls, A.D. 1294 to A.D. 1307. The exchequer subsidy roll of A.D. 1327,* with BRIDGEMAN, G.T.O., ed. *Pt. 2: A history of the family of Swynnerton of Swynnerton, and of the younger branches of the same family settled at Eccleshall, Hilton, and Butterton.* 6 fiche. Reprint; originally published 1886. £42.00.
9(1-2). WROTTESLEY, G., ed. *Pt. 1: Extracts from the plea rolls of the reign of Edward II, A.D. 1307 to A.D. 1327. Extracts from the fine rolls of the reign of Edward II;* with GRAZEBROOK, H.S. *The barons of Dudley.* 4 fiche. Reprint; originally published 1888. £28.00.
10(2). *Extracts from the plea rolls of the reign of Edward II;* with WROTTESLEY, G., ed.*The subsidy roll of 6 Edward III, A.D. 1332-33,* and GRAZEBROOK, H.SYDNEY, ed. *Junior branches of the family of Sutton, alias Dudley.* 4 fiche. Reprint; originally published 1889. £28.00.
11. *Extracts from the plea rolls of Edward III and Richard II, A.D. 1360 to A.D. 1387. The final concords, or feet of fines, Staffordshire, A.D.1327 to A.D. 1547 ...* and PARKER, F., ed. *A chartulary of the Augustine priory of Trentham.* 5 fiche. Reprint; originally published 1890. £35.00.
15. WROTTESLEY, G., ed. *Extracts from the plea rolls of Richard II and Henry IV, A.D. 1387 to A.D. 1405,* with *Final concords ... Elizabeth, A.D. 1580 to A.D. 1589,* and *The Staffordshire muster of A.D. 1640.* 4 fiche. Reprint; originally published 1894. £28.00.

Staffordshire Record Society (*cont.*)
New Series
1. MADAN, FALCONER. *The Gresleys of Drakelowe; an account of the family and notes of its connexions by marriage and descent from the Norman conquest to the present day.* 4 fiche. Reprint; originally published 1898. £28.00.
5. WROTTESLEY, GEORGE. *The Giffards from the Conquest to the present time,* and *The muster roll for Staffordshire, A.D. 1539, hundreds of Cuttlestone and Pyrehill.* 4 fiche. Reprint; originally published 1902. £28.00.
6(2) WROTTESLEY, GEORGE. *A history of the family of Wrottesley of Wrottesley, co. Stafford.* Reprinted from *The Genealogist,* vols. xv-xix. 5 fiche. Originally published 1903. £35.00.
28. WROTTESLEY, GEORGE. *An account of the family of Okeover of Okeover, co. Stafford, with transcripts of the ancient deeds of Okeover,* with *Final concords ... Staffordshire, 16 James I to 19 James I,* and WROTTESLEY, GEORGE. *Early Chancery proceedings, Richard II to Henry VII.* 4 fiche. Reprint; originally published 1904. £28.00.
8. WILSON, ROWLAND A., ed. *The registers or act books of the bishops of Coventry and Lichfield. Book 5, being the second register of Bishop Robert de Stretton, A.D. 1360-1385.* 5 fiche. Reprint; originally published 1905. £35.00.
10(2). WILSON, ROWLAND A., ed. *The registers or act books of the bishops of Coventry and Lichfield. Book 4, being the register of the guardians of the spiritualities during the vacancy of the see, and the first register of Bishop Robert de Stretton, 1358-1385.* 3 fiche. Reprint; originally published 1907. £21.00.
12. PARKER, F., ed. *Collections for a history of Pirehill hundred, by Walter Chetwynd of Ingestre, esq., A.D. 1679.* 4 fiche. Reprint; originally published 1909. £28.00.

Third Series
42, 44, 46. WEDGWOOD, JOSIAH. *Staffordshire parliamentary history from the earliest times to the present day.* 3 vols. Reprint; originally published 1920. vol.1. 6 fiche. £42.00. vol.2(1). 3 fiche. £21.00. vol.2(2). 2 fiche. £14.00. See below for vol.3.

45. CORNFORD, M.E., & MILLER, E.B., ed. *Calendar of the manuscripts in the William Salt library, Stafford,* and *Lay subsidy 256/31, hearth tax, Pyrehill hundred, co. Stafford [part].* 3 fiche. Reprint. Originally published 1921. £21.00.
48. SAVAGE, H.E., ed. *The great register of Lichfield cathedral known as Magnum registrum album.* 5 fiche. Reprint; originally published 1924. £35.00.
49. *Notes on Staffordshire families,* with *Lay subsidy 256/31, hearth tax, Totmonslow hundred.* 4 fiche. Reprint; originally published 1925. £28.00.
53. BURNE, S.A.H., ed. *The Staffordshire Quarter Sessions rolls. Vol. i: 1581-1589.* 5 vols. Reprint; originally published 1929-40. Vol.1. 1581-1589. 5 fiche. £35.00. Vol.2. 1590-1593. 5 fiche. £35.00. Vol.3. 1594-97. 5 fiche. £35.00. Vol.4. 1598-11602. 6 fiche. £42.00. Vol.5. 1603-1606. 5 fiche. £35.00.
57. WEDGWOOD, JOSIAH. *Staffordshire parliamentary history from the earliest times to the present day. Vol. iii: 1780-1841,* with CAVENAGH-MAINWARING, J.G. *The Mainwarings of Whitmore and Biddulph in the county of Stafford. An account of the family and its connections by marriage and descent; with special reference to the manor of Whitmore.* 4 fiche. Reprint; originally published 1933. £28.00.
67. BURNE, S.A.H., ed. *Parrott's Audley survey, 1733,* with MIDGLEY, L. MARGARET, ed. *A terryar for Audley parish for 1708 and the manner of tytheing with the vicar.* 2 fiche. Reprint; originally published 1944. £14.00.
70. SALT, D.H.G., ed. *Staffordshire quarter sessions rolls, Easter 1608-Trinity 1609.* 3 fiche. Reprint; originally published 1948-49. £21.00.

Fourth Series
1. PENNINGTON, D.H., & ROOTS, I.A., ed. *The Committee at Stafford, 1643-1645. The order book of the Staffordshire County Committee.* 5 fiche. Reprint; originally published 1957. £35.00.
2. KIDSON, RUTH M. *The gentry of Staffordshire, 1662-63,* with *Active Parliamentarians during the Civil War,* and GREENSLADE, MICHAEL. *List of Staffordshire recusants.* 2 fiche. Reprint; originally published 1958. £14.00.

3. DONALDSON, BARBARA, ed. *The registrations of dissenting chapels and meeting houses in Staffordshire, 1689-1852.* 2 fiche. Reprint; originally published 1960. £14.00.
75. SALTMAN, AVROM, ed. *The cartulary of Tutbury Priory.* 4 fiche. Reprint; originally published 1962. £28.00.
76. VALSEY, D.G., ed. *Probate inventories of Lichfield and district, 1568-1680.* 4 fiche. Reprint; originally published 1969. £28.00.

Sussex

Sussex Record Society

Orders for microfiche reprints to: Chadwyck-Healey Ltd., The Quorum, Barnwell Road, Cambridge, CB5 8SW
Phone: (01223) 215512
Email: mail@chadwyck.co.uk
Http://www.chadwyck.co.uk

1. DUNKIN, EDWIN H.W., ed. *Calendar of Sussex marriage licences recorded in the Consistory Court of the bishop of Chichester for the Archdeaconry of Lewes, August 1586 to March 1642/3.* 4 fiche. Reprint; originally published 1902. £28.00.
2. SALZMAN, L.F., ed. *An abstract of feet of fines relating to the county of Sussex, from 2 Richard I to 33 Henry III.* 2 fiche. Reprint; originally published 1903. £14.00.
3. SALZMAN, L.F., ed. *A calendar of post mortem inquisitions relating to the county of Sussex, 1 to 25 Elizabeth.* 3 fiche. Reprint; originally published 1904. £21.00.
5. RICE, R. GARRAWAY, ed. *West Sussex protestation returns, 1641-2.* 3 fiche. Reprint; originally published 1906. £21.00.
6. DUNKIN, EDWIN H.W., ed. *Calendar of Sussex marriage licences ... for the Archdeaconry of Lewes, August 1670 to March 1728/9, and in the peculiar court of the Archbishop of Canterbury for the Deanery of South Malling, May 1620 to December 1732.* 5 fiche. Reprint; originally published 1907. £35.00.
7. SALZMAN, L.F., ed. *An abstract of feet of fines ... from 34 Henry III to 35 Edward I.* 3 fiche. Reprint; originally published 1908. £21.00.

8, 11. DEEDES, CECIL, ed. *The episcopal register of Robert Rede, ordinis predicatorum, lord bishop of Chichester, 1397-1415.* 2 vols. Reprint; originally published 1908-10. Vol.1. 3 fiche. £21.00. Vol.2. 4 fiche. £28.00.
9. DUNKIN, EDWIN H.W., ed. *Calendar of Sussex marriage licences ... for the Archdeaconry of Chichester, June 1575 to December 1730.* 5 fiche. Reprint; originally published 1909. £35.00.
10. HUDSON, WILLIAM, ed. *The three earliest subsidies for the county of Sussex in the years 1296, 1327, 1332. With some remarks on the origin of local administration in the county through 'borowes' or tithings.* 5 fiche. Reprint; originally published 1910. £35.00.
12. DUNKIN, EDWIN H.W., ed. *Calendar of Sussex marriage licences recorded in the peculiar courts of the Dean of Chichester and of the Archdeaconry of Canterbury: Deanery of Chichester, January 1582/3 to December 1730; Deaneries of Pagham and Tarring, January 1579/80 to November 1730.* 4 fiche. Reprint; originally published 1911. £28.00.
13. RENSHAW, W.C., ed. *The parish registers of Cuckfield, Sussex, 1598-1699.* 3 fiche. Reprint; originally published 1911. £21.00.
14. ATTREE, F.W.T., ed. *Notes of post mortem inquisitions taken in Sussex, 1 Henry VII to 1649 and after.* 4 fiche. Reprint; originally published 1912. £28.00.
15. HUTH, EDWARD, ed. *The parish registers of Bolney, Sussex, 1541-1812.* 3 fiche. Reprint; originally published 1912. £21.00.
16. MUNDY, PERCY D., ed. *Abstracts of Star Chamber proceedings relating to the county of Sussex, Henry VII to Philip and Mary.* 2 fiche. Reprint; originally published 1913. £14.00.
17. LODER, GERALD W.E., ed. *The parish registers of Ardingly, Sussex, 1558-1812.* 3 fiche. Reprint; originally published 1913. £21.00.
18. PENFOLD, EDWARD W.D., ed. *The first book of the parish registers of Angmering, Sussex, 1562-1687.* 2 fiche. Reprint; originally published 1913. £14.00.
19. DUNKIN, EDWIN W.H., ed. *Sussex manors, advowsons, etc., recorded in the feet of fines, Henry VIII to William IV, 1509-1833.* 2 vols. 4 fiche per vol. Reprint; originally published 1914. £28.00 per vol.

Sussex Record Society (*cont.*)

21. RICE, R. GARRAWAY, ed. *The parish register of Horsham in the county of Sussex, 1541-1635.* 6 fiche. Reprint; originally published 1915. £42.00.
22. GODMAN, P.S., ed. *The parish register of Cowfold, Sussex, 1558-1812.* 4 fiche. Reprint; originally published 1916. £28.00.
23. SALZMAN, L.F., ed. *An abstract of feet of fines relating to the county of Sussex from 1 Edward II to 24 Henry VII.* 4 fiche. Reprint; originally published 1916. £28.00.
24. CRAWFORD, R.P., ed. *The parish register of East Grinstead, 1558-1661.* 3 fiche. Reprint; originally published 1917. £21.00.
25. PENFOLD, E.W.D., ed. *Calendar of Sussex marriage licences ... for the Archdeaconry of Lewes, and in the peculiar court of the archbishop of Canterbury for the Deanery of South Malling, 1772-1837.* 3 fiche. Reprint; originally published 1917. £21.00.
26. PENFOLD, E.W.D., ed. *Calendar of Sussex marriage licences ... for the Archdeaconry of Lewes, and in the peculiar court of the archbishop of Canterbury for the deanery of South Malling, 1772-1837. Pt. 2: M-Z.* 3 fiche. Reprint; originally published 1919. £21.00.
27. THOMAS-STANFORD, CHARLES, ed. *An abstract of the court rolls of the manor of Preston (Preston Episcopi).* 2 fiche. Reprint; originally published 1921. £14.00.
28. RICE, R. GARRAWAY, ed. *Sussex apprentices and masters, 1710 to 1752, extracted from the apprenticeship books.* 3 fiche. Reprint; originally published 1924. £21.00.
29. BUDGEN, W., ed. *Abstracts of Sussex deeds and documents from the muniments of the late H.C. Lane, esq., of Middleton Manor, Westmeston, Sussex.* 3 fiche. Reprint; originally published 1924. £21.00. Estate records of the Dobell family.
30. SALZMAN, L.F., ed. *The parish register of Glynde, Sussex, 1558-1812.* 2 fiche. Reprint; originally published 1924. £14.00.
31. PECKHAM, W.D., ed. *Thirteen custumals of the Sussex manors of the bishop of Chichester, and other documents, from libri P and C of the episcopal manuscripts.* 2 fiche. Reprint; originally published 1925. £14.00.
32. DUNKIN, EDWIN H.W., & MACLEOD, D., ed. *Calendar of Sussex marriage licences ... for the Archdeaconry of Chichester. January 1731 to December 1774.* 3 fiche. Reprint; originally published 1926. £21.00.
33. HOLGATE, MARY S., ed. *Sussex inquisitions. Extracts from Rawlinson ms. B.433 in the Bodleian Library, Oxford, described as inquisitiones post mortem relating to Sussex.* 2 fiche. Reprint; originally published 1927. £14.00.
34. GODFREY, WALTER H., ed. *The book of John Rowe, steward of the manors of Lord Bergavenny, 1597-1622, comprising of twenty-seven manors in Sussex, manorial customs and information concerning the borough of Lewes, the hundreds within the rape of Lewes, etc.* 4 fiche. Reprint; originally published 1928. £28.00.
35. MACLEOD, D., ed. *Calendar of Sussex marriage licences ... for the Archdeaconry of Chichester, January 1775 to December 1800. Index to vols. 32 and 35, 1731-1800.* 3 fiche. Reprint; originally published 1929. £21.00.
36. RAY, JOHN E., ed. *Sussex chantry records, extracted from documents in the Public Record Office relating to the dissolution of the chantries, colleges, free chapels, fraternities, brotherhoods, guilds and other institutions.* 3 fiche. Reprint; originally published 1931. £21.00.
37. COURTHOPE, ELINOR JOAN, & FORMOY, BERYL E.R., ed. *Lathe court rolls and views of frankpledge in the rape of Hastings, A.D. 1387 to 1474.* 4 fiche. Reprint; originally published 1934. £28.00.
38, 40. SALZMAN, L.F., ed. *The chartulary of the priory of St. Pancras of Lewes.* 2 vols. 3 fiche. Reprint; originally published 1933-5. Vol.1. 3 fiche. £21.00. Vol.2. 2 fiche. £14.00.
39. STRAKER, ERNEST, ed. *The Buckhurst terrier, 1597-1598.* 2 fiche. Reprint; originally published 1934. £14.00.
41-3, 45. GODFREY, WALTER H., ed. *Transcripts of Sussex wills as far as they relate to ecclesiological and parochial subjects, up to the year 1560.* 4 vols. Reprint; originally published 1935. £35.00. Vols.1-3. 5 fiche per vol. £35.00 per vol. Vol.4. 6 fiche. £42.00.

44. TAYLOR, ARNOLD J., ed. *Records of the barony and honour of the Rape of Lewes.* 2 fiche. Reprint; originally published 1940. £14.00.

46. PECKHAM, W.D., ed. *The chartulary of the high church of Chichester.* 5 fiche. Reprint; originally published 1946. £35.00.

47. D'ELBOUX, R.H., ed. *Surveys of the manors of Robertsbridge, Sussex, and Michelmarsh, Hampshire, and of the demesne lands of Halden in Rolvenden, Kent, 1567-1570.* 3 fiche. Reprint; originally published 1946. £21.00.

48. SALZMAN, L.F., ed. *The town book of Lewes, 1542-1701.* 2 fiche. Reprint; originally published 1947. £14.00.

49. JOHNSTONE, HILDA, ed. *Churchwardens' presentments (17th century). Pt. i: Archdeaconry of Chichester.* 2 fiche. Reprint; originally published 1949. £14.00.

50. JOHNSTONE, HILDA, ed. *Churchwardens' presentments (17th century). Pt. ii: Archdeaconry of Lewes.* 2 fiche. Reprint; originally published 1950. £14.00.

51. SALZMAN, L.F., ed. *Record of deputations of gamekeepers.* 3 fiche. Reprint; originally published 1951. £21.00.

52. PECKHAM, W.D., ed. *The acts of the dean and chapter of the cathedral church of Chichester, 1472-1544 (the white act book).* 2 fiche. Reprint; originally published 1952. £14.00.

53. VIVIAN, SYLVANUS P., SIR, ed. *The manor of Etchingham cum Salehurst.* 4 fiche. Reprint; originally published 1953. £28.00.

54. REDWOOD, B.C., ed. *Quarter sessions order book, 1642-1649.* 4 fiche. Reprint; originally published 1954. £28.00.

55. SALZMAN, L.F., ed. *Ministers' accounts of the manor of Petworth, 1347-1353.* 2 fiche. Reprint; originally published 1955. £14.00.

56. CORNWALL, JULIAN, ed. *The lay subsidy rolls for the county of Sussex, 1524-25.* 3 fiche. Reprint; originally published 1956. £21.00.

57. REDWOOD, B.C., & WILSON, A.F., ed. *Custumals of the Sussex manors of the Archbishop of Canterbury.* 3 fiche. Reprint; originally published 1958. £21.00.

58. PECKHAM, W.D., ed. *The acts of the dean and chapter of the cathedral church of Chichester, 1545-1642.* 4 fiche. Reprint; originally published 1959. £28.00.

59. FLEMING, LINDSAY, ed. *The chartulary of Boxgrove Priory.* 3 fiche. Reprint; originally published 1960. £21.00.

60. WILSON, A.E., ed. *Custumals of the manors of Laughton, Willingdon and Goring.* 2 fiche. Reprint; originally published 1961. £14.00.

61. STEER, FRANCIS W., ed. *A catalogue of Sussex estate and tithe award maps.* 3 fiche. Reprint; originally published 1962. £21.00.

62. STEER, FRANCIS W., ed. *Minute book of the Common Council of the city of Chichester, 1783-1826.* 3 fiche. Reprint; originally published 1963. £21.00.

63. CLOUGH, MARIE, ed. *The book of Bartholomew Bolney.* 2 fiche. Reprint; originally published 1964. £14.00. Estate record, 15th c.

64. DELL, R.F., ed. *Rye shipping records, 1566-1590.* 3 fiche. Reprint; originally published 1965. £21.00.

65. SEARLE, ELEANOR, & ROSS, BARBARA, ed. *The cellarers' rolls of Battle Abbey, 1275-1513.* 3 fiche. Reprint; originally published 1967. £21.00.

67. CLOUGH, MARIE, ed. *Two estate surveys of the Fitzalan Earls of Arundel.* 3 fiche. Reprint; originally published 1969. £21.00.

68. BIRD, RUTH, ed. *The journal of Giles Moore (1617-1679).* 4 fiche. Reprint; originally published 1970. £28.00. Rector of Horsted Keynes.

Additional volume
The chartulary of Lewes Priory. The portions relating to counties other than Sussex. 4 fiche. Reprint; originally published 1943. £28.00.

Wiltshire
Wiltshire Record Society
Orders for microfiche reprints to:
Chadwyck-Healey Ltd., The Quorum, Barnwell Road, Cambridge, CB5 8SW
Phone: (01223) 215512
Email: mail@chadwyck.co.uk
Http://www.chadwyck.co.uk

1. SWAYNE, HENRY JAMES FOWLE, ed. *Churchwardens' accounts of S. Edmund and S. Thomas, Sarum, 1443-1702, with other documents.* 5 fiche. Reprint; originally published 1896. £35.00.

3. WORDSWORTH, CHR., ed. *The fifteenth century cartulary of St. Nicholas's hospital, Salisbury, with other records.* 6 fiche. Reprint; originally published 1902. £42.00.

Worcestershire Historical Society

Orders for microfiche reprints to:
Chadwyck-Healey Ltd., The Quorum,
Barnwell Road, Cambridge, CB5 8SW
Phone: (01223) 215512
Email: mail@chadwyck.co.uk
Http://www.chadwyck.co.uk

1. BUND, J.W. WILLIS, & AMPHLETT, JOHN, eds. *Lay subsidy roll for the county of Worcester, circ.1280.* 2 fiche. Reprint; originally published 1893. £14.00.
2. BUND, J.W. WILLIS, ed. *The inquisitiones post mortem for the county of Worcester. Part 1: From their commencement in 1242 to the end of the 13th c.* 2 fiche. Reprint; originally published 1894. £14.00.
3. AMPHLETT, JOHN, ed. *An index to Dr Nash's 'collections for a history of Worcestershire'.* 5 fiche. Reprint; originally published 1894-5. £35.00.
4. ELD, F.J., ed. *Lay subsidy roll for the county of Worcester, 1 Edward III.* 2 fiche. Reprint; originally published 1895. £14.00.
5. AMPHLETT, JOHN, ed. *A survey of Worcestershire, by Thomas Habington (died 1647).* 12 fiche. Reprint; originally published 1895-9. £84.00.
6. AMPHLETT, JOHN, ed. *An index to Worcestershire fines, 1649-1714.* 5 fiche. Reprint; originally published 1896. £35.00.
7. AMPHLETT, JOHN, ed. *The churchwardens' accounts of St. Michael's in Bedwardine, Worcester, from 1539 to 1603. To which are prefixed the churchwardens' accounts of the church of St. Helen, Worcester, for the years 1519 and 1520.* 3 fiche. Reprint; originally published 1896. £21.00.
8. BUND, J.W. WILLIS, ed. *The register of the diocese of Worcester during the vacancy of the see, usually called registrum sede vacante, 1301-1435.* 8 fiche. Reprint; originally published 1897. £56.00.
9. BURTON, J.R., & PEARSON, F.S., eds. *Bibliography of Worcestershire ...* 5 fiche. Reprint; originally published 1898-1907. £35.00.
10. AMPHLETT, JOHN, ed. *Lay subsidy roll, 1332-3, and nonarum inquisitiones, 1340, for the county of Worcester.* 1 fiche. Reprint; originally published 1899. £7.00.
11. BUND, J.W. WILLIS, ed. *Worcester county records. Calendar of the quarter sessions papers, 1591-1643.* 13 fiche. Reprint; originally published 1899-1900. £91.00.
12. AMPHLETT, JOHN, ed. *Lay subsidy rolls, A.D.1346 and A.D.1358, for the county of Worcester.* 1 fiche. Reprint; originally published 1900. £7.00.
13. AMPHLETT, JOHN, ed. *Lay subsidy roll, 1603, for the county of Worcester.* 1 fiche. Reprint; originally published 1901. £7.00.
14. AMPHLETT, JOHN, ed. *Lay subsidy rolls, 6 and 7 Henry VI, 1427-9, for the county of Worcester.* 1 fiche. Reprint; originally published 1902. £7.00.
15. BUND, J.W. WILLIS, ed. *Episcopal registers, Diocese of Worcester. Register of Bishop Godfrey Giffard, Sept. 23rd 1268 to Aug. 15th 1301.* 10 fiche. Reprint; originally published 1902. £70.00.
16. ROBERTSON, DAVID, ed. *Diary of Francis Evans, secretary to Bishop Lloyd, 1699-1706.* 3 fiche. Reprint; originally published 1903. £21.00.
17. ROBERTSON, DAVID, ed. *The old order book of Hartlebury Grammar School, 1556-1752.* 3 fiche. Reprint; originally published 1904. £21.00.
18. FRY, EDW. ALEX., ed. *Calendar of wills and administrations in the consistory court of the bishop of Worcester. Also marriage licences and sequestrations now deposited in the probate registry at Worcester.* 9 fiche. Reprint; originally published 1904-11. £63.00.
19. AMPHLETT, JOHN, ed. *The Kyre Park charters.* 3 fiche. Reprint; originally published 1905. £21.00.
20. HAMILTON, S.G., ed. *Catalogue of manuscripts preserved in the chapter library of Worcester Cathedral.* 3 fiche. Reprint; originally published 1906. £21.00.
21. WILSON, J.M., & HAMILTON, S.G., ed. *Accounts of the priory of Worcester for the year 13-14 Henry VIII, 1521-2, and a catalogue of the rolls of the obedientiaries.* 2 fiche. Reprint; originally published 1907. £14.00.
22. BUND, J.W.W., ed. *The register of William de Geynesborough, bishop of Worcester, 1302-1307.* 3 fiche. Reprint; originally published 1907. £21.00.
23. WILSON, J.M., & GORDON, C., ed. *Early compotus rolls of the Priory of Worcester.* 2 fiche. Reprint; originally published 1908. £14.00.
24. *The inquisitiones post mortem for the county of Worcester. Pt ii: From 28 Edward I to 19 Edward II, A.D.1300 to A.D.1326.* 2 fiche. Reprint; originally published 1909. £14.00.

25. BLOOM, J.H., ed. *Original charters relating to the city of Worcester in possession of the dean and chapter.* 3 fiche. Reprint; originally published 1909. £21.00.
26. HAMILTON, S.G., ed. *Compotus rolls of the Priory of Worcester of the 14th and 15th centuries.* 2 fiche. Reprint; originally published 1910. £14.00.
27. BLOOM, J.H., ed. *Liber elemosinarii: the almoner's book of the priory of Worcester.* 1 fiche. Reprint; originally published 1911. £7.00.
28. BLOOM, J.H., ed. *Liber ecclesiae Wigorniensis: a letter book of the priors of Worcester.* 1 fiche. Reprint; originally published 1912. £7.00.
30. AMPHLETT, JOHN, & HAMILTON, SIDNEY GRAVES, ed. *Court rolls of the manor of Hales, 1270-1307.* 8 fiche. Reprint; originally published 1912. £56.00.
31. LEACH, A.F., ed. *Documents illustrating early education in Worcester, 685 to 1700.* 5 fiche. Reprint; originally published 1913. £35.00.
32. FEGAN, ETHEL S., ed. *Journal of Prior William More.* 5 fiche. Reprint; originally published 1914. £35.00.
33. WILSON, JAMES M., & JONES, ETHEL C., ed. *Corrodies at Worcester in the 14th century. Some correspondence between the Crown and the priory at Worcester in the reign of Edward II concerning the corrody of Alicia Conan, with a summary of the correspondence.* 1 fiche. Reprint; originally published 1917. £7.00.
34. ATKINS, IVOR, ed. *The early occupants of the office of organist and master of the choristers of the cathedral church of Christ and the Blessed Virgin Mary, Worcester.* 1 fiche. Reprint; originally published 1918. £7.00.
35. WILSON, J.M., ed. *The liber albus of the priory of Worcester, parts 1 and 2, Priors John de Wyke, 1301-1317, and Wulstan de Bransford, 1317-1339, folios 1 to 162.* 2 fiche. Reprint; originally published 1919. £14.00.
36. BUND, J.W.W., ed. *Diary of Henry Townshend of Elmley Lovett, 1640-1663.* 5 fiche. Reprint; originally published 1920. £35.00.
37. CAVE, T., & WILSON, R.A., ed. *The Parliamentary survey of the lands and possessions of the Dean and Chapter of Worcester, made in or about the year 1649 in pursuance of an ordinance of Parliament for the abolishing of deans and chapters.* 4 fiche. Reprint; originally published 1924. £28.00.
38. PRICE, CLEMENT, ed. *Liber pensionum prioratus Wigorn: being a collection of documents relating to pensions from appropriated churches and other payments receivable by the prior and convent of Worcester and to the privileges of the monastery.* 1 fiche. Reprint; originally published 1925. £7.00.
39. WILSON, ROWLAND ALWYN, ed. *The register of Walter Reynolds, bishop of Worcester, 1308-1313.* 3 fiche. Reprint; originally published 1927. £21.00.
40. PEARCE, ERNEST HAROLD, ed. *The register of Thomas de Cobham, bishop of Worcester, 1317-1327.* 4 fiche. Reprint; originally published 1930. £28.00.
41. WILSON, R.A., ed. *Court rolls of the manor of Hales, pt.iii, containing additional courts of the years 1276-1301, and Romsley courts, 1280-1303.* 3 fiche. Reprint; originally published 1933. £21.00.
42. HOLLINGS, MARJORY, ed. *The red book of Worcester, containing surveys of the bishop's manors and other records, chiefly of the twelfth and thirteenth centuries.* 8 fiche. Reprint; originally published 1934. £56.00.
43. SOMERS, FRANK, ed. *Halesowen churchwardens' accounts, 1487-1582.* 2 fiche. Reprint; originally published 1952-1957. £14.00.

Yorkshire
see also Durham

Yorkshire Archaeological Society
Claremont, 23, Clarendon Road, Leeds LS2 9NZ
Phone: (0113) 2457910
Email: j.heron@shef.ac.uk
Members are entitled to substantial discounts.
Parish Register Section
Map of ancient parishes and chapelries of Yorkshire. Sheet map. £5.00 + p&p £1.50.
Addingham
129. LUMB, GEORGE DEVISON, ed. *The register of the parish church of Addingham, Co. York, 1612-1812.* 1920. Fiche reprint £8.00 (inc. p&p).

Yorkshire Archaeological Society (*cont.*)

Aldborough
110. LAWSON-TANCRED, T., ed. *The parish register of Aldborough (W.R.), vol. 1. 1538-1611.* 1940. Fiche reprint £8.00 (inc. p&p).

Atwick
111. CHARLESWORTH, JOHN, ed. *The parish register of Atwick (E.R.) 1538-1708.* 1941. Fiche reprint £8.00 (inc. p&p).

Aughton
86. CHARLESWORTH, JOHN, ed. *The parish register of Aughton in the County of York.* 1928. Fiche reprint £8.00 (inc. p&p). Covers 1610-1813, with marriages to 1825.

Bentham
91. CHIPPINDALL, W.H., ed. *The parish register of Bentham (1666-1812).* 1932. Fiche reprint £8.00 (inc. p&p).

Bingley
9. STAVERT, W.J., ed. *The parish register of Bingley in the county of York 1577-1686.* 1901. Fiche reprint £8.00 (inc. p&p).

Blacktoft
8. WEDDALL, GEORGE EDWARD, ed. *The registers of the parish church of Blacktoft, East Yorkshire, 1700-1812.* 1900. Fiche reprint £8.00 (inc. p&p).

Bolton by Bowland
19. STAVERT, W.J., ed. *The parish register of Bolton-by-Bolland in the County of York, 1558-1724.* 1904. Fiche reprint £8.00 (inc. p&p).

22. STAVERT, W.J., ed. *The parish register of Bolton-by-Bowland in the County of York, 1725-1812.* 1905. Fiche reprint £8.00 (inc. p&p).

Bowes
127. ALDERSON, BASIL ROXBY, ed. *The parish register of Bowes, 1670-1837 (bishops transcripts 1615-1700).* 1964. Fiche reprint. £8.00 (inc. p&p.)

Brantingham
12. WEDDALL, GEORGE EDWARD, ed. *The registers of the parish church of Brantingham, East Yorkshire, 1653-1812.* 1902. Fiche reprint. £8.00 (inc. p&p).

Brodsworth
104. WHITING, C.E., ed. *The parish register of Brodsworth, 1538-1813.* 1937. Fiche reprint £8.00 (inc. p&p).

Burton Fleming
2. PARK, G.E., & LUMB, G.D., eds. *The register of the parish church of Burton Fleming, otherwise North Burton, 1538-1812.* 1899. Fiche reprint £8.00 (inc. p&p).

Cherry Burton
15. WINN, ARTHUR T., ed. *The registers of the parish church of Cherry Burton, Co. York, 1561-1740.* 1903. Fiche reprint £8.00 (inc. p&p).

Clapham
67. CHARLESWORTH, JOHN, ed. *The parish register of Clapham, Co. York. Part 1. 1595-1683.* 1921. Fiche reprint £8.00 (inc. p&p).

Coxwold
120. LLOYD, R.L.H., ed. *The parish registers of Coxwold (part 1): 1583-1666.* 1955. Fiche reprint £8.00 (inc. p&p).

Crofton
62. TOWNEND, WILLIAM, ed. *The parish registers of Crofton, Co. York, 1615-1812.* 1918. Fiche reprint £8.00.

Danby in Cleveland
43. COLLINS, F., ed. *The registers of Danby-in-Cleveland, 1585 to 1812.* 1912. Fiche reprint £8.00 (inc. p&p).

Drypool
125. INGRAM, M. EDWARD, ed. *The parish register of Drypool, vols 1-5. Baptisms and burials 1572-1812; marriages 1572-1807.* 1961. Fiche reprint £8.00 (inc. p&p).

Easingwold
56. LUMB, GEORGE DENISON, ed. *The register of the parish church of All Saints, Easingwold, co.York. Vol. 1. 1599-1812.* 1916. Fiche reprint £8.00 (inc. p&p).

East Rounton
54. ROBSON, WILLIAM THOMAS, ed. *The register of the chapelry of East Rounton in the parish of Rudby-in-Cleveland, Co. York, 1595-1837.* 1916. Fiche reprint £8.00 (inc. p&p).

Eston

76. KAYE, WALTER J., ed. *The parish register of Eston (1590-1812)*. 1924. Fiche reprint £8.00 (inc. p&p).

Frickley cum Clayton

95. WHITING, C.E., ed. *The parish register of Frickley-with-Clayton (1577-1812)*. 1933. Fiche reprint £8.00 (inc. p&p).

Garforth

46. LUMB, GEORGE DENISON, ed. *The register of the parish church of Garforth, Co. York, 1631-1812*. 1913. Fiche reprint £8.00 (inc. p&p).

Gargrave

28. STAVERT, W.J., ed. *The parish register of Gargrave in the County of York, 1558-1812*. 1907. Fiche reprint £8.00 (inc. p&p).

Gilling

113. HUDSON, E.C., ed. *The parish register of Gilling, York, 1573-1812*. 1942. Fiche reprint £8.00 (inc. p&p).

Gisburne

114. SIMPSON, STEPHEN, & CHARLESWORTH, J.N.O., eds. *The parish register of Gisburne (part I), Yorks., 1558-1745*. 1943. Fiche reprint £8.00 (inc. p&p).

118. LONG, A.E., ed. *The parish register of Gisburne (part II), Yorks., 1745-1812*. 1952. Fiche reprint £8.00 (inc. p&p).

Great Ayton

90. KAYE, WALTER J., ed. *The parish register of Great Ayton (1600-1812)*. 1931. Fiche reprint £8.00 (inc. p&p).

Grinton in Swaledale

23. SLINGSBY, F. WILLIAM, ed. *The registers of the parish church of Grinton in Swaledale, Co. York*. 1905. Fiche reprint £8.00 (inc. p&p). Baptisms and burials, 1640-1807; marriages 1640-1802.

Hackness

25. JOHNSTONE, CHARLES, & HART, EMILY J., eds. *The register of the parish of Hackness, Co. York, 1557-1783*. 1906. Fiche reprint £8.00 (inc. p&p).

Halifax

37. CROSSLEY, E.W., ed. *The parish registers of Halifax, Co. York. Vol. I. Baptisms, 1538 to 1593*. 1910. Fiche reprint £8.00 (inc. p&p).

45. CROSSLEY, E.W., ed. *The parish registers of Halifax, Co. York. Vol. II. Marriages and burials, 1538-1593*. 1912. Fiche reprint £8.00 (inc. p&p).

Hampsthwaite

13. COLLINS, FRANCIS, ed. *The registers of Hampsthwaite, Co. York. Marriages 1603-1807; baptisms 1603-1794; burials 1603-1794*. 1902. Fiche reprint £8.00 (inc. p&p).

Harewood

50. BRIGG, WILLIAM, ed. *The parish registers of Harewood, Co. York. Part I: baptisms, 1614 to 1812; marriages 1621 to 1812*. 1914. Fiche reprint £8.00 (inc. p&p).

Hartshead

17. ARMYTAGE, EDITH B., ed. *The parish register of Hartshead in the County of York, 1612-1812*. 1903. Fiche reprint £8.00 (inc. p&p).

Heptonstall

78. HORSFALL, EDITH, ed. *The parish registers of Heptonstall, in the County of York. Vol. 1. 1593-1660 ...* 1925. Fiche reprint £8.00 (inc. p&p).

Hooton Pagnell

87. WHITING, C.E., ed. *The parish registers of Hooton Pagnell (1538-1812)*. 1929. Fiche reprint £8.00 (inc. p&p).

Horbury

3. CHARLESWORTH, JOHN. *The registers of the chapel of Horbury, in the parish of Wakefield in the County of York, 1598-1812*. 1900. Fiche reprint £8.00 (inc. p&p)

Ilkley

83. COOPER, WILLIAM, ed. *The parish register of Ilkley (1597-1812)*. 1927. Fiche reprint £8.00 (inc. p&p).

Ingleton

94. CHIPPINDALL, W.H., ed. *The parish registers of the churches of Ingleton and Chapel-le-Dale 1607-1812*. 1933. Jointly published with the Lancashire Parish Register Society. Fiche reprint £8.00 (inc.p&p).

Keighley

77. BRIGG, WM. ANDERTON, ed. *The parish registers of St. Andrew's, Keighley. Vol. I: baptisms, marriages and burials April 1562 - September 1649*. 1925. Fiche reprint £8.00 (inc p&p.)

Yorkshire Archaeological Society (*cont.*)

82. BRIGG, WM. ANDERTON, ed. *The parish registers of St. Andrew's, Keighley. Vol. II: baptisms, marriages and burials October 1649 - March 1688.* 1927. Fiche reprint £8.00 (inc. p&p.)

98. LIVETT, RONALD G.C., ed. *The parish registers of St. Andrew's, Keighley, part III: baptisms, marriages and burials, March 1689 - March 1735/6.* 1935. Fiche reprint £8.00 (inc. p&p).

Kildwick in Craven

47. BRIGG, WM. ANDERTON, ed. *The parish registers of St. Andrew's, Kildwick in Craven. Vol. I. Baptisms, deaths and marriages, 1575-1622.* 1913. Fiche reprint £8.00 (inc. p&p).

55. BRIGG, WM. ANDERTON, ed. *The parish registers of St. Andrew's Kildwick in Craven, vols. II and III. Baptisms, marriages and burials April 1623 - August 1678.* 1916. Fiche reprint £8.00 (inc. p&p).

69. LIVETT, RONALD G.C., ed. *The parish registers of St. Andrew's, Kildwick in Craven, vols. IV, V, and VI. Baptisms, marriages and burials September 1678 - March 1743.* 1922. Fiche reprint £8.00 (inc. p&p).

92. LIVETT, RONALD G.C., ed. *The parish register of Kildwick in Craven, IV [vols VII and VIII (in part)]. Baptisms March 1744 - April 1789; marriages March 1744 - March 1754; burials March 1744 - June 1771.* 1932. Fiche reprint £8.00 (inc. p&p).

Kippax

10. LUMB, GEORGE DENISON, ed. *The registers of the parish church of Kippax, Co. York, 1539-1812.* 1901. Fiche reprint £8.00 (inc. p&p).

Kirkby Malham

106. OLIVER, W., ed. *The parish register of Kirkby Malham. Vol. 1. 1597-1690.* 1938. Fiche reprint £8.00 (inc. p&p).

Kirkleatham

59. CHARLESWORTH, JOHN, ed. *The parish register of Kirkleatham, Co. York, 1559-1812.* 1917. Fiche reprint £8.00 (inc. p&p).

Ledsham

26. CLAY, J.W., ed. *The parish registers of Ledsham in the County of York 1539-1812.* 1906. Fiche reprint £8.00 (inc. p&p).

Linton in Craven

5. SHARPE, F.A.C, ed. *The registers of the parish church of Linton in Craven, Co. York. Two volumes, 1562-1812. Vol. I (1562-1779).* 1900. Fiche reprint £8.00 (inc. p&p).

18. SHARPE, F.A.C, ed. *The registers of the parish church of Linton in Craven, Co. York. Two volumes, 1562-1812. Vol. II (1779-1812).* 1903. Fiche reprint £8.00 (inc. p&p).

Marske in Cleveland

16. WOOD, HERBERT MAXWELL, ed. *The registers of Marske in Cleveland, Co. York. Baptisms 1570-1812; marriages 1570-1812; burials 1569-1812.* 1903. Fiche reprint £8.00 (inc. p&p).

Mirfield

64. BRIGG, WILLIAM, ed. *The registers of the parish of Mirfield. Part I. Baptisms, marriages, burials, 1559-1700.* 1919. Fiche reprint £8.00 (inc. p&p).

Otley

33. BRIGG, WILLIAM, ed. *The parish registers of Otley, Co. York. Part 1. 1562 to 1672.* 1908. Fiche reprint £8.00 (inc. p&p).

44. BRIGG, WILLIAM, ed. *The parish registers of Otley, Co. York. Part 2. Bap., April 1672 to June 1753; Marr., April 1672 to June 1750; Bur., April 1672 to March 1751-2.* 1912. Fiche reprint £8.00 (inc. p&p).

Patrington

6. MADDOCK, HENRY EDWARD, ed. *The registers of Patrington, Co. York, 1570-1731.* 1900. Fiche reprint £8.00 (inc. p&p).

Pontefract

122. WILLIS, THOMAS B., ed. *The parish register of Pontefract, 1585-1641.* 1958. Fiche reprint £8.00 (inc. p&p).

Richmondshire

101. WAINE, W.G., ed. *The register of the civil marriages, 1653-1660, belonging to Richmondshire in the County of York.* OLIVER, W., ed. *Index to the parish register transcripts belonging to the Archdeaconry of Richmond (the ancient deaneries of Boroughbridge, Catterick and Richmond) from their commencement to 1848.* 1936. Fiche reprint £8.00 (inc. p&p).

Rillington

117. WHITING, C.E., ed. *The parish registers of Rillington, 1638-1812.* 1946. Fiche reprint £8.00 (inc. p&p).

Rothwell

27. LUMB, GEORGE DENISON, ed. *The registers of the parish church of Rothwell, Co. York. Part I. 1538-1689.* 1906. Fiche reprint £8.00 (inc. p&p).

34. LUMB, GEORGE DENISON, ed. *The registers of the parish church of Rothwell, Co. York. Part II. 1690-1763, baptisms and burials; 1690-1812 marriages.* 1909. Fiche reprint £8.00 (inc. p&p).

51. LUMB, GEORGE DENISON, ed. *The registers of the parish church of Rothwell, Co. York. Part III. 1763-1812. Baptisms and burials. Index.* 1914. Fiche reprint £8.00 (inc. p&p).

Saxton in Elmet

93. LUMB, GEORGE DENISON, ed. *The parish register of Saxton-in-Elmet, 1538-1812.* 1932. Fiche reprint £8.00 (inc. p&p).

Sculcoates

123. INGRAM, M. EDWARD, ed. *The parish register of Sculcoates (part 1) 1538-1772.* 1959. Fiche reprint £8.00 (inc. p&p).

Snaith

57. BRIGG, WILLIAM, ed. *The parish registers of Snaith, Co. York. Part I. Baptisms 1558-1657. Marriages 1537-1657.* 1917. Fiche reprint £8.00 (inc. p&p).

63. BRIGG, WILLIAM, ed. *The parish registers of Snaith, Co. York. Part II. Burials 1537-1656.* 1919. Fiche reprint £8.00 (inc. p&p).

Stokesley

7. HAWELL, JOHN, ed. *The registers of the parish church of Stokesley, Co. York, 1571-1750.* 1900. Fiche reprint £8.00 (inc. p&p).

Swillington

115. GEORGE, E., ed. *The parish register of Swillington, Yorks. Baptisms 1543-1812. Marriages 1540-1812. Burials 1539-1812.* 1944. Fiche reprint £8.00 (inc. p&p).

Thornhill

30. CHARLESWORTH, JOHN, ed. *The register of the parish of Thornhill, part I. Baptisms 1580 to 1742; marriages 1580 to 1745; burials 1580 to 1678.* 1907. Fiche reprint £8.00 (inc. p&p).

40. CHARLESWORTH, JOHN, ed. *The register of the parish of Thornhill, part II. Baptisms 1743 to 1812; marriages 1746 to 1753; burials 1678 to 1812; Flockton baptisms, marriages and burials, 1713 to 1812.* 1911. Fiche reprint. £8.00 (inc. p&p).

53. CHARLESWORTH, JOHN, ed. *The register of the parish of Thornhill, part III. Marriages 1754 to 1812; banns 1788 to 1812; baptisms and burials 1717 to 1812.* 1915. Fiche reprint £8.00 (inc. p&p).

Thornton in Lonsdale

89. CHIPPINDALL, W.H., ed. *The parish register of Thornton-in-Lonsdale (1576-1812).* 1931. Fiche reprint £8.00 (inc. p&p).

Waddington

88. PARKER, JOHN, ed. *The parish registers of Waddington, Yorkshire (1599-1812).* 1930. Fiche reprint £8.00 (inc. p&p).

Wath upon Dearne

14. CLAY, J.W., ed. *The registers of Wath-upon-Dearne, Yorkshire. Baptisms and burials, 1598-1778; marriages 1598-1779.* 1902. Fiche reprint £8.00 (inc. p&p).

Whitby

84. CHARLESWORTH, JOHN, ed. *The parish register of Whitby 1600-1676. Part I.* 1928. Fiche reprint £8.00 (inc. p&p).

Winestead in Holderness

4. MILLER, NORMAN J., ed. *The registers of Winestead in Holderness, Co. York, 1578-1812.* 1899. Fiche reprint £8.00 (inc. p&p).

Wintringham

71. CHOLMLEY, ALFRED J., ed. *The parish register of Wintringham (1558 to 1812).* 1922. Fiche reprint £8.00 (inc. p&p).

Wragby

105. CHARLESWORTH, JOHN, ed. *The parish register of Wragby vol. I. 1538-1704 ...* 1938. Fiche reprint £8.00 (inc. p&p).

CHARLESWORTH, JOHN, ed. *The parish register of Wragby in the County of York. Vol. II. 1704-1812.* 1939. Fiche reprint £8.00 (inc. p&p).

York. Goodramgate

41. COOK, ROBERT BEILBY, ed. *The parish registers of Holy Trinity church, Goodramgate, York, 1573-1812.* 1911. Fiche reprint £8.00 (inc. p&p).

Yorkshire Archaeological Society (*cont.*)
York. St.Lawrence
97. HUDSON, EGBERT CLAUD, ed. *The parish register of St. Lawrence, York (1606-1812).* 1935. Fiche reprint £8.00 (inc. p&p).

York. St.Martin
36. COOK, ROBERT BEILBY, ed. *The parish registers of St. Martin, Coney Street, York.* 1909. Fiche reprint £8.00 (inc. p&p). For 1557-1812.

York. St.Michael le Belfrey
1. COLLINS, FRANCIS, ed. *The registers of St. Michael le Belfrey, York. Part I. 1565-1653.* 1899. Fiche reprint £8.00 (inc. p&p).
11. COLLINS, FRANCIS, ed. *The register of St. Michael le Belfrey, York. Part II. Marriages 1653-1772; baptisms and burials 1653-1778.* 1901. Fiche reprint £8.00 (inc. p&p).

York. St.Olave
73. HARRISON, F., & KAYE, WALTER J., eds. *The parish register of St. Olave, York. Part I (1538-1644).* 1923. Fiche reprint £8.00 (inc. p&p).

Bradford Historical and Antiquarian Society
Orders for microfiche reprints to:
Chadwyck-Healey Ltd., The Quorum, Barnwell Road, Cambridge, CB5 8SW
Phone: (01223) 215512
Email: mail@chadwyck.co.uk
Http://www.chadwyck.co.uk

1. PRESTON, WILLIAM E., ed. *Wills proved in the court of the manor of Crosley, Bingley, Cottingley and Pudsey, in co. York, with inventories and abstracts of bonds.* 2 fiche. Reprint; originally published 1929. £14.00.
2. ROBERTSHAW, WILFRID, ed. *West Yorkshire deeds.* 3 fiche. Reprint; originally published 1936. £21.00.
3. WHONE, CLIFFORD, ed. *Court rolls of the manor of Haworth.* 2 fiche. Reprint; originally published 1946. £14.00.
4. ROBERTSHAW, WILFRID, ed. *Registers of the independent chapel of Kipping in Thornton, parish of Bradford.* 2 fiche. Reprint; originally published 1953. £14.00.

North Riding Record Society
Orders for microfiche reprints to:
Chadwyck-Healey Ltd., The Quorum, Barnwell Road, Cambridge, CB5 8SW
Phone: (01223) 215512
Email: mail@chadwyck.co.uk
Http://www.chadwyck.co.uk

1. ATKINSON, J.C., ed. *Quarter sessions records 1605-1612.* 4 fiche. Reprint; originally published 1884. £28.00.
2. ATKINSON, J.C., ed. *Quarter sessions records 1612-1620.* 5 fiche. Reprint; originally published 1884. £35.00.
3. ATKINSON, J.C., ed. *Quarter sessions records 1621-1634.* 5 fiche. Reprint; originally published 1885. £35.00.
4. ATKINSON, J.C., ed. *Quarter sessions records 1634-1647.* 4 fiche. Reprint; originally published 1886. £28.00.
5. ATKINSON, J.C., ed. *Quarter sessions records 1647-1658.* 4 fiche. Reprint; originally published 1887. £28.00.
6. ATKINSON, J.C., ed. *Quarter sessions records 1658-1677.* 4 fiche. Reprint; originally published 1888. £28.00.
7. ATKINSON, J.C., ed. *Quarter sessions records 1677-1716.* 4 fiche. Reprint; originally published 1889. £28.00.
8. ATKINSON, J.C., ed. *Quarter sessions records.* 4 fiche. Reprint; originally published 1890. £28.00. 18th c.
9. ATKINSON, J.C., ed. *Quarter sessions records.* 4 fiche. Reprint; originally published 1892. £28.00. 18th c.

New Series
1-4. TURTON, ROBERT BELL, ed. *The honor and forest of Pickering.* 4 vols. 4 fiche per vol. Reprint; originally published 1897. £28.00 per vol.

Thoresby Society
Orders for microfiche reprints to:
Chadwyck-Healey Ltd., The Quorum, Barnwell Road, Cambridge, CB5 8SW
Phone: (01223) 215512
Email: mail@chadwyck.co.uk
Http://www.chadwyck.co.uk

1. MARGERISON, S., ed. *Leeds parish church registers. 1572-1612.* 6 fiche. Reprint; originally published 1891. £42.00.
3. LUMB, GEORGE DENISON, ed. *The registers of the parish church of Leeds, from 1612 to 1639.* 5 fiche. Reprint; originally published 1895. £35.00.

5. LUMB, GEORGE DENISON, ed. *The registers of the parish church of Adel, in the county of York, from 1606 to 1812; and monumental inscriptions.* 3 fiche. Reprint; originally published 1895. £21.00.
6. BAILDON, WILLIAM PALEY, & MARGERISON, SAMUEL, eds. *The Calverley charters presented to the British Museum by Sir Walter Calverley Trevelyan, Baronet.* 5 fiche. Reprint; originally published 1904. £35.00.
7. *The registers of the parish church of Leeds, from 1639 to 1667.* 6 fiche. Reprint; originally published 1897. £42.00.
8. LANCASTER, W.T., & BAILDON, W.PALEY, eds. *The coucher book of the Cistercian Abbey of Kirkstall, in the West Riding of the county of York.* 5 fiche. Reprint; originally published 1904. £35.00.
10. *The registers of the parish church of Leeds, from 1667 to 1695.* 5 fiche. Reprint; originally published 1901. £35.00.
12. LUMB, G.D., ed. *The registers of the parish church of Methley, in the county of York, from 1560 to 1812.* 4 fiche. Reprint; originally published 1903. £28.00.
13. *The registers of the parish church of Leeds, from 1695 to 1722, with Armley chapel, 1665 to 1711, and Hunslet chapel, 1686 to 1724.* 5 fiche. Reprint; originally published 1909. £35.00.
14. WILSON, EDMUND, ed. *Leeds Grammar School admission books, from 1820 to 1900.* 5 fiche. Reprint; originally published 1906. £35.00.
19. LUMB, GEORGE DENISON, ed. *Testamenta Leodiensia. Wills of Leeds, Pontefract, Wakefield, Otley, and district, 1539 to 1553.* 5 fiche. Reprint; originally published 1913. £35.00.
20. *The registers of the parish church of Leeds, from 1722 to 1757.* 7 fiche. Reprint; originally published 1914. £49.00.
21. LANCASTER, W.T., ed. *Letters addressed to Ralph Thoresby, F.R.S.* 4 fiche. Reprint; originally published 1912. £28.00.
23. LUMB, GEORGE DENISON, ed. *The registers of the chapels of the parish church of Leeds, from 1724 to 1763, with a few earlier years. St. John's, Holy Trinity, Armley, Beeston, Bramley, Chapel Allerton, Farnley, Headingley, Holbeck, and Hunslet.* 5 fiche. Reprint; originally published 1916. £35.00.

25. SINGLETON, JAMES, & HARGRAVE, EMILY, eds. *The registers of the parish church of Leeds. Baptisms and burials, 1757-1776; marriages 1754-1769.* 6 fiche. Reprint; originally published 1923. £42.00.
27. LUMB, GEORGE DENISON, ed. *Testamenta Leodiensia. Wills of Leeds, Pontefract, Wakefield, Otley, and district, 1553-1561.* 5 fiche. Reprint; originally published 1930. £35.00.
29. LUMB, GEORGE DENISON, ed. *The registers of the chapels of St. John, Holy Trinity, Headingley, Bramley, Beeston, Chapel Allerton, and Farnley, all in the parish of Leeds, from 1763 to 1812, and in some cases later years.* 6 fiche. Reprint; originally published 1928. £42.00.
31. LUMB, GEORGE DENISON, ed. *The registers of the chapels of the parish of Leeds, from 1764 to 1812: Holbeck, Armley, and Hunslet.* 7 fiche. Reprint; originally published 1934. £49.00.
34. CLARK, J.G., ed. *The court books of the Leeds Corporation. First book: January 1662 to August 1705.* 3 fiche. Reprint; originally published 1936. £21.00.
LUMB, GEORGE DENISON, ed. *The parish register of Aberford, co. York, 1540-1812.* 3 fiche. Reprint; originally published 1937. £21.00.
38. *Jubilee index to the publications of the Thoresby Society issued during the half-century 1889-1939.* 1 fiche. Reprint; originally published 1941. £7.00.

Isle of Man
Manx Society
Orders for microfiche reprints to: Chadwyck-Healey Ltd., The Quorum, Barnwell Road, Cambridge, CB5 8SW
Phone: (01223) 215512
Email: mail@chadwyck.co.uk
Http://www.chadwyck.co.uk

14. HARRISON, WILLIAM, ed. *Memorials of 'God's acre', being monumental inscriptions in the Isle of Man, taken in the summer of 1797.* 2 fiche. Reprint; originally published 1868. £14.00.
24. HARRISON, WILLIAM. *Bibliotheca Monensis. A bibliographical account of works relating to the Isle of Man.* 4 fiche. Reprint; originally published 1876. £28.00.

Manx Society (*cont.*)

28. HARRISON, WILLIAM, ed. *Records of Saint Mark's chapel in the parish of Malew, Isle of Man, from its foundation in 1771 to 1864, compiled from original documents and papers of the Rev. John Thomas Clarke.* 2 fiche. Reprint; originally published 1878. £14.00.

29. HARRISON, WILLIAM. *An account of the diocese of Sodor and Man and St. German's cathedral; also a record of the bishops of Sodor and Man and a tabular statement of the rectors, vicars, and chaplains in the seventeen parishes in said diocese with the date of their appointment and cause of vacancy.* 2 fiche. Reprint; originally published 1879. £14.00.

Scotland

East Ayrshire Family History Society

Hon. Secretary, c/o The Dick Institute, Elmbank Avenue, Kilmarnock, KA1 3BU.

Ardrossan poor index, 1859-1900. 4 fiche. £10.00.

Glasgow & West of Scotland Family History Society

Unit 5, 22, Mansfield Street, Glasgow, G11 5QP.

1851 census for the Lanarkshire parish of Old Monkland. 5 fiche. £7.70.

MILLER, S. *A guide to Glasgow addresses, 1837-1945.* 1993.

Index to the births, marriages and deaths in the Glasgow Herald, 1851. 3 fiche. £3.50 + p&p 20p.

PART 3
Libraries and Record Offices

Public Record Office,
Sales and Marketing, Kew, Surrey,
TW9 4DU
Phone: (0181) 3925271
Email: bookshop@pro.gov.uk
http://www.pro.gov.uk
Guide to the Public Record Office.
Microfiche. 1-873162-62-6. Forthcoming,
January 1999. £50.00 (institutions £75.00).

Bedfordshire
Bedfordshire County Record Office
County Hall, Bedford, MK42 9AP
BRIGGS, WILLIAM, ed. *Haynes parish register
1596-1812.* Fiche reprint; originally
published 1891. £7.50.
Marriage licences 1747-1790. Fiche. £13.50.
Marriage licences 1578-1618 & 1791-1812.
Fiche. £13.50.

Bedfordshire parish registers series
Many of these are also available in hard
copy; see *British genealogical books in
print* for details.
Ampthill. **17.** Fiche £5.00.
Astwick. **26.** Fiche £3.00.
Barton le Clay. **4.** Fiche £5.00.
Battlesden. **37.** Fiche £3.00.
Bedford. St. Cuthbert. **1.** Fiche £5.00.
Bedford. St. John. **1.** £9.00. Fiche £5.00.
Bedford. St. Mary. **35.** £11.50. Fiche £5.00.
Bedford. St. Peter. **40.** Fiche £3.00.
Biddenham. **16.** Fiche £3.00.
Biggleswade. **30.** Fiche £5.00.
Billington. **33.** Fiche £3.00.
Bletsoe. **24.** Fiche £3.00.
Blunham. **19.** Fiche £5.00.
Edworth. **2.** Fiche £3.00.
Eggington (with Leighton Buzzard).
31-3. Fiche £10.00.
Elstow. **1.** Fiche £5.00.
Eyeworth. **2.** Fiche £3.00.
Felmersham. **9.** Fiche £3.00.
Flitton. **18.** Fiche £5.00.
Flitwick. **21.** Fiche £3.00.

Goldington. **40.** Fiche £3.00.
Great Barford. **5.** Fiche £5.00.
Harlington. **20.** Fiche £3.00.
Harrold. **34.** Fiche £3.00.
Hatley Cockayne. **2.** Fiche £3.00.
Henlow. **26.** Fiche £3.00.
Highham Gobion. **13.** Fiche £3.00.
Hockcliffe. **33.** Fiche £3.00.
Houghton Conquest. **41.** Fiche £5.00.
Hulcote. **29.** Fiche £3.00.
Kempston. **39.** Fiche £5.00.
Knotting. **7.** Fiche £3.00.
*Leighton Buzzard (including the
chapelries of Heath, Reach and
Eggington).* **31-3.** Fiche £10.00.
Lidlington. **29.** Fiche £3.00.
Little Barford. **6.** Fiche £3.00.
Lower Gravenhurst. **13.** Fiche £3.00.
Marston Moretaine. **44.** Fiche £5.00.
Maulden. **22.** Fiche £5.00.
Melchbourne. **7.** Fiche £3.00.
Meppershall. **38.** Fiche £3.00.
Millbrook. **20.** Fiche £5.00.
Milton Bryan. **37.** Fiche £3.00.
Milton Ernest. **11.** Fiche £3.00.
Northill. **13.** Fiche £5.00.
Oakley. **16.** Fiche £3.00.
Odell. **11.** Fiche £3.00.
Old Warden. **10.** Fiche £5.00.
Pavenham. **9.** Fiche £3.00.
Potsgrove. **37.** Fiche £3.00.
Pulloxhill. **22.** Fiche £3.00.
Renhold. **5.** Fiche £3.00.
Riseley. **28.** Fiche £3.00.
Roxton. **5.** Fiche £3.00.
Salford. **29.** Fiche £3.00.
Sandy. **6.** Fiche £7.50.
Sharnbrook. **24.** Fiche £3.00.
Shelton. **7.** Fiche £3.00.
Shillington. **36.** Fiche £5.00.
Souldrop. **7.** Fiche £3.00.
Southill. **12.** Fiche £7.50.
Stanbridge. **33.** Fiche £3.00.
Steppingley. **51.** Fiche £3.00.
Stevington. **9.** Fiche £3.00.
Stotfold. **38.** Fiche £3.00.
Streatley. **4.** Fiche £3.00.

Bedfordshire County Record Office
  (cont.)
Sundon. **4.** Fiche £3.00.
Sutton. **2.** Fiche £5.00.
Swineshead. **7.** Fiche £3.00.
Tempsford. **19.** Fiche £3.00.
Thurleigh. **28.** Fiche £3.00.
Tilsworth. **33.** Fiche £3.00.
Tingrith. **17.** Fiche £3.00.
Toddington. **23.** Fiche £5.00.
Upper Gravenhurst. **13.** Fiche £3.00.
Upper Stondon. **26.** Fiche £3.00.
Westoning. **20.** Fiche £3.00.
Whipsnade. **25.** Fiche £3.00.
Wilden. **46.** Fiche £5.00.
Willington. **10.** Fiche £3.00.
Wilshampstead. **49.** Fiche £7.50.
Woburn. **3.** Fiche £10.00.
Wootton. **43.** Fiche £5.00.
Wrestlingworth. **2.** Fiche £5.00.
Yelden. **7.** Fiche £3.00.

CHESHIRE

Cheshire Record Office
Duke Street, Chester, CH1 1RL
Phone: (01244) 602574

*Cheshire parish register transcription
  project: burial register transcripts and
  indexes:*
  Cheadle 1558-1870. Fiche. £18.00 + p&p
    31p.
  Heswall 1558-1872. Fiche. £12.00 + p&p
    31p.
  Knutsford 1582-1872. Fiche. £15.00 + p&p
    31p.
  Neston 1574-1891. Fiche. £27.00 + p&p
    31p.
  West Kirby 1561-1971. Fiche. £24.00 +
    p&p 31p.
  Whitegate 1665-1870. Fiche. £12.00 + p&p
    31p.

DEVON

Devon County Council
County Local Studies Librarian, Exeter
  Central Library, Castle Street, Exeter.
  EX4 3PQ.

*Moger's typescript transcripts of Devon
  wills.* 108 fiche. Code WIL/MOG. £108.00
  + p&p £5.00.
CHICHESTER, A.B.P. *History of the family of
  Chichester.* 3 fiche. Code CHI/1871.
  £30.00 + p&p £5.00

CRESSWELL, BEATRIX. *Notes on Devon churches.*
  147 fiche. Code CRE £147.00 + p&p £5.00.
  Also available separately by deanery.
DAVISON, JAMES. *Church notes.* 4 pts.
  East Devon. 11 fiche. DAV/E £11.00 + p&p
    £5.00.
  North Devon. 14 fiche. DAV/N £14.00 +
    p&p £5.00.
  South Devon. 14 fiche. DAV/S £14.00 +
    p&p £5.00.
  West Devon. 15 fiche. DAV/W £15.00 +
    p&p £5.00.
DRAKE, WILLIAM R. *Notes, genealogical,
  historical and heraldic, of the family of
  Chichester.* 4 fiche. Code DRA/1886.
  £4.00 + p&p £5.00.
FURSDON, C.A.T. *Devon parishes.* 39 fiche.
  Code FUR. £39.00 + p&p £5.00.
  Typescript transcripts of rate assessments
  and other records.
TUCKETT, J. *Devonshire pedigrees.* 5 fiche.
  Code TUC/1859.
VIVIAN, J.L. *Visitations of Devon.* 10 fiche.
  Code VIV/DEV. £14.00 + p&p £5.00.
VIVIAN, J.L. *Visitations of Cornwall.* 10
  fiche. Code VIV/COR. £10.00 + p&p £5.00.

Directories
Trewman's Exeter directory. Available on
  one or two fiche for 1791, 1796, 1816, 1822,
  1825, 1827, 1828 and most years from 1830
  to 1857. £1.00 per fiche + p&p £5.00.
Besley's Exeter directory. Available on 2 or
  3 fiche for 1828, 1835, 1845, 1847, 1853,
  and most years from 1858 to 1927. £1.00
  per fiche + p&p £5.00.
Rees & Curtis' Plymouth directory, 1812. 3
  fiche. Code DIR/PLY/1812. £3.00 + p&p £5.00.
Taperell's Plymouth directory, 1822. 2 fiche.
  Code DIR/PLY/1822. £2.00 + p&p £5.00.
Brindley's Plymouth directory, 1830. 4 fiche.
  Code DIR/PLY/1830. £4.00 + p&p £5.00.
Thomas's Plymouth directory, 1836. 3 fiche.
  Code DIR/PLY/1836. £2.00 + p&p £5.00.
William's Plymouth directory, 1847. 4 fiche.
  Code DIR/PLY/1847. £4.00 + p&p £5.00.
Brendon's Plymouth directory, 1852. 5 fiche.
  Code DIR/PLY/1852. £5.00 + p&p £5.00.
Elvin's Plymouth directory, 1862. 4 fiche. Code
  DIR/PLY/1862. £4.00 + p&p £5.00.
Three towns directory, 1875. 7 fiche. Code
  DIR/PLY/1875. £7.00 + p&p £5.00.
Eyre's Plymouth directory, 1882. (11 fiche),
  1890 (8 fiche), 1900 (6 fiche) and 1904 (6
  fiche). £1.00 per fiche + p&p £5.00.

Swiss's Plymouth directory 1911. 8 fiche. Code DIR/PLY/1911. £8.00 + p&p £5.00.
Swiss's Plymouth directory 1920. 6 fiche. Code DIR/PLY/1920. £6.00 + p&p £5.00.
Daw's Torbay directory, 1891. 5 fiche. Code DIR/TOR/1891. £5.00 + p&p £5.00.
McKenzie's Torbay directory 1910. 7 fiche. Code DIR/TOR/1910. £7.00 + p&p £5.00.
Torquay Times directory 1923. 5 fiche. Code DIR/TOR/1923.

ESSEX
Essex Record Office
PO Box 11, County Hall, Chelmsford, SM1 1LY

Name index to poor law settlement papers. 4 fiche. Essex family history series **3**. 1-898529-05-1. (Cat no. 133). 1996. £8.00. Jointly published with Essex Society for Family History.
Parish census listings, 1797-1831. 3 fiche. Essex family history series **2**. 1-898529-04-3. (Cat no. 133). 1996. £4.50. Jointly published with Essex Society for Family History.
Return of owners of land in Essex, 1873. 1 fiche. 1-898529-03-5. Essex family history series **1**. (Cat no. 131). 1996. £2.50. Jointly published with Essex Society for Family History.

GLOUCESTERSHIRE AND BRISTOL
Bristol Historical Databases Project
University of the West of England, St. Matthias Campus, Oldbury Court Road, Fishponds, Bristol, BS16 2JP
Phone: (0117) 9655384 ext. 4487

Please specify whether you require computer disks in ASCII format, or in *Idealist for Windows*. The latter requires Microsoft Windows 3.1 or above, a 386 processor, at least 1.5 Mb free space, and at least 4 MB RAM.
Bibliography of Bristol and Bath. Disc. £3.00.
Matthews' commercial directory, 1792. Disc. £3.00.
Reed's commercial directory, 1794. Disc. £3.00.
Matthews' commercial directory, 1801. Disc. £3.00.

Matthews' commercial directory, 1851. Disc. £3.00.
Bristol obituaries, 1871-1921. Disc. £3.00.
Bristol poll book, 1722. Disc. £3.00.
Bristol poll book, 1774. Disc. £3.00.
Guide to the Port of Bristol archives. Disc. £3.00.
Bristol business archives. Disc. £3.00.

HAMPSHIRE
Hampshire Record Office
Sussex Street, Winchester, Hampshire, SO23 8TH
Phone: (01962) 846154

Microfiche reprints:
Hampshire allegations for marriage licences. Fiche. £5.00.
Will index (names, occupations, places) 1571-1858. Fiche. £15.00.
Phillimores Hampshire marriage registers vols 1-16. 16 fiche. £8.00.
Kelly's directory, 1895. Fiche. £7.00.
White's directory, 1859. Fiche. £5.00.

KENT
Folkestone Library
Heritage Room, 2, Grace Hill, Folkestone, Kent, CT20 1HD

1871 Dover, Folkestone directory. 1 Fiche £1.00 + vat.
Creed's Folkestone directory, 1873. 2 fiche £.50 + vat.
Sinnock's Folkestone, Dover & district directory, 1875. 6 fiche. £4.00 + vat.
Russell's Folkestone directory, 1885. 2 fiche. £1.00 + vat.
Pike's Folkestone & district directory, 1887. 5 fiche. £3.50 + vat.
Pike's Folkestone & district directory, 1888-9. 5 fiche. £3.50 + vat.
Pike's Folkestone & district directory, 1889-90. 5 fiche. £3.50 + vat.
Pike's Folkestone & district directory, 1890-91. 5 fiche. £3.50 + vat.
Pike's Folkestone & district directory, 1892-3. 5 fiche. £3.50 + vat.
Pike's Folkestone & district directory, 1893-4. 5 fiche. £3.50 + vat.
Pike's Folkestone & district directory, 1894-5. 4 fiche. £3.00 + vat.
Pike's Folkestone & district directory, 1895-6. 5 fiche. £3.50 + vat.

Folkestone Library (cont.)
Pike's Folkestone & district directory, 1897-8. 5 fiche. £3.50 + vat.
Pike's Folkestone & district directory, 1898-9. 5 fiche. £3.50 + vat.
Kelly's Folkestone & district directory, 1898-9. 5 fiche. £3.50 + vat.
Pike's Folkestone & district directory, 1899-1900. 5 fiche. £3.50 + vat.
Pike's Folkestone & district directory, 1900-1901. 4 fiche. £3.00 + vat.
Pike's Folkestone & district directory, 1901-2. 5 fiche. £3.50 + vat.
Pike's Folkestone & district directory, 1902-3. 5 fiche. £3.50 + vat.
Pike's Folkestone & district directory, 1903-4. 5 fiche. £3.50 + vat.
Kelly's Folkestone & district directory, 1903-4. 5 fiche. £3.50 + vat.
Parson's Folkestone & district directory, 1926. 5 fiche. £3.50 + vat.
Kelly's Folkestone & district directory, 1927. 5 fiche. £3.50 + vat.
Kelly's Folkestone & district directory, 1928. 5 fiche. £3.50 + vat.
Kelly's Folkestone & district directory, 1929. 5 fiche. £3.50 + vat.
Kelly's Folkestone & district directory, 1930. 5 fiche. £3.50 + vat.
Kelly's Folkestone & district directory, 1931. 5 fiche. £3.50 + vat.
Kelly's Folkestone & district directory, 1932. 5 fiche. £3.50 + vat.
Kelly's Folkestone & district directory, 1933. 5 fiche. £3.50 + vat.
Kelly's Folkestone & district directory, 1934. 5 fiche. £3.50 + vat.
Kelly's Folkestone & district directory, 1935. 6 fiche. £4.00 + vat.
Kelly's Folkestone & district directory, 1936. 6 fiche. £4.00 + vat.
Kelly's Folkestone & district directory, 1937. 6 fiche. £4.00 + vat.
Kelly's Folkestone & district directory, 1938. 6 fiche. £4.00 + vat.

NORTHUMBERLAND

Berwick upon Tweed Record Office

Council Offices, Wallace Green, Berwick upon Tweed TD15 IED
Phone: (01289) 330044, ext.230.
Email: Archives@berwickc.demon.co.uk
1891 census, Berwick upon Tweed. Fiche. £4.50 + p&p 50p. Full transcript.

Belford West Street Presbyterian Church: Baptisms 1774-1848. Fiche. £3.00 + p&p 50p. Indexed transcript.
Berwick High Meeting Presbyterian Church: baptisms 1761-1879. Fiche. £3.00 + p&p 50p. Indexed transcript.
Berwick Low Meeting Presbyterian Church: baptisms 1780-1849, 1864-66; marriages 1838-48, 1874; deaths 1831-49. Fiche £2.50 + p&p 50p. Indexed transcript.
Lowick Scotch Presbyterian Church: baptisms 1804-49. Fiche. £3.50 + p&p 50p. Indexed transcript.
Berwick-upon-Tweed Methodist Circuit: baptisms 1837-83. Fiche. £2.50 + p&p 50p. Indexed transcript.
Berwick-upon-Tweed Golden Square Presbyterian Church: baptisms 1771-1919 & marriages 1782-1812, 1838-1920. Fiche. £4.00 + p&p 50p. Indexed transcript.
Wooler, Cheviot Street Presbyterian Church: baptisms 1752-1837. Fiche. £4.00 + p&p 50p. Indexed transcript.
Tweedmouth parish church monumental inscriptions. Fiche. £2.50 + p&p 50p.
Berwick-upon-Tweed Roman Catholic baptisms 1804-40. Fiche. £2.00 + p&p 50p.
Lowick parish census. 1841, 1851 & 1861. Fiche. £3.00 + p&p 50p.
Berwick-upon-Tweed Shaws Lane Protestant Relief Congregation: baptisms 1779-1858; marriages 1778-1810. Fiche. £3.00 + p&p 50p. Indexed transcript.
Coldstream Bridge marriages, 1793-97. Fiche. £2.00 + p&p 50p. Indexed transcript.
Lowick parish census 1871, 1881 and 1891. Fiche. £3.50 + p&p 50p.
Bamburgh monumental inscriptions. Fiche £3.50 + p&p 50p.
Good's directory of Berwick upon Tweed, 1806. Fiche. £3.50 + p&p 50p.
Royal Cheviot Legion muster rolls, 1799-1814. Fiche. £2.50 + p&p 50p.
Berwick freemasons' list, 1799-1814. Fiche. £2.50 + p&p 50p.
Bamburgh parish: baptisms 1758-1812. Fiche. £3.50 + p&p 50p.
Bamburgh parish: baptisms 1813-1902. Fiche. £3.50 + p&p 50p.
Berwick Holy Trinity: baptisms 1813-1829. Fiche. £3.50 + p&p 50p.
Berwick Holy Trinity: baptisms 1829-1844. Fiche. £4.00 + p&p 50p.

Berwick Charity School admissions, 1757-1860. Fiche. £2.50 + p&p 50p.
Berwick Holy Trinity: baptisms 1844-1856. Fiche. £3.50 + p&p 50p.
Berwick Holy Trinity: baptisms 1856-1874. Fiche. £4.00 + p&p 50p.
Berwick Holy Trinity: burials 1813-1841. Fiche. £5.00 + p&p 50p.
Bamburgh parish: marriages 1837-1875. Fiche. £2.50 + p&p 50p.
Bamburgh parish: burials 1810-1902. Fiche. £4.00 + p&p 50p.
Bamburgh parish: burials 1810-1902. Fiche. £4.00 + p&p 50p.

Northumberland Record Office

Melton Park, North Gosforth, Newcastle upon Tyne, NE3 5QX
http://www.swinhope.c
/NBL/NorthumberlandRO

Rothbury Congregational Church: baptisms 1840-56. Thorneycroft Presbyterian Church baptisms, 1804-32. Fiche. £2.00 + p&p 50p. Indexed transcript.
Thropton Presbyterian Church baptisms, 1799-1847. Fiche. £2.00 + p&p 50p. Indexed transcript.
Hairpowder tax return for Northumberland, 1795, 1796 & 1797. Fiche. £2.50 + p&p 50p.
Robinson's penny almanac and Blyth directory, 1871. Fiche. £3.00 + p&p 50p.
Robinson's penny illustrated household almanac for 1882, general local year book, directory for Blyth, Amble & Warkworth & maritime register for Blyth and Amble. Fiche. £3.50 + p&p 50p.
Longframlington Presbyterian Church: baptisms 1757-1859. Fiche. £3.50 + p&p 50p.
Morpeth St. George Presbyterian Church: baptisms 1747-1806. Fiche. £2.50 + p&p 50p. Indexed transcript.
Northumberland poll books 1747-8, 1774. Fiche. £2.00 + p&p 50p.

Northumberland poll book 1826. Fiche. £2.00 + p&p 50p.
Northumberland poll book 1841. Fiche. £2.00 + p&p 50p.
Northumberland poll books 1710, 1721. Fiche. £2.00 + p&p 50p.
Northumberland poll books, 1722-1734. Fiche. £2.00 + p&p 50p.
Morpeth Herald births marriages, deaths and obituaries, April 1854-March 1860. Fiche. £4.50 + p&p 50p.
Morpeth St. George Presbyterian Church: baptisms 1806-1848. Fiche. £3.50 + p&p 50p.
Calendar of Northumberland alehouse licences 1822-26. Fiche. £4.00 + p&p 50p.
Otterburn Presbyterian: baptisms 1863-1930; marriages 1887-1930. Fiche. £2.50 + p&p 50p.
Alnwick Roman Catholic baptisms, 1794-1840; marriages 1846-1855. Fiche. £2.50 + p&p 50p. Indexed.
Bellingham Roman Catholic baptisms 1794-1925. Fiche. £3.50 + p&p 50p. Indexed.
Felton Roman Catholic baptisms, 1792-1858. Fiche. £2.50 + p&p 50p. Indexed.
1871 census, Newbiggin by the Sea [RG10/5168, f.80-104]. Fiche. £2.50 + p&p 50p. Indexed.
1891 census, North Seaton (RG12/4260, f.43-75). Fiche. £3.50 + p&p 50p. Indexed.
1891 census, Tynemouth Union Workhouse, Northumberland; Northumberland Village Homes Industrial School for Girls, Whitley Bay (RG12/4230, f.127-134). Fiche. £2.00 + p&p 50p. Indexed.

Sussex

West Sussex Record Office

County Hall, Chichester, West Sussex PO19 1RN
Phone: (01243) 533911

MCCANN, TIMOTHY J. *West Sussex probate inventories, 1521-1834.* 24pp + 4 fiche. 0-86260-005-7. 1981. £15.00.

Author Index

Place Name Index

103

104

106

107

110

111

Surname Index

Subject Index

Counties are indicated in accordance with the Chapman system of county codes.

116

118

120

122